INSIDERS' GUIDE®

OFF THE BEATE...

Off the Beaten Path®

EIGHTH EDITION

wisconsin

A GUIDE TO UNIQUE PLACES

MARTIN HINTZ

AND

DANIEL HINTZ

INSIDERS' GUIDE®

GUILFORD, CONNECTICUT
AN IMPRINT OF THE GLOBE PEQUOT PRESS

The prices, rates, and hours listed in this guidebook
were confirmed at press time. We recommend,
however, that you call establishments to obtain
current information before traveling.

To buy books in quantity for corporate use
or incentives, call **(800) 962–0973, ext. 4551,**
or e-mail **premiums@GlobePequot.com.**

INSIDERS' GUIDE®

Text design by Linda Loiewski
Maps created by Equator Graphics © Morris Book Publishing, LLC
Illustrations by Carole Drong
Spot photography throughout © Siede Preis/Getty

ISSN 1540-2134
ISBN-13: 978-0-7627-4057-4
ISBN-10: 0-7627-4057-4

Manufactured in the United States of America
Eighth Edition/First Printing

To the family, travelers all

NORTHERN

Superior

Eau Claire

Wausau

Green Bay

La Crosse

CENTRAL

Oshkosh

EASTERN

WESTERN

Madison

Milwaukee

MILWAUKEE
AND ENVIRONS

Racine

Contents

Acknowledgments

Special gratitude to all our friends throughout Wisconsin who helped with this book, especially Paula Runde, Gary Knowles, Ronda Allen, and the staff of the Wisconsin Division of Tourism. Visitor bureaus, historical societies, and local information offices around the state were particularly helpful as well. The people of Wisconsin themselves also deserve a rousing hand clap: from the guy who told us where to find the best pie in his hometown to the volunteer at the local historical site. Thanks also to Mario Raspanti and Pam Percy for their assistance.

Introduction

Wisconsin is a state of imagery: cows, woods, beer, fish.

Sure enough.

But the state has a lot more to offer. For instance, think of Wisconsin in superlatives: It has the world's largest four-sided clock, the biggest penny, and most massive loon. It offers a giant, five-story leaping muskie in whose massive mouth avid fisherfolk can even be married. The state cradles the nation's most comprehensive collection of works by beloved artist Norman Rockwell and the world's largest carousel. The country's only whooping crane preserve is in Wisconsin, and so is a record-size black bear. The cranes are alive and flopping. The bear is stuffed.

Wisconsin is a place for doing and seeing. It hosts regattas, ice fishing competitions, one-act play festivals, and Civil War reinactments.

There are lead mines, cornfields, and superconductors. There are ship manufacturers, goats on top of restaurants, and milk-carton raft races. One city boasts of its own submarine; another hosts the world's busiest airstrip during a summertime fly-in of experimental and private aircraft.

Wisconsin is a state tailor-made for off-the-beaten-path adventures. You can discover some of the secrets in a corridor of Madison's stately Capitol Building, on the rocky tip of foggy Door County, in a pine-scented North Woods glade, on a narrow Milwaukee side street.

Wisconsin Off the Beaten Path ranges from urban to rural and back again. Dan and I hope that this book will lighten your travel planning, heighten your sensibilities, and increase your fun.

The enthusiastic explorer can use this poke-along guide to uncover secluded hideaways as well as to discover hints about getting around the more well-known tourist attractions.

Care has been taken to ensure accuracy as much as possible. Over time, however, ticket prices, phone numbers, and hours of operation may change; establishments may close for one reason or another; and personnel may move on. Subsequently, there may be a few discrepancies in this edition that will have to wait for the next update. So please be patient and let the publisher know of any necessary adjustments, because you, as reader, can also be a great scout. Who knows what neat new Wisconsin discoveries you will find to share with other readers!

On your journeys, always, *always* remember to verify lodging arrangements before arrival. It pays to call ahead. Even that most off-the-beaten-path bed-and-breakfast could be booked the night you wish to register.

Resident admission stickers for Wisconsin state parks cost $20.00 annually, $5.00 daily, and $3.00 for one hour. For resident senior citizens (sixty-five and older), stickers are $10.00 annually and $3.00 daily. For nonresidents, the cost is $30.00 annually, $10.00 daily, and $3.00 for one hour. Stickers are required on all motor vehicles entering and stopping in state parks. They can be purchased at the parks, at local Department of Natural Resources (DNR) offices, or by writing the DNR, Bureau of Parks and Recreation, Box 7921, Madison 53707 (888–WIPARK or 608–947–2757; www.dnr.state.wi.us). Half-price annual tickets are available for additional vehicles in a resident family.

One thing you'll notice as you journey through the state is that Wisconsinites have a way with slogans and nicknames. Almost every city, town, and hamlet has a booster phrase posted along the roads leading to Main Street. Abbotsford brags about being "Wisconsin's First City." Albany is the "Sweetest Village on the Sugar River." You can pedal like crazy in Brodhead, "The Bicycle Gateway to Wisconsin" or in Sparta, which is the "Bicycling Capital of America." Be sure to shake hands in Cumberland, "Famous for Friendliness," and in Middleton because it's the "Good Neighbor City." Don't stop now because Marion is "Where Strangers Are Friends We'd Like to Meet" and "You're Always Welcome" in Holmen. You'll never get away from Monroe because "We Bring You Back." Yet don't forget that Frederic is "A Beautiful Place to Visit, A Great Place to Live."

You'll have to come to the state to find who is "Tops in Wisconsin," "The Gem City," and "Home of the World's Largest Sauerkraut Plant."

Wisconsin is also the capital of self-proclaimed "capitals." Almost every community worth its civic salt has given itself some municipal distinction. Onalaska is the Sunfish Capital. Birchwood is the Bluegill Capital. Algoma is the Trout and Salmon Capital. Bayfield is the Lake Trout Capital. And a fierce battle to retain the Walleye Capital tag is constantly being waged by Presque Isle, Stone Lake, and Long Lake (depends on the size and amount of the annual sportfishing catch, and, by the way, it takes an average of one hundred hours to catch a 33.4-inch muskie). With all these titles, don't think that there's something fishy about Wisconsin. After all, Sheboygan is the Bratwurst Capital. Racine is the Kringle Capital. Green Bay is the Toilet Paper Capital (because of its paper products industry). Bloomer is the Rope Jumping Capital. Monroe is the Swiss Cheese Capital. Elmwood and Belleville each claim to be the UFO Capital of the World.

Consequently, it's quite obvious that visiting Wisconsin is a capital idea, whether we're on or off the beaten path. But much of the fun in Wisconsin comes in discovery, in finding the little known and the really unexpected. You can find that out for yourself.

Restaurant cost categories refer to the price of entrees without beverages, desserts, taxes, and tips. Those listed as inexpensive are $10 or less; moderate, between $10 and $15; and expensive, $20 and over. Places to stay listed as inexpensive are up to $100 per double night; moderate, $101 to $200 per night; and expensive, $200 and up per night.

Fast Facts about Wisconsin

HOW TO OBTAIN ADDITIONAL INFORMATION

There's a lot of help available for planning an off-the-beaten-path expedition. In fact, the most recent tourism department mottos have been "You're Among Friends" in Wisconsin and "Stay Just a Little Bit Longer." Believe them. After all, any state that hosts the U.S. Watermelon Seed Spitting Championships has to have a lot of affable neighborliness going for it and a lot of fun and interesting events and attractions for you to enjoy.

INFORMATION CENTERS

Wisconsin has six year-round and three seasonal information centers at its borders with Illinois, Iowa, and Minnesota. You may wish to pull into any one of them for a driving break and to browse through brochure racks, check on maps, and discover what's going on in nearby communities. Bathrooms are readily accessible.

Open all year are facilities at Beloit (I 90, Rest Area 96); Hudson (I–94, Rest Area 25); Hurley (Highways 2 and 51, Rest Area 103); Kenosha (I–94, Rest Area 26); La Crosse (I–90, Rest Area 31); and Madison (123 Washington Street).

Open May 1 through October are Kieler (Grant County, Highway 51); Marinette (on Bridge Street at Menominee River crossing); Genoa City (Highway 12, Rest Area 24); Prairie du Chien (at the Highway 18 bridge); and Superior (Highways 2 and 53, Rest Area 23).

For the convenience of travelers, the state has thirty-two year-round, heated toilet stops along major highways and 163 primitive sites. The latter are closed in the off-season, so plan to accommodate your carload of kids accordingly. Look for the red triangle on state road maps for locations.

Aside from being functional, most of the sites offer the bonus of exceptional views of the countryside. One of the best is about 5 miles west of Fennimore on Highway 18. On both sides of the road, deep valleys roll toward the horizon. Currier & Ives farmsites dot the oak-shrouded hills, their red barns and white houses dappling the scenery. A tired traveler can lie on a sun-drenched summer hillside there and count clouds before meandering eastward toward Madison or west toward the Mississippi River. Unfortunately, area bathrooms are among those locked in the winter, although the access road is plowed. I've always wanted to stop there on our holiday trips to see Iowa relatives, but for one reason or another, we've always had to forgo the thrill of swooshing down the steep hillsides.

HISTORICAL MARKERS AND RUSTIC ROADS

Historical sites abound in Wisconsin. There's the usual selection of baronial mansions, rough-hewn pioneer settlements, and George-Washington-slept-here sort of places—not that the famous founding father ever actually visited Wisconsin according to anyone's tall tale, but many other presidents and other notables have stopped by since then, either simply to say hello or to do some fishing.

Don't whiz past the numerous historical markers scattered along Wisconsin's highways. Nobody has ever kept an accurate total of the state, county, and local signposts, but 3,000 is a conservative estimate. They'll tell you of famous personalities, famous fires, famous floods, famous Native American battles, and famous industries. Roadway signs about 0.5 mile before each marker alert motorists that such a monument is just down the pike.

One prime way to wander Wisconsin is to follow any of the fifty officially designated paved or gravel Rustic Roads at key points around the state. The program started in 1973, with the first designation made in 1975. The roadways range from 2.5 to 10 miles long and are marked by easily identifiable brown-and-yellow signs that are highlighted by an outline of the state's boundaries to indicate the appropriate routes. For a free map and brochure telling about these "less-traveled roads," write to the *Rustic Roads Program, Wisconsin Department of Transportation,* Box 7913, Madison 53707 (608–266–0649).

To have one of its byways so designated, a community or county submits an application to the board, which reviews the proposal and determines if it fits the following criteria: The road should have outstanding natural attributes such as native vegetation, scenic vistas, or historical significance; it should be lightly traveled; no widening or other improvement can be scheduled to detract from the original condition of the road upon application; and the road should be at least 2 miles long.

TRAVEL INFORMATION BUREAUS AND CONTACTS

For the latest general information on the state's travel scene, contact the *Wisconsin Department of Tourism,* Department of Development, 201 West Washington Avenue, Box 8690, Madison 53708 (608–266–2161, 800–432–8747; www.travelwisconsin.com).

Bureaus for the state's primary tourism regions can provide details about specific areas, so write or call:

- **Visit Milwaukee,** 648 North Plankinton Avenue, Suite 425, Milwaukee 53203. (800–231–0903 or 414–273–3950; www.visitmilwaukee.org).
- **Wisconsin Indian Head Country,** Box 628, Chetek 54728 (800–472–6654 or 715–924–2970; http://wisconsinindianhead.org).

For information about specific lodgings, attractions, or parks, contact:

- **Wisconsin Association of Campground Owners (WACO),** Box 130, Galesville 54630 (800–843–1821 or 608–582–2092; wisconsincampgrounds .com). To receive a directory of the 154 WACO members, send $2.00 to cover postage. Otherwise, directions are free at tourist information centers, travel shows, chambers of commerce, and campgrounds.
- **Wisconsin Department of Natural Resources,** Bureau of Parks & Recreation, Box 7921, Madison 53707 (608–266–2621 or 888–947–2757; www.dnr.state.wi.us).
- **Wisconsin Historical Society,** 816 State Street, Madison 53706 (608–264–6400; www.wisconsinhistory.org or 608–264–6535 [UW Library reference desk]).
- **Wisconsin Innkeepers Association,** 1025 South Moorland Road, Suite 200, Brookfield 53005 (414–782–2851 or 262–782–2851; www.lodging-wi.com).
- **Wisconsin Restaurant Association,** 2801 Fish Hatchery Road, Madison 53713 (608–270–9950; www.wirestaurant.org).
- **Wisconsin Society of Ornithology,** 2022 Sheryl Lane, Waukesha 53188 (262–547–6128; www.uwgb.edu/birds/wso).
- **Wisconsin State Horse Council,** 132A South Ludington Street, Columbus 53925 (920–623–0393; www.wisconsinstatehorsecouncil.org).

Remember that most communities have a chamber of commerce or tourist office eager to help with drop-in requests. They'll load you down with printed material or describe the best place in town for pecan pie. Or simply stop in at the corner pub, ask at the local gas station, or inquire of a passerby. Most likely, you'll get some friendly suggestions and lots of advice on what to see and do locally.

WISCONSIN TRAVEL PUBLICATIONS

For a look at what Wisconsin has to offer, especially in the nooks and crannies of the state, subscribe to *Wisconsin Trails.* The glossy, comprehensive magazine is published bimonthly ($24.95 a year for six issues or $4.95 per issue on the newsstand). Articles range from folksy pieces on how to bake onion-dill bread to reports on the latest bed-and-breakfast facility. I've written features for the magazine on subjects such as kringle bakers in Racine and Milwaukee's best ethnic eateries. My subsequent paunch proclaims proudly that "somebody has to do it." (For a list of other Wisconsin publications, see page xiv.)

For a selection of excellent maps of the state, secure a copy of the *Wisconsin Atlas & Gazetteer* ($19.95), published by the DeLorme Mapping Company (2 DeLorme Drive, P.O. Box 298, Yarmouth, ME 04096; 800–642–0970; www.delorme.com). The state is broken into eighty-one quadrangular topographical sections, which show every bump and less-traveled path in the Badger State. There are also listings of bike routes, canoe trips, lighthouses, waterfalls, and a ton of other handy information for anyone into hard-core meandering.

WISCONSIN TRIVIA

Although half the fun is in getting here, you may need some time-fillers for the tykes in the backseat. So here are some background statistics and little details to use when, for the umpteenth time, the youngsters ask, "Are we there yet?" Have them guess these facts:

- Population: 5,363,675
- State tree: maple
- State bird: robin
- State animal: badger
- State fish: muskie
- State capital: Madison
- State cheese: Colby
- Length of Wisconsin: 302 miles
- Width of Wisconsin: 291 miles
- Annual average snowfall: 45 inches

- Forest area: 14,487,000 acres
- Lakes: 14,927 (the largest is Lake Winnebago, at 137,708 acres)
- Golf courses: 463
- Bike trails: 10,000 miles
- Off-road bike trails: 155 miles
- Camping sites: 51,748
- Cross-country skiing: 20,835 miles
- Snowmobile trails: 22,000 miles
- State parks: 59
- State trails: 17

Had enough? Aw, how about a few more for the record? Wisconsin has 500 different types of soils; 108,000 miles of roads; 2,444 fantastic trout streams and a couple that aren't so good (those are the ones where we don't bag our limit); the Fox River flows north (one of the few in the country to do so); and Beatles recording luminary Paul McCartney owns the rights to the rousing state song, "On, Wisconsin."

CLIMATE OVERVIEW

- Average July temperature: 70°F (21°C)
- Average January temperature: 14°F (-10°C)
- Record high temperature: 114°F (146°C) at Wisconsin Dells on July 13, 1936

- Record low temperature: -54°F (-48°C) at Danbury on January 24, 1922
- Average yearly precipitation: 31 inches (79 centimeters)

POPULATION FIGURES

- Population: 5,363,675 (2000 census)
- Population in 1840: 30,945
- Density: 99 persons per square mile (38 per square kilometer); the United States average is 80 persons per square mile (30 per square kilometer)
- Distribution: 66 percent urban, 34 percent rural
- Rank among states: 18th

WISCONSIN CITIES WITH THE LARGEST POPULATIONS

- Milwaukee: 596,974
- Madison: 208,054
- Green Bay: 102,313
- Racine: 81,855
- Kenosha: 90,352
- Appleton: 70,087

FAMOUS WISCONSINITES

- Don Ameche (1908–1993), actor
- August Derleth (1909–1971), author of more than 150 books
- Edna Ferber (1887–1968), best-selling novelist, Pulitzer prize winner
- Robert M. LaFollette (1855–1921), United States senator and progressive political leader
- Zona Gale (1874–1938), Pulitzer prize–winning author of *Miss Lulu Bett*
- Hamlin Garland (1860–1938), Pulitzer prize–winning author of *Main Traveled Roads* and numerous novels
- Eric Heiden (1958–   ), five-time Olympic gold-medal winner in skating
- Tom Hulce (1953–   ), actor
- Garrison Keillor (1942–   ), public radio personality (host of *Prairie Home Companion*), author
- Aldo Leopold (1886–1948), conservationist, ecologist, author
- Liberace (1919–1987), born Wlaziv Valentino Liberace, noted pianist and flashy showman
- Joseph McCarthy (1909–1957), conservative Republican U.S. senator
- Agnes Moorehead (1906–1974), actress
- John Muir (1838–1914), geologist, naturalist, author
- John Norquist (1949–   ), world's tallest (6'7") singing mayor of Swedish heritage, mayor of Milwaukee (1988–2003)

- Patrick O'Brien (1899–1983), actor
- Georgia O'Keeffe (1887–1981), noted painter
- Carl Sandburg (1878–1967), poet, essayist, Pulitzer prize–winning author of *Abraham Lincoln: The War Years*
- Spencer Tracy (1900–1967), actor
- Gene Wilder (1934–   ), actor
- Laura Ingalls Wilder (1867–1957), author of Little House books
- Thornton Wilder (1897–1975), Pulitzer prize–winning author of *Our Town*
- Frank Lloyd Wright (1869–1959), architect
- Frank Zeidler (1912–   ), historian, political activist, Socialist mayor of Milwaukee (1948–1960), Socialist candidate for president in 1976
- David Zucker (1947–   ) and Jerry Zucker (1950–   ), film producers

WISCONSIN NEWSPAPERS AND OTHER PUBLICATIONS

Major Dailies

Green Bay Press Gazette
435 East Walnut
Green Bay 54307
(920) 431–8355

Janesville Gazette
1 South Parker Drive
Janesville 53547-5001
(608) 754–3311

Madison Capitol Times
1901 Fish Hatchery Road
Madison 53708
(608) 252–6100

Marshfield News-Herald
111 West Third Street
Marshfield 54449
(715) 384–3131

Milwaukee Journal-Sentinel
333 West State Street
Milwaukee 53203
(414) 224–2000

Oshkosh Northwestern
224 East State Street
Oshkosh 54901
(920) 235–7700

Rhinelander Daily News
314 Courtney Street
Rhinelander 54501
(715) 365–6397

Shawano Leader
1464 East Green Bay Street
Shawano 54166
(715) 526–2121

Sheboygan Press
632 Center Avenue
Sheboygan 53081
(920) 457–7711

Watertown Daily Times
113-115 West Main Street
Watertown 53094
(920) 261–4949

Waukesha Freeman
801 North Barstow
Waukesha 53187
(262) 542–2501

Wausau Daily Herald
800 Scott Street
Wausau 54402
(715) 842–2101

West Bend Daily News
100 South Sixth Street
West Bend 53095
(262) 306–5000

Wisconsin Rapids Daily Tribune
200 First Avenue South
Wisconsin Rapids 54494
(715) 423–7200

Wisconsin State Journal
1901 Fish Hatchery Road
Madison 53713
(608) 252–6100

Major Weeklies

CNI Newspapers
15700 West Cleveland Avenue
New Berlin 53131
(262) 938–5000

(twenty-two newspapers in the
greater Milwaukee suburban area)

Alternative Publications

Madison Isthmus
101 King Street
Madison 53703
(608) 251–5627
(published on Friday)

Shepherd Express
413 North Second Street
Milwaukee 53203
(414) 276–2222
(published on Wednesday)

City Magazines

These monthlies are available at
newsstands and by subscription:

Madison Magazine
P.O. Box 44965–53744
7025 West Raymond Road
Madison 53719
(608) 270–3600

Milwaukee Magazine
417 East Chicago Street
Milwaukee 53202
(414) 273–1101

HELPFUL WISCONSIN WEB SITES

- General Wisconsin information: www.welcometraveler.com
- Maps of Wisconsin: www.northwoodmap.com; www.delorme.com
- Wisconsin Department of Tourism: www.travelwisconsin.com
- Wisconsin Innkeepers Association: www.lodging-wi.com
- Wisconsin Restaurant Association: www.wirestaurant.org

Western Wisconsin

The rolling, muddy waters of the Mississippi form most of the western boundary of Wisconsin. The river edges a slow way from where it first touches the state at Prescott, meandering 200 miles south to the rural southwestern corner of the state near Dubuque, Iowa. The Great River Road, Highway 35, skirts the rim of the river, crawling through sloughs, up over the ridgebacks, and along short straightaways that end much too soon in a sweeping curve. The road has consistently been voted one of the country's most scenic routes by everyone from motorcycle clubs to travel editors. The route is well marked by white signs with a green riverboat pilot's wheel.

For a map of the entire Great River Road, covering the 3,000 miles from Canada to the Gulf of Mexico, contact the Mississippi River Parkway Commission, P.O. Box 59159, Minneapolis 55459-8207; (763) 212–2560; www.mississippiriverinfo.com.

Muscular tugboats, with their roaring diesel engines, shove blocks of barges loaded with coal, oil, lumber, and other goods. They make these runs almost year-round between Minnesota's Twin Cities, Minneapolis and St. Paul, to the Gulf of Mexico. Only the freezing cold of midwinter forces closing of the river traffic. The river is then turned over to hardy anglers who brave the blustery winds in search of the

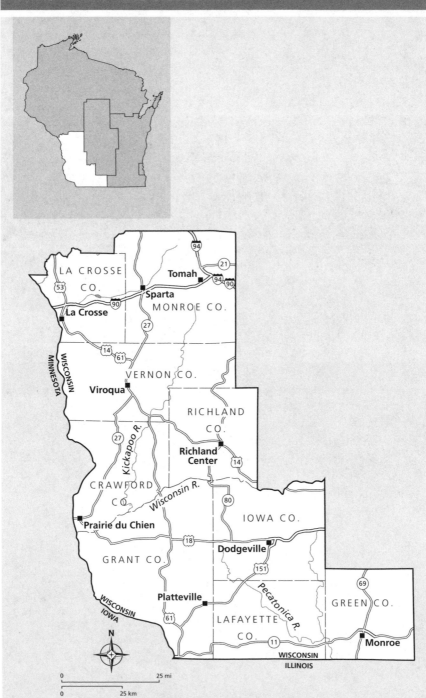

Midwest's best-tasting bluegills and catfish. The hapless fish are plucked through holes chopped in ice that can be 2 or more feet thick.

Trappers range along the riverbanks, bringing in dozens of muskrat, beaver, and fox pelts each year to satisfy the demands of the national and international markets.

Passengers get rides straight out of Mark Twain days on riverboats—such as the steam-spitting *Delta Queen* and her sisters—that still ply the waters. The vessels call at quays in Prairie du Chien and La Crosse. The boats' appearances are often surprising. I remember camping on a riverfront sandbar one summer and being awakened in the predawn hours to the crash of paddle wheels storming downriver. A quick glance out the tent flap revealed what seemed to be a sky-high bank of lights surging south on the blackness of the river. Waltz music wafted through the humid night air, just audible over the roar of machinery. Then it was gone, like a nineteenth-century dream.

The river is dotted with islands, fringed with marshlands, and speckled with drowned trees, which are the reminders of the Mississippi's many spring run-off tantrums. But on decent days, canoeists can paddle along the backwater sloughs in search of great, flapping herons and slithery muskrats. Houseboaters can drift along in tune with seasons.

WESTERN WISCONSIN'S TOP HITS

American Players Theater	Nelson Dewey State Park
Badger Mine Museum	Norskedalen
Elroy-Sparta Trail	Pendarvis
Fennimore Doll Museum	Prairie du Chien Museum at Fort Crawford
First Capitol State Park and Museum	Spurgeon Vineyards and Winery
Fur-Traders' Rendezvous	
Grand Army of the Republic Hall	Stonefield Village
Grant County Courthouse	Sugar River Trail
House on the Rock Golf Club Resort	Swiss Historical Village
Jos. Huber Brewing Company	Villa Louis
Kickapoo Indian Caverns	Wisconsin High School Rodeo Association Championships
Mount La Crosse	

Crawford County

This is a county of rivers. The Wisconsin bisects the landscape, meandering downstream from the state's northlands. Its importance in history is marked by a sign in Portage (Columbia County) that reads: ON JUNE 14, 1673, JACQUES MARQUETTE AND LOUIS JOLIET STARTED THE 1.28 MILE PORTAGE FROM HERE TO THE WISCONSIN RIVER, WHICH LED TO THEIR DISCOVERY OF THE UPPER MISSISSIPPI JUNE 17, 1673, AT PRAIRIE DU CHIEN.

Other markers in the county should be perused as well. While you are in Gays Mills for the annual **Blossom Day Festival** in May, read the marker on Highway 171 east of town. It tells of the early lives of the pioneers who developed the apple industry there. A marker commemorating early governor James Davidson is on Highway 61 near the village of Soldiers Grove. A marker on Highway 35 south of Lynxville describes the log rafts that used to float down the Mississippi in the 1800s. The Prairie du Chien marker is at the tourist information center on the Mississippi River, memorializing the building of the third frontier fort in the Wisconsin Territory. Another marker in Prairie du Chien, located at Villa Louis, outlines the importance of Fort Crawford in protecting the American frontier during the War of 1812. A Marquette-Joliet marker at the state's tourism information center where Highway 18 crosses the Mississippi honors the two French explorers and their five French-Canadian *voyageur* companions as being the first whites to travel the Upper Mississippi.

After the Mississippi and the Wisconsin, Crawford County's third major waterway is the Kickapoo, a name derived from the Winnebago Indian term *kwigapawa,* which means "moves about from here to there." The Winnebagos knew what they were talking about. The Kickapoo offers more twists and turns than a dish of spaghetti on its crooked north and south route, joining the Wisconsin River at Wauzeka.

On Highway 60, just before entering Wauzeka from the west, are the **Kickapoo Indian Caverns,** discovered by lead miners in the early 1800s. The caves are the state's largest, once used by local Native Americans as a shelter. Forty-minute guided tours can be taken through the caverns, formed by an

Old Abe

The "Eagle Regiment," the Eighth Wisconsin, took its name from Old Abe, a tamed bald eagle that the unit carried into battle during the Civil War. During the fighting, the bird would perch on a cannon or fly overhead, taking part in twenty-two battles and sixty skirmishes. After the war he lived in the basement and yard of the state capitol.

AUTHORS' FAVORITES

Badger Mine Museum, Shullsburg	**St. John Mine,** Potosi
Dickeyville Grotto	**Spurgeon Vineyards & Winery,** Highland
Fennimore Doll Museum	
Kickapoo Indian Caverns, Wauzeka	**Swiss Historical Village Museum,** New Glarus
	Yellowstone Lake State Park, Blanchardville
Pendarvis, Mineral Point	

underground river. Be sure to wear comfortable walking shoes and a sweater or jacket. The caverns are open from 9:00 A.M. to 4:15 P.M. daily from May 15 to October 31. The last tour starts at 4:15 P.M. After Labor Day, the caverns open at 10:00 A.M., and the last tour is at 4:00 P.M. For details on the rock formations, contact the Kickapoo Indian Caverns in Wauzeka at (608) 875–7723 or www .kickapooindiancaverns.com.

Lovely as it is, the Kickapoo can be nasty. The angry river waters flooded so often that the town of *Soldiers Grove* moved from its base along the cliffs to high ground in 1978. Originally called Pine Grove, the town of 680 was an encampment for troops during the Black Hawk War in 1832 and subsequently changed its name in honor of the soldiers.

All buildings in the rebuilt community, now high above the floodline, receive 50 percent or more of their power supply from the sun. The solar panels over the bank, supermarkets, clinic, stores, and homes give the town a futuristic look. The site of the former village has been turned into a riverside park with a ball diamond, a campground, tennis courts, and a picnic spot. Tourist information is available at the Solar Town Pharmacy, Box 95, Passive Sun Drive (608–624–5217).

The *Old Oak Inn* in Soldiers Grove offers comfortable accommodations, a heated pool, and a restaurant that has some of the best sage-stuffed chicken in western Wisconsin. Room rates range from $48.00 to $62.00, with meals in the $5.00 to $17.50 spread. The restaurant is open from 5:00 P.M. to 2:00 A.M. Monday and Wednesday through Friday, 8:00 A.M. to 2:00 P.M. Sunday, and is closed Tuesday.

Nearby is the *Country Garden Restaurant,* which offers, as the counter girl says, "great home cookin'." The Country Garden is usually just open for weekday lunches from 11:00 A.M. to 1:00 P.M., but it does have an all-you-can-eat fish fry on Friday evenings.

There are two explanations of how **Prairie du Chien** was named. One legend says the place was called "Field of the Dogs" by French trappers who gathered here and saw acres of prairie dog mounds. Another version says the town was named after "Big Dog," a local tribal leader. Whatever the true story, the city that evolved from the early frontier encampments has been a major Wisconsin trading center and river port for generations. Wisconsin's first millionaire, fur dealer Hercules Dousman, put the place on the map when he built his mansion, **Villa Louis,** in 1843. That original house was razed in 1870, and the current Italianate building was constructed. The richly appointed building and its grounds are now owned by the State Historical Society of Wisconsin.

There's a bit of personal history attached to the Villa Louis. My maternal great-grandmother, Bridget O'Malley, was a linen maid there when she came from Ireland to the United States around the time of the Civil War.

Her beau, Louie Larson, was a young Norwegian shopkeeper who lived in Marquette, on the Iowa side of the Mississippi. In the winter Louie would ice-skate across the river to court Bridget.

In the summer he would take his sailboat, *The Bluebird,* across the river to pitch woo to his lady love. Naturally Bridget was quite smitten with all this attention, and the couple eventually married and moved to Iowa. Viola! Without them, *Wisconsin Off the Beaten Path* might never have been written—at least not by yours truly.

Great-grandma Bridget was always hospitable, according to reliable family memories, so she probably wouldn't mind the guests who come to the Villa each June to try their hand at preparing breakfast in a Victorian kitchen. Up to sixteen adults can sign up for a hands-on cooking class in the mansion's kitchen. Reservations are required; call the historic site. But as Bridget would have admonished, "Just clean up after yourselves and put everything back in the proper drawer."

The Villa Louis, 900 West Bolvin Street (608–326–2721), is open from 9:00 A.M. to 5:00 P.M. daily May 1 to October 31. Admission is $8.50 for adults, $7.50 for seniors, and $3.50 for children. To get to the Villa from downtown Prairie, take Main Street north to Washington Street West.

Prairie du Chien annually hosts a **Fur-Traders' Rendezvous** on St. Feriole Island near the Villa Louis on the third weekend in June. Grizzled mountain men, Native American trappers, and appropriately garbed military men from the era fill the grounds with their tents and tepees. This is the place to pick up skins, beads, blankets, tomahawks, flintlock rifles, traps, and similar frontier accoutrements for the suburban homestead. As I've always said, "You never know when you might need a bolt of cloth or a kettle." The participants lay out trade goods, talk shop, cook over open fires, scratch, and look at us twenty-first-century types with bemusement. But when the weekend is over, they all go back to being bank presidents, mechanics, nurses, shop owners, and lawyers. For details contact the Prairie du Chien Chamber of Commerce and Tourism Council, 211 South Main Street, Prairie du Chien 53821-0326 (608–326–8555; www.prairieduchien.org).

Prairie du Chien also played another part in our family history. Great-uncle Charlie (one of the sons of the aforementioned Louie and Bridget) and a couple of his friends sneaked across the old railroad pontoon bridge that linked Iowa and Wisconsin at the turn of the twentieth century. They had hitched an all-night ride on an eastbound freight train from their hometown to see the Buffalo Bill Wild West Show in Prairie du Chien. They got more than their money's worth in that hot summer of 1901.

The show folk and the townspeople began brawling in the streets, a brouhaha that resulted in calling out the Wisconsin militia. Uncle Charlie and his frightened young pals hid in an old boiler next to a tavern as they watched the

TOP ANNUAL EVENTS

Ice Rally Cross (auto racing on ice),
West Salem, early January,
(608) 785–1773

Bald Eagle Month,
Cassville, January,
(608) 725–5855;
www.cassville.org

Vintage Snowmobile Drag Racing,
Friendship, February,
(608) 339–3749

Home Show,
Monroe, mid-March,
(608) 325–7648

Fur-Traders' Rendezvous,
Prairie du Chien, late June,
(608) 732–1673

Horse & Colt Show,
Viola, late September,
(608) 627–1831

Cranberry Festival,
Warrens, late September,
(608) 378–4200

Oktoberfest,
La Crosse, early October,
(608) 784–3378

Oktoberfest Car Races,
West Salem, early October,
(608) 786–1525

Centerfest,
Richland Center, early October,
(608) 647–6205

Shihata Orchard Fest,
Prairie du Chien, October,
(608) 326–2785

Potter Tour,
Pierce, St. Croix, Dunn counties,
October,
(715) 426–7637

Hmong New Year Festival,
La Crosse, mid-October,
(608) 781–5744

Picnic, Parks, and Mounds

Wyalusing State Park, on Grant County Highway VV along the Mississippi, is a prime location for camping sites, hiking trails, and picnic areas. Native American mounds dating back a thousand years can be found on the bluff overlooking the river. From the vantage point on the Sentinel Ridge Walk, you can see where the Mississippi and Wisconsin Rivers converge. The park, sprawling over 2,700 acres, is a wildlife haven. I've spotted white-tailed deer, bald eagles, Canada geese, muskrats, raccoons, wild turkeys, turkey vultures, and possums.

Here are some of the best hiking trails in the park:

Bluff, Indian, and Flint Ledge Trails. Take the 2-mile walk down the bluff side for great views of the Mississippi. These paths are not recommended for toddlers.

Mississippi Ridge Trail. Hikers do not have any difficulty getting across the 3.5-mile trail overlooking the river.

Old Immigrant, Old Wagon Road, and Sand Cave Trails. The trails run for more than 3 miles through heavy oak and maple groves and have some steep slopes, so watch your step. As the names imply, these tracks were used by early settlers moving overland into the river valley.

Sentinel Ridge Trail. The 1.6-mile trail runs south from the park's main campground along the high ridge. It offers some of the best views of the river.

Walnut Springs Trail. This 2.6-mile grassy pathway is a two-hour-long walk.

boisterous fight. Buffalo Bill managed to round up his crew before the militia arrived and scurried westward across the river to the safety of Iowa.

It's a lot quieter now in Prairie du Chien. Down the street from the Villa Louis is the *St. Feriole Train Depot,* a tavern in an old railroad passenger car that claims to serve the best Bloody Marys on the Mississippi River.

Judge for yourself at 220 Water Street (608–326–8548). If you need to use the facilities, a tank car serves as a rest room. Other railroad cars on the siding at *St. Feriole Island* house the Gift Box and a dangerously delightful place called Confection Connection. The latter's homemade fudge is guaranteed to add happy tonnage to hips. The cars, however, are open only from May through October.

The island is actually a spit of land jutting into the Mississippi on the west side of the city. The cars are parked south of the quay used by the riverboat *Delta Queen* when it docks in *Lawler Park.* The site is at the end of Blackhawk Avenue, where the railroad pontoon bridge used to link Wisconsin to Iowa.

Each Father's Day, a rendezvous that brings alive memories of the fur-trapper days is held on St. Feriole Island. Hundreds of reenactors portray traders, *voyageurs,* soldiers, and Native Americans in a large encampment of tents and huts. Interested in a skunk pelt? Tomahawk? Flintlock? Everything a frontier family could use is for sale. Even a contemporary suburban home can probably do with an iron kettle or two. There are black-powder musket firings, dances, fiddling, tall tales, and plenty of rough-and-ready types to photograph. In mid-July a War of 1812 military reenactment is held featuring British-Canadian and U.S. troops. The pageant is held on the lawn of the Villa Louis.

While in Prairie du Chien, stop at the **Prairie du Chien Museum at Fort Crawford,** 717 South Beaumont Road (608–326–6960; www.fortcrawford museum.com), and view its extensive collection of frontier surgical instruments and medical devices. Seen in today's light, they look more like inquisitor's tools than anything else. Dr. William Beaumont, whose studies on the digestive system revolutionized the medical world, was once stationed at Fort Crawford. While there he conducted some of his experiments on a French-Canadian trapper who had been wounded in the stomach. Beaumont would put food, tied onto a string, into the man's stomach and withdraw it for study. The doctor published a book about his experiences in 1853.

The fort, built by Zachary Taylor and Jefferson Davis, was one of the most important outposts in the young United States, especially during the Black Hawk War. Hours are 10:00 A.M. to 4:00 P.M., May, September, and October; 10:00 A.M. to 5:00 P.M., June, July, and August. Admission is $4.00 for adults; $3.25 for seniors; $2.25 for children six to twelve; five and under free; and $12.00 for families.

Grant County

Grant County is tucked into the far southwestern corner of Wisconsin, where the Mississippi joins the state with Iowa and Illinois. The county has some 49 miles of prime river frontage on its western border and 42 miles of Wisconsin River on

OTHER ATTRACTIONS WORTH SEEING

A. D. German Warehouse,
Richland Center

Cassville Car Ferry

Hamlin Garland Homestead,
West Salem

La Crosse River State Trail

Painted Forest Folk Art Museum,
Valton

Palmer-Bullickson Octagon House,
West Salem

Pump House Regional Center for the Arts,
La Crosse

its northern rim. To capitalize on this watery connection, the county operates ten boat landings on the rivers, augmenting the dozens of private put-in sites.

The landscape consists of rolling ridges and deep valleys, with thick stands of oak and maple overlooking the waterways. **Nelson Dewey State Park** and **Wyalusing State Park** offer the best scenic overviews. Each perches some 400 to 500 feet on the limestone crests towering above the valley floors. Excellent views of the confluence of the Wisconsin and the Mississippi can be had at Wyalusing on Highway X near Bagley.

Native American mounds dot both sides of the **Sentinel Ridge Trail** in Wyalusing State Park along the Mississippi River. The park is only 2 miles south of Prairie du Chien off U.S. Highway 18. After studying the mounds, many is the time we perched on the rocks high above the river and looked over the sprawling river valley below. This vista is especially great during October, when the oaks and maples are in full glory. Daughter Kate and elder Hintz even did an early spring look-see, at a time when ice still coated the shaded trails. But it was time for spring's new life to peek through the snow patches. And it did: skunk cabbage, morel mushrooms, jack-in-the-pulpit, and trillium were everywhere. You also can take this trail from the top of the bluffs at Point Lookout to a boat landing on the Mississippi. The area here is part of the **Upper Mississippi Wildlife and Fish Refuge.** Stay on the trail because the adjoining ground is marshy. Yet despite the mushiness, the bird-watching opportunities make this side trip worthwhile.

In addition to bird-watching possibilities, Nelson Dewey State Park (named after Wisconsin's first governor) near Cassville offers a good view of the **Stonefield Village** historic site (608–725–5210; www.cassville.org/stonefield.html). Take County Trunk Road VV north of town to the village (across the highway from the entrance to the state park), operated by the state historical society.

The community is a re-creation of an 1890s village, complete with railroad station, shops, firehouse, and school. The facility is open Memorial day to Labor day, 10:00 A.M. to 4:00 P.M., and then open weekends only until October 16, 10:00 A.M. to 4:00 P.M. Stonefield is a good place to bring kids, who can talk with costumed interpreters portraying characters of the period.

A moody color photo of Stonefield, taken from the Nelson Dewey bluffs just as the morning fog was shredded by the oaks, captured the grand prize in a Wisconsin tourism division photo contest. Needless to say, the place is photogenic . . . with or without the mist. So bring cameras and plenty of color and black-and-white film.

After visiting Stonefield, head into **Cassville,** the "doorway to nature's wonders and historic past." The Cassville Historical Society has drawn out a map that guides you on a walking tour of buildings constructed by early Cassville residents. The sites and buildings that are included were chosen for their architectural and/or historical significance to the development of Cassville.

The first stop on the map is the **Denniston House,** which was built in 1836. It was first constructed by a New York company, Daniels-Denniston Co., and later was purchased by Nelson Dewey, who converted the building into a hotel. This beautiful brick building has been standing tall for more than 160 years and is worth admiring. Feel free to pack a lunch and stop at Riverside Park for a picnic if you wish. It has been a village park since the 1890s. The 1889 **St. Charles Borromeo Church,** a Victorian Gothic structure built of solid brick laid upon a limestone foundation, has a steeple that soars 137 feet in the air. Open doors welcome you to enter and see the Gothic decor.

Take the tour on foot, hop on your bicycle, or cruise in your automobile.

Continue east on Highway 60 to **Boscobel** and the yellow limestone **Boscobel Hotel,** where the Gideon Bible Society was founded in 1898. A group of local businessmen formed the Christian Commercial Men's Association of America, more commonly known as the Gideons, International. They thought it would be important to place Bibles in hotel rooms to keep traveling salesmen on the straight and narrow. Since that time, the society has distributed more than ten million Bibles to lodgings around the country.

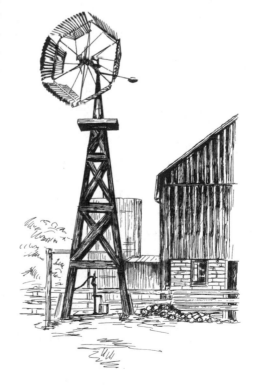

The hotel is a funky, comfortable old place that was recently remodeled with period antiques. The owners, however, decided to move back home to California and put the place up for sale. But you can still drive past the hotel with its high arched windows and plain facade at 1005 Wisconsin Avenue. And, yes, there are—or were—Gideon Bibles in each room. If you wish to stop, the hotel now houses only a tavern and most of the rest of the building is

Stonefield Village

Farm Fun

Looking for a good getaway with the clan? Spend a few days at the **Life O'Riley Farm & Guesthouse** where Jean Murphy and her family run an operating farm. Visiting parents and kids can feed chickens, pet the pig, and generally see how crops are raised and harvested. Guests stay in a renovated one-hundred-year-old-plus schoolhouse that has its own kitchen, with a fridge well stocked with homemade goodies and farm-raised eggs.

Life O'Riley has a great picnic spot on a rise overlooking the farm, where everyone can commune with nature. Little signage marks the place. "That way, people think they are the only ones who've discovered us," laughs Jean. "It's nothing fancy, but quiet and fun." It isn't really that hard to reach. Just take Riley Road, south 6 miles out of Boscobel. The farm is located at 15706 Riley Road, Boscobel (608–375–5798 or e-mail at mjmurphy@mwt.net).

closed. Room 19, where the Gideon idea was launched, can be visited if one of the bartenders is able to take a break from serving patrons.

Immediately off Wisconsin Avenue in Boscobel is the last remaining **Grand Army of the Republic (GAR) Hall** in the state. Built in the 1880s, the building has been left as it was when Civil War veterans met there to reminisce about their salad days in uniform. Plenty of memorabilia and regimental documents pack the display cases.

The hall is open at irregular hours, so it's a hit-or-miss proposition. Yet for any Civil War fan, an attempt is worth it. You'll probably be lucky.

From Boscobel, take off to Highland, driving southeast via County Roads S to T to M to Q. From Highland, go west 4 miles on Highway Q to Pine Tree Road, then north to the **Spurgeon Vineyards and Winery** for a sample of its various vintages (608–929–7692; www.spurgeonvineyards.com). The vineyards also host June Festival, a free, one-day cheese and wine tasting—and—October 8 and 9, a Fall Harvest Festival wine and cheese tasting, $1.00 hay rides, live music, and free tours. The vineyards are open 10:00 A.M. to 5:00 P.M. daily year-round except for Christmas and Easter.

Spurgeon grows such American grape varieties as the Concord and Delaware, in addition to French hybrids such as Rosette and Aurora. Prices of the distinctively labeled wines range from $7.15 to $9.95, a dollar less per bottle if you purchase by the case. Tours are $3.00, and tasting is free.

From the vineyards return to Highland and drive south on Highway 80 to the tiny community of Cobb. Go west from Cobb to **Fennimore** (www.fennimore .com). Drive through town, heading west on Highway 18 to the **Fennimore Railroad Historical Society Museum.** You can't miss the little park that features, of course, a little train. The locomotive, made by the late Vern Wilkinson, a local train buff, took several years to build. Kids love riding along the operational 15-inch gauge rail line with its 700 feet of track at the facility. An appropriately small-scale depot and water tower finish off the layout. A ticket booth has old-time telegraph equipment and a potbellied stove. Plenty of memorabilia and photos from Fennimore's railroad past can also be perused. A real narrow-gauge engine on display is appropriately known as the Dinky, which operated between Fennimore and Woodman from 1878 to 1926, meandering through the scenic Green River Valley. The museum is open daily from Memorial weekend through Labor Day from 10:00 A.M. to 4:00 P.M. and weekends only through September and October. The facility is located at 610 Lincoln Avenue (608–822–6144; railmuseum@fennimore.com).

The **Fennimore Doll Museum** (608–822–4100) has more than 5,000 dolls representing a span of generations. The dolls are made of wood, cloth, plastic, ceramic, and even stone, collected over the years by a local farm woman who wanted them to be available for viewing in her hometown, rather than in some big-city museum. Anyone who thinks dolls are too feminine will get a kick out of the display of *Star Wars* figurines and John Wayne and Roy Rogers action characters. But the biggest attraction is probably the Barbie collection, which covers the thirty-plus years from the first leggy, buxom doll to the most contemporary. All her friends and accoutrements are shown as well. The museum, on the city's main street opposite the parking lot for the Silent Woman Restaurant, is open daily from spring through late autumn. Hours vary, so it is best to call ahead. A group rate for four or more is $3.00 for adults and $1.00 for children; or $1.50 for students five to eighteen, and $3.50 for adults.

The **Fenmore Hills Motel,** 2 miles west of town on Old Highway 18, boasts "unique bridal suites." If you want to try out the circular waterbed, give the place a call at (608) 822–3281. That room costs weekend guests $125, but the rate is a mere $100 Sunday through Thursday. A regular room, with steam bath, runs $60. Add a bathroom with a whirlpool for $64. Take some cheese along, and don't forget the Spurgeon wine.

After lolling on the waterbed, continue south out of Fennimore on Highway 61 to **Lancaster** for a peek at the **Grant County Courthouse.** The imposing structure, in the middle of the

nationallyknown rockbandsfrom wisconsin

Bodeans

Little Blue Crunchy Things

The Gufs

Violent Femmes

town square, has a copper and glass double dome modeled after St. Peter's Basilica in Rome. The building was constructed in 1905, following a design by architect Armand Koch. Inside the dome are four beautiful murals painted by Franz Edward Rohrbeck. Another town landmark is the City Hall, which now includes a movie theater. Built in 1922, the building was designed by architects Claude and Starck, emphasizing a fashionable, prairie-style look. The Lancaster Chamber of Commerce (608–723–2820; lanchamber@pcii.net) can help tell of building tours and other activities around town.

The square is also the site of the first Civil War monument erected in the United States, according to local lore. The statue was dedicated on July 4, 1867, after a private and county fund drive.

Recommended Reading for Families

Alden, Sharyn. *Historical Wisconsin Getaways: Touring the Badger State's Past.* Black Earth, WI: Trails Books, 2001. 168 pp.

Bie, Michael. *Classic Wisconsin Weekends.* Black Earth, WI: Trails Books, 2003. 240 pp.

Brown, Harriet. *Madison Walks.* Madison: Jones Press, 2003. 124 pp.

Davenport, Don. *Natural Wonders of Wisconsin.* Castine, ME: Country Roads Press, 1995. 158 pp.

Hintz, Martin. *Hiking Wisconsin.* Champaign, IL: Human Kinetics, 1997. 212 pp.

Hintz, Martin, and Daniel Hintz. *Day Trips from Milwaukee.* Guilford, CT: The Globe Pequot Press, 2002. 288 pp.

Hintz, Martin, and Stephen Hintz. *Fun with the Family Wisconsin.* Guilford, CT: The Globe Pequot Press, 2004. 272 pp.

Hintz, Martin, and Bob Rashid. *Backroads of Wisconsin: Your Guide to Wisconsin's Most Scenic Backroad Adventures.* Stillwater, MN: Voyageur Books, 2002. 160 pp.

Johnson, Steve. *Biking Wisconsin: 50 Great Road and Trail Rides.* Black Earth, WI: Trails Books, 2004. 120 pp.

Knowles, Gary. *The Great Wisconsin Touring Book.* Black Earth, WI: Trails Books, 2000. 162 pp.

McGrath, Chad. *Great Cross-Country Ski Trails.* Black Earth, WI: Trails Books, 2001. 240 pp.

Smith, Susan Lampert. *Wisconsin Family Weekends.* Black Earth, WI: Trails Books, 2000. 160 pp.

Stuttgen, Joanne Raetz. *Café Wisconsin: A Guide to Wisconsin's Down-Home Cafes.* Madison, WI: University of Wisconsin Press, 2004. 392 pp.

The "great, big, tall" monument (as proudly described by Lancaster citizens) is on the northeast side of the square and consists of a central marble pillar surrounded by eight smaller pillars. The memorial is inscribed with the names of 755 Grant County soldiers who either died or were injured during the Civil War. Don't confuse that monument with the one erected in 1906 by the ladies' auxiliary of the Grand Army of the Republic, a soldier atop a pedestal on the northwest side of the courthouse.

funfacts

The Wisconsin state song is "On, Wisconsin," with words by J. S. Hubbard and Charles D. Rose. The music was composed by William T. Purdy.

On the southeast corner is a statue of Grant County resident Nelson Dewey, who was the county's first clerk of courts in 1836 and Wisconsin's first governor in 1848. Dewey is perched importantly in a chair, looking appropriately governor-like. Dewey's Lancaster home is located at 147 West Hickory Street, now occupied by an insurance agency. I've been told the folks there will probably let you peek around a bit, if you come during business hours.

Look at the display on the first floor of the courthouse featuring the county's collection of Civil War memorabilia. Much of it was donated by the family of Gen. John Clark, the town's resident Civil War general- long deceased, of course. Among the artifacts is a captured Confederate battle flag.

After spending an hour or two wandering around Lancaster and admiring the older homes and commercial buildings, follow Highway 61 south to 133, which leads to Potosi, an old lead-mining boomtown tucked into a deep, skinny valley.

Around the War of 1812 most of the lead mined in the country came from this region. Several of the villages were larger than Chicago and Milwaukee at the time. Today all you see are the remains of pits and furnaces where the mostly Welsh and Cornish miners set up camp. The state's nickname, "The Badger State," came from these early miners. Let me explain: When the men first moved to the vicinity, prior to building barracks, they dug shallow trenches in the hillsides to get away from the rain. The holes served as protection from marauding Native Americans as well, since they were always dug near another miner's hideaway for a musket crossfire. In calmer days visitors saw these holes in the slopes and likened them to badger burrows, hence the state's nickname. Some of these pits, framed by low stone barricades, can be seen on the hillsides around *Potosi.*

The workmen who went south in the winter, when some of the mines closed for the season, were called "suckers," after a type of Mississippi River fish.

There are about forty crumbled old buildings, open pit mines, smelters, and huts scattered around the vicinity of the one-street town, once the leading port on the northern Mississippi. By 1833, more than 237 steamboats were making regular stops at Potosi. River towns along this stretch of the Mississippi all the way to Fort Snelling in St. Paul, Minnesota, used the town as a storage facility for whiskey, flour, trade goods, bacon, and munitions. The boats would leave the docks laden with lead, heading for New Orleans and ocean-bound freighters. Hard-swearing teamsters picked up the supplies the paddle wheelers dropped off and hauled them inland, using huge carts pulled by ten oxen at a time over muddy trails.

Years ago, a "Ripley's Believe It or Not" column said that Potosi's main street was the longest in the world without an intersection. It extended some 5 miles through the valley, linking the scattered mining sites and ethnic enclaves such as British Hollow (built by the English) and Van Buren (home for Dutch settlers). There's not much there now, except for scattered gas stations and several antiques stores. Developers have considered refurbishing the battered but still serviceable Potosi Brewery building into a complex of crafts shops or even reopening it as a brewery. Several local residents established a foundation in 1999 to attempt preserving what is left of the dilapidated old facility and reconnect the town with its brewing heritage. To accomplish this, they sponsor dinners and raffles to raise funds for a restoration. To help, contact the Potosi Brewery Foundation, Inc., Box 177, 209 South Main Potosi, 53820 (www.potosi brewery.com).

The *St. John Mine* (608–763–2121) in Potosi is open for summer touring, after a succession of owners attempted to make it a tourist attraction. Stories about the mine date from 1640, when French explorers found Winnebagos living there and mining lead for trade. After a peace treaty was signed with local Winnebago tribes in 1827, miners poured into southwestern Wisconsin. One intrepid soul who became rich during those rough-and-tumble lead-mining days was Willis St. John, after whom the largest mine was named. Mining in the vicinity died out during the Gold Rush of 1849, but there was a resurgence throughout the Civil War. In that conflict, Wisconsin's mines provided most of the lead for the Northern armies. The lead deposits eventually petered out, and the St. John Mine officially closed in 1870.

Today, watch your step in walking up the steep slope to the cavern, and be sure to take comfortable walking shoes if you plan to enter the mine. Once inside, you can still see on the walls the pick and chisel marks made in those early days. It's an eerie feeling.

There's good canoeing along the Grant, Big Platte, and Little Platte Rivers near Potosi. It's best to bring your own equipment because of the difficulty in finding an outfitter that stays in business from year to year. Among the better put-in spots along the Grant is one at Klondike Springs on the left bank of County Trunk K, which can give you a nineteen-hour run downstream to the Potosi boat landing on the Mississippi if your muscles are so inclined.

Louthain Bridge on the right bank of County Trunk B is a fine set-off on the Big Platte. For the Little Platte, try the Church Road Bridge (right bank on Church Road), Shinoe Bridge (where Highways 61 and 35 intersect—use the right bank), or the Banfield Bridge public boat landing.

If you need a break from canoeing, make a stop at a funky museum. Rollo Jamison, a Beetown farmer/repair-shop owner/tavernkeeper/janitor, had a fever for collecting just about anything. He filled sheds with "valuables," organizing his finds into categories: stoves, vending machines, farm machinery, and so on. When the ninety-three-year-old Jamison died in 1981, the city of Platteville took over the assemblage of oddities and moved everything to the old high school, where it can currently be viewed.

Now called the **Rollo Jamison Museum,** the school building at 405 East Main Street is open daily May 1 through October 31 from 9:00 A.M. to 5:00 P.M. It also is open November through April from 9:00 A.M. to 4:00 P.M. Monday through Friday.

Next door to the Jamison place is the **Mining Museum,** where visitors can descend ninety, count 'em, ninety steps down into a shaft of the **Bevans Lead Mine,** reopened in 1976. Above ground, rides are given on a train of ore cars pulled by a restored mine locomotive. For those with phobias about knocking their heads on the ceiling, hard hats are standard issue at the entrance. From May 1 until the end of October, the museum is open from 9:00 A.M. to 5:00 P.M. Monday through Friday. From November 1 to April 30, it's open daily 9:00 A.M. to 4:00 P.M. Tours of the mine are offered only May through October, with the exception of reserved groups. There is a small admission charge. The museum, located in a refurbished schoolhouse, is at 405 East Main Street (608–348–3301).

The mine was discovered in 1845 by Lorenzo Bevans, who had used his life's resources and was in debt up to his high-brow nose while searching for lead. On a mid-July day of that year, he could afford to pay his hired hand only until noon. But the fellow agreed to stay on until the end of the day. At 2:00 that afternoon, the two men broke into one of the richest veins of lead ever discovered in southwestern Wisconsin.

Before leaving Grant County, check out the **Dickeyville Grotto,** built by parish priest Father Mathias Wernerus. The dedicated clergyman assembled bottles, stone, glass, and other cast-off artifacts to make his shrine, spending the years 1925 to 1929 collecting, hauling, and cementing the whole thing together. "We built better than we knew" was his motto. About seven carloads of rock were taken from quarries around the Midwest, with other stones coming from every state and from the Holy Land. Some Chippewa Indians from northern Wisconsin even donated arrowheads and axes for inclusion in one section. The grotto, on the east and south sides of Holy Cross Church, is located at 305 Main Street (608–568–3119). Hours are 9:00 A.M. to 5:00 P.M. daily, April 15 through October. Donations are accepted. Father Wernerus's grave is in the rear of the church.

In addition to Father Wernerus's glittering, ponderous masterpiece, Dickeyville is noted for its more secular May and September motorcycle and four-wheel-drive hill climbs and tractor pulls.

Not that all roads lead to Dickeyville, but most do in this corner of Wisconsin. To get to this old German farming community, take either Highways 61, 35, or 151.

Green County

Folks in Green County brag that their landscape is a Little Switzerland. They certainly are correct when it comes to driving over hills and dales that could easily pass for alpine meadows. For this reason, thousands of Swiss émigrés settled here in the 1800s. Their tidy homesteads dot the countryside, where cows outnumber people five to three.

In 1986 Green County celebrated its 150th anniversary, a fete topped off by the opening of the refurbished courthouse in **Monroe,** the county seat. The town's fund-raisers, "The Steeple People," collected nearly $50,000 for the restoration of the building's ornate tower and its four-sided clock.

But Monroe isn't just a place to sit on your hands in the town square and watch the time pass. The community hosts the annual county fair, something it has been doing since 1853. In late July the exposition of giant vegetables, nose-wriggling rabbits, beefy cattle, rounds of delicious cheese, grandma's pickles, and 4-H crafts creates a lot of hoopla for celebrating farm life.

A must-see attraction to visit in Monroe is the **Jos. Huber Brewing Company,** in business since Wisconsin became a state in 1848. Free tours are offered daily here, at one of the few small, privately owned breweries remaining in the state. Samples of the clear, light Huber brews are de rigueur, of course.

Say *Lactobacillus bulgaricus* in Monroe, and nobody's eyebrows will go up. The bacteria is one of the ingredients in manufacturing Swiss cheese, an economic mainstay in the Monroe area with its twenty-three factories (a total of thirty-six are in the county).

The limestone subsoil makes this heart of Wisconsin's dairyland rich in the

Green County Tours

Green County is an antiques lovers' paradise, with nooks and crannies in several towns offering "the stuff 'o grannies" that make for charming home decorating. Dedicated treasure hunters claim they can spend upwards of a week scouring the area's shops for that "perfect find." As always, call ahead to confirm times and to see if the proprietors have any specialties, whether furniture, jewelry, farm equipment, photos, or related items. Here are several places from which to start that search: **Bev's Attic Treasures,** 1018½ 17th Avenue (608–325–6200) and **The Recovery,** 1204 19th Street (608–325–5916), both in Monroe; **Glarnerladen Antiques & Collectibles,** 101 6th Avenue, New Glarus (608–527–6325); **Ott To Recover,** 203 North Main Street, Monticello 53570 (608–938–4124); and **Center Avenue Antique Mall,** 1027 1st Center Avenue, Brodhead (608–897–2696). Happy hunting.

right kind of milk for Muenster, Limburger, and other cheese varieties, as well as Swiss. The county's Holsteins and Brown Swiss are truly contented cows.

Many of the plants in the county allow visitors, but you have to be on hand by noon or most of the day's work will be over. The factories kick into gear around 5:00 A.M. For a list of licensed outlets, write Cheese Days, Box 606, Monroe 53566. The plants, all members of the Foreign Type Cheesemakers Association (FTCA), are headquartered in town. The members sponsor the Monroe Cheese Days, held in September every even-numbered year. These Big Cheeses of the county's agricultural community offer an average of eleven tons of the stuff for nibbling at these events. When they say "cheese," they mean it! The festival features a Cheesemaker's Kickoff Ball, Cheese Day Chase marathon run, cheese-making demonstrations, factory tours, and, of course, lots of cheese sandwiches.

After the festivities, go on a cheese hunt throughout Green County, concentrating on the Monroe area. But first, cheese-seekers need a bit of history, so stop at the *Historic Cheesemaking Center,* 2108 Seventh Avenue, Monroe. The center is in a restored depot, with exhibits on cheese-making and its impact on Green County. The building is open daily from March to mid-November, 10:00 A.M. to 4:00 P.M.; December on Friday only, 10:00 A.M. to 4:00 P.M.; and is closed January and February. Contact Jim Glessner at (608) 325–4636 for more information.

Now everyone should be set to explore the rolling hills around the city. Here are a few production plants that offer fun tours or a place to pick up a wheel of Edam. *Chalet Cheese Cooperative* (608–325–4343); *Chula Vista Cheese Company* (608–439–5211); *Decatur Dairy* (608–897–8661); *Deppeler Cheese Factory* (608–325–6311); *Franklin Cheese Cooperative* (608–325–3725); *Klondike Cheese*

Biking and Cheese

Located in the heart of dairy country, the Cheese Country Trail links Monroe, Browntown, South Wayne Gratiot, and Mineral Point. The trail system accommodates horseback riders, hikers, snowmobilers, bikers, all-terrain vehicles, and skiers. There are at least thirty cheese factories in the three counties—Green, Lafayette, and Iowa—that incorporate the trail system. Some sections of the Cheese Country Trail have included elements of the Pecatonica Trail. Links are marked for the appropriate use: ATVs, for example, aren't allowed where horses can be ridden, so be alert for signage. A $6.00 trail-user fee is required and can be purchased at most gas stations near the trail and at other businesses in towns along the way.

Company (608–325–3226); *Maple Leaf Cheese Factory Outlet* (608–934–1237); *Roth Kase USA* (608–328–3355); *Swiss Heritage Cheese Factory* (608–938–4455); and *Torkelson's Prairie Hill Cheese Plant* (608–325–2918). For more information, contact Green County Tourism (608–328–1838; www.greencounty.org).

One of the top bike jaunts in Wisconsin is along the 23.5-mile **Sugar River Trail,** which meanders through the county along an abandoned railroad right-of-way. Even though the route opened in 1986, it has yet to "be discovered" by hordes of outsiders.

Cyclists eighteen and older need a trail permit, however, which can be obtained at Sugar River headquarters at the New Glarus Woods State Park, Box 781, New Glarus 53574 (608–527–2335 or 888–222–9111). Bikes can be rented at the park, but car shuttle service is not available.

The gently rolling grade is barely 1 percent, making it a great trip for short-legged kids. For puffing oldsters there are plenty of pit stops along the way in **New Glarus,** Monticello, Albany, and Brodhead. Better than Epsom salts is a foot soak in the Sugar River, where a covered bridge spans the stream near Brodhead. It's also a good place to hunker down while waiting out a rainstorm. The ford is one of fourteen along the route as the trail zigzags back and forth across the river and its tributaries. The route is also excellent for fervid cross-country skiers during Wisconsin's blustery winters. Midway between connecting points of New Glarus on the north and Brodhead on the south is the **Albany Wildlife Refuge.** Look for the herons and other bird life that inhabit the reeds and woodlands. The Sugar River Trail is also part of the 1,000-mile-long **Ice Age National Scenic Trail** that connects routes throughout Wisconsin.

Pause while biking and take in the **New Glarus Woods**—with its 350 acres of woods, farmland, and prairie—a favorite picnic spot for area families. Check out the following park trails: The **Basswood Nature Trail** is less than 0.5 mile long, running from the picnic area near the park office to the north of County Highway NN. *Chattermark Trail* loops from the campgrounds through an oak and maple grove. Pick up the *Great Oak Trail* for a short stroll around the north end of the park, departing from the edge of the primitive camping area. The *Walnut Trail* proceeds south from the west end of the campground and links with the *Havenridge Nature Trail.* The latter is the most extensive system in the park with loops north and south of County NN. It leads through heavy groves of oak and maple and past extensive prairie plantings. Redwing blackbirds, turkey vultures, sparrows, wrens, and other birds swoop and soar overhead as you trek along trails framed by the tall bluestem and swaying buffalo grass. It makes for a special time, especially on a hot August afternoon. A cool drink back in the shade of oak groves will be truly appreciated.

For information on the park, contact the Park Superintendent, c/o Wisconsin Department of Natural Resources, Pleasant View Annex, Monroe 53593. In the summer, call (608) 527-2335; winter, (608) 325-4844 or www.dnr.state.wi. To find the site, take State Highway 69, 4 miles south of New Glarus.

New Glarus probably epitomizes all those Green County placemat images of Switzerland. Settled by pioneers from the Swiss canton of Glarus in 1845, the town remains small. Only about 1,700 citizens live here, so it's not hard to find your way around. In the summer, downtown shops and many homes feature window boxes exploding with crimson geraniums.

Many of the houses in the community date from the turn of the twentieth century, and a *Swiss historical village* on the west side of town shows how life was on the Wisconsin frontier prior to the Civil War. The cluster of buildings at

biketouring

Bill Howda of Bike Wisconsin offers two major tours in the summer pedaling season. He can be reached at wisbike@mhtc.net, call toll-free at (888) 575-3640, or write to Bike Wisconsin, P.O. Box 310, Spring Green 53588. One of the most popular tours is the weeklong Great Annual Bike Adventure Along the Wisconsin River (GRABAAWR; www.grabaawr.com). Usually more than 1,000 riders puff, pant, and pedal in early June on a 490-mile run from Eagle River near the Wisconsin-Michigan border to Prairie du Chien, where the Wisconsin and Mississippi rivers link. Then, in early August, the Sprocket's Annual Great Bicycle Ride Across Wisconsin (SAGBRAW; www.grabaawr.com/sagbraw-main page.html) is another weeklong ride over mostly flat terrain. Between 1,000–1,200 dedicated cyclists participate. There are three ways to do this 340-mile run: use the provided motor coach and bike transport to the start, make your own way to the kickoff site, or merely register for daily portions of the jaunt.

612 Seventh Avenue (608–527–2317) is open daily 10:00 A.M. to 4:00 P.M., May through October. No designated time for last tour. Admission is $7.00 for adults, $3.00 for ages six through thirteen and free for age five and under.

The townspeople harken back to their heritage with locally staged summertime productions of *Heidi,* the famed folktale of the Swiss mountain girl, and *Wilhelm Tell,* of apple-shooting fame. Women from New Glarus made all the costumes for the shows, staged in the town's outdoor amphitheater. Don't despair in case of rain—with inclement weather, the shows are readily moved to the high school auditorium.

Need a rest? Outgoing Swiss-born hosteler Hans Lenzlinger owns and manages the New Glarus Hotel (608–527–5244), a chalet-style hostelry bedecked with flowers hanging from heavy wooden balconies.

For a varied New Glarus/Green County munch other than cheese, try Flannery's **Wilhelm Tell Supper Club,** featuring a respectably extensive Swiss menu. The club is located at 114 Second Street. You will need to call for weekend reservations (608–527–2618).

You can load up on typical souvenirs at the town's several gift shops, but for a special keepsake, the **Swiss Miss Lace Factory and Textile Mart** has some out-of-this-world embroideries and lace.

Iowa County

Nope, you aren't in the wrong state when you come to Iowa. The county is in the heart of the Hidden Valleys tourism area of southwestern Wisconsin. **Mineral Point,** a prime jumping-off spot for an off-the-beaten-path adventure, is one of the oldest communities in the state. It was founded in 1827 by lead miners who easily scooped up the precious metal from surface pits near the town. Evidence of their digging can be spotted from any backcountry road in the vicinity.

Peek into the miners' past at Mineral Point's **Pendarvis,** a complex of restored cabins built by settlers from Cornwall more than 150 years ago, when the streets of southwestern Wisconsin were paved with zinc and lead, not gold. The new arrivals immediately began quarrying Galena limestone for use in their cottages.

Walking along Tamblyn's Row, a stretch of rowhouses, you'd think you were back in England. Shake Rag Alley is typical of the street names. Its moniker is derived from the practice of the miners' wives waving their aprons or dish towels from the house windows when lunch was ready. The Pendarvis property was acquired by the state historical society in 1971. It is open daily 10:00 A.M. to 5:00 P.M., May through October. Guided tours are offered as well (608–987–2122; www.wisconsinhistory.org/sites/pend). The last tour leaves at 4:00 P.M. The facility is administered by the State Historical Society of Wisconsin.

Admission is $8.00 for adults, $7.20 for seniors, and $4.00 for youngsters ages five to twelve. Discount rates are offered for children's groups. Families (two adults and two or more dependent children) can pay $22.00.

While in the neighborhood, try a Cornish pasty (*past-ee*), a meat pie with a thin crust that a worker would take with him to the mine facing. Most of the town's bakeries and restaurants offer these ethnic delicacies. Try one at the **Red Rooster Cafe,** 158 High Street, in Mineral Point (608–987–9936). The cafe has been a local favorite for more than thirty years. Prices are moderate.

Take Highway 151 from Mineral Point to **Dodgeville,** seat of Iowa County and home of the state's oldest courthouse, which dates from 1859. South of Dodgeville about 2 miles, just off Highway 18, is the **Folklore Village** (608–924–4000; www.folklorevillage.org), which offers regular Saturday-night folk dancing and singing programs in the old Wakefield Schoolhouse. The place is the brainchild of Jane Farwell, who usually is on hand wearing Tyrolean peasant clothing. Since the 1940s Jane has set up folk-dance camps and seminars around the country, bringing that expertise with her to Wisconsin in the mid-1960s. Throughout the week, craft demonstrations, programs for youngsters, and music lessons are held. Holiday time has ongoing fun. Scandinavian midsummer feasts, Ukrainian and Greek Easters, Israeli Purim, husking bees, and other events fill the calendar.

Drive north of Dodgeville on Highway 23 to the **FantaSuite Don Q Resort.** You'll know that you've arrived after spotting the grounded Boeing prop C-97 parked alongside the highway. The ninety-ton beast was flown to the site, parked there, and left as is by the resort's flamboyant former owner, Ron Dentinger. A 67-foot-high tree made of steel wagon wheels also has been erected outside the building, just in case somebody misses the plane while driving past.

The Don Q is one of the kinds of places that make a weekend away a something-else eyebrow-raising treat. One of the rooms is in a spire from an old Methodist church adjacent to the main complex. On the bottom floor of the steeple are the bathroom facilities; on the second level is a queen-size bed; on the third is a stereo complex, a pile of pillows, and windows for the best view (if you're looking) of the countryside around Dodgeville. It's a great place to try an in-spire-ed "let down your long hair" routine on your lady love. Sixteen of the Don Q's forty-six suites have hanging beds, baths made from copper cheese vats, and assorted similar, delightfully quirky wonders. Try the Float Room, with a queen-size bed set in a Viking ship, a heart-shaped hydrotherapy tub, and mirrors on the wall ($105 Sunday through Thursday and $125 Friday and Saturday). Or how about Tranquillity Base, featuring a re-creation of a Gemini space capsule and a ten-sided waterbed? The rates differ for each type of suite. The FantaSuite suites range from $149 during the week to $199 on weekends. The Original Theme suites are $105 Sunday through Wednesday and $125 on Friday and Saturday. Deluxe suites are $174 during the week, $224 on weekends. Call (800) 666–7848. The restaurant on the premises is in a salvaged barn.

Just before the Don Q is the ***Walnut Hollow Farm*** (608–935–2341), which turned a cottage corporation into a national business, growing from 5 employees to 129 in fifteen years. Walnut Hollow is on Highway 23 North.

Using cross sections of tree limbs harvested in the state, Walnut Hollow makes several hundred products for the wood craft industry. The first week of August holds the annual Warehouse Clearance Sale. Walnut Hollow has won many awards for its environmental activities. As much of the wood waste as possible is recycled or used to fire the company's two boilers. In addition, a lot is peddled as bedding for livestock. The firm's employees have also planted more than 250,000 trees and shrubs around the area.

Walnut Hollow is open 9:00 A.M. to 5:00 P.M. Monday through Saturday and 11:00 A.M. to 4:00 P.M. Sunday. It's closed on Sunday from November through April (800–950–5101; 608–935–2341; www.walnuthollow.com). Ordering can be done via catalog.

Immediately to the north of the Don Q is the entrance to ***Governor Dodge State Park,*** a sprawling preserve of 5,000 acres with two lakes, camping sites, hiking trails, and fishing spots.

Nearby is Spring Green's ***House on the Rock,*** a home perched on a pinnacle of stone called Deershelter Rock, 450 feet above the floor of Wyoming Valley near the Baraboo Range. The home was built in the 1940s by Alex Jordan, a noted Wisconsin sculptor and art collector. It was opened to the public in 1961.

A musical museum and the world's largest carousel (weighing in at thirty-five tons and standing 80 feet high) are located at the base of the rock. Most of the home is open for touring, with passageways cut through the rock and neat nooks and crannies set aside for reading, loafing, or peering out over the countryside far below.

Jordan had a penchant for doing big things. The central fire pit is large enough to roast a woolly mammoth (critters that actually roamed the valley a few millennia before the House on the Rock was built).

The buildings are open for tours March 15 to October 31. Tickets go on sale at 9:00 A.M., with the last tickets being sold about one hour prior to early evening closing, due to the time it takes to tour the complex. Hours vary from spring to summer; call (608) 935–3639 or www.thehouseontherock.com for more information. Admission is $19.50 for adults ages thirteen and up, and $10.50 for ages five to twelve; four and under are free. A group of twenty or more can get a discounted tour rate. Sales tax will be added to the admission price.

The Spring Green area (Iowa and Sauk Counties along the Wisconsin River) was called home by famed architect *Frank Lloyd Wright,* who worked there on his uncle's farm as a kid. The crusty, eccentric, and brilliant Wright built his home, *Taliesin,* into the brow of a hill near the Wisconsin River (Iowa County). The building is not open to the public, but other Wright structures in the area are.

Before the junction of Highway 23 and County Road C is the Wright-designed *Hillside Home School* (Iowa County), which includes a drafting studio and galleries displaying some of the builder's notable designs. The school is open for visitors from late June through Labor Day. Tours are at 10:30 A.M.; and 12:30, 2:30, and 4:30 P.M. Admission is charged. For information call (608) 588–7900.

A wide range of tour prices is available, depending on the length of time a guest wishes to spend at the facility, which buildings are toured, the number of visitors in a group, and the ages of the participants. We recommend that you call or check Taliesin's comprehensive Web site to determine which program is best for you (www.taliesinpreservation.org).

The Right Place at the Wright Time

Famed architect Frank Lloyd Wright made central Wisconsin his home base during the peak of his career. A visitors center (open 9:00 A.M. to 6:00 P.M.; 608–588–7900; www.taliesinpreservation.org) and restaurant at the corner of Highway 23 and County Road C is the starting point for tours. Many Wright-connected buildings are in Jones Valley, 3 miles south of Spring Green on Highway 23. Hillside tours are held daily May through October every hour on the half hour between 10:30 A.M. and 4:30 P.M. Tours range from $15 to $80 per person. From April to November, shuttle tours are offered for $20 a person.

This natural getaway was at least one reason why Wright loved this area so much. He established his *Taliesin* studio as a "hope and a haven" for creative thinking; it became a complex of buildings that shaped design for generations. At Taliesin, Wright developed plans for the Imperial Hotel in Japan, the Johnson Wax administration building in Racine, and other marvelous structures. Tours of his former home, now a national landmark, are regular components of the tourist scene in the area. Wright designed the elaborate, 300-foot-long visitors center, as well. Tell the kids that the trusses throughout the center were made from the skeleton of the *Ranger,* a World War II aircraft carrier, and they should be impressed.

Folks in Spring Green still reminisce about the master architect's strolling about the town as if he owned it. Although Wright died in 1959, the town of Spring Green in Sauk County remains the headquarters for Taliesin Associated Architects and the Frank Lloyd Wright School of Architecture. Buildings designed by the architectural firm include the Valley Bank in downtown Spring Green. To see other Wright buildings, stop at the *Riverview Terrace Cafe* inside the Frank Lloyd Wright Center at Taliesin on Highway 23 along the banks of the Wisconsin River (608–588–7937) or swing past *Wyoming Valley School,* 4 miles south of Taliesin on Highway 23. The last two are in Iowa County.

While in the Spring Green area, turn east on County Road C off Highway 14 to get to the *American Players Theater.* Its resident troupe presents Shakespearean productions and other classics during the summer.

Bring bug repellent and dress for the weather, because seating is under the open sky. There's something fantastic about watching *A Midsummer Night's Dream* under an umbrella of stars. The theater was constructed by Korean-American actor Randall Duk Kim and his associates in 1980. For a time the company was treading thin financial ice, but a concerted marketing effort and aggressive ticket promotions saved the day. With the crowds you'll now need to have reservations. Contact the theater at Box 819, Spring Green 53588 (608–588–7401) for the year's production lineup.

For the best in relaxation, try the *House on the Rock Golf Club Resort* (800–822–7774; www.thehouseontherock.com), across the country road from the American Players Theater. It is one of the classiest resorts in western Wisconsin, with a gourmet chef, family health-club programs, and—of course —golf, golf, golf. There is a Wright feel to the place, with its rooms and interior furnishings that bespeak comfort without overstating it. And there is space for skis, golf clubs, and other outdoor gear as well, along with a microwave, refrigerator, and kitchen nook in each suite. The resort hosts a gourmet nature trek each autumn (call for the date), where wine might be served with a pheasant pâté and Wisconsin cheese at one trail stop, a cold cucumber soup and black bread at another, chocolate-covered strawberries and mile-

franklloydwright– designedbuildings

A. D. German Warehouse, Richland Center

Annunciation Greek Orthodox Church, Milwaukee

S. C. Johnson Wax Administration Building, Racine

Seth Petterson Cottage, Lake Delton (available for vacation rentals)

Unitarian Meeting House, Madison

Seek and Ye Shall Find Old Stuff

The Wisconsin Department of Tourism has developed *The Wisconsin Heritage Traveler,* a guide to the state's Heritage Sign Program. The project is the nation's first to identify historic sites for the traveling public through uniform directional road signs.

The Wisconsin Historic Traveler lists 121 historic sites, districts, museums, and heritage areas that offer opportunities to poke around the state's history and culture. The sites are referenced by number so they can be easily found in the book and on the road . . . a great idea.

The free, one-hundred-page publication is available to the public at each of the eleven Wisconsin Travel Information Centers, participating historic sites, or by calling (800) 432–8747 or (800) 372–2737 or visiting www.travelwisconsin.com.

The historical importance of each location, along with the address, phone number, hours of operation, and services available, are provided in the guide. Easy-to-read maps illustrate site locations.

When on the road, look for the brown-and-white signs that feature an outline of the state and the word Heritage along with the reference number of the site.

high cheesecake at the next. And so it goes for the entire length of the trudge across the maple-shrouded ridges behind the resort. Eat as much as you want; you will work off any calories picked up along the way.

La Crosse County

La Crosse County marks the northwestern boundary of the Hidden Valleys tourism region. The city of **La Crosse,** population 50,000, is the largest in the western part of Wisconsin. The French named the site after watching a rough-and-tumble Native American game that utilized long-handled racquets.

The competition reminded the trappers of the aristocratic game of tennis, called *la crosse.* A statue by Elmer Peterson in front of the La Crosse Radisson Hotel depicts several Native Americans swinging into action during a spirited match.

A good place to keep an eye on all the folks in town is from atop the 500-foot **Grandad's Bluff** on the east side of the city. From the sharp drop-off, the flatlands leading to the Mississippi look like a slightly rumpled bedsheet covered with toy houses and crisscrossed by tiny cars.

To get to the bluff, take Main Street through town toward Hixon Forest. It's quite a drive up to the parking lots near the crest, but some tough bikers always seem to be puffing their way upwards.

Not me. I've always preferred to drive and arrive refreshed. Telescopes at the far end of the observation platform can be used to spot La Crosse landmarks, such as the city's meeting center, the G. Heileman Brewery grain elevators, and the playing fields of the University of Wisconsin–La Crosse. As for the last, you'll get better seats for viewing athletic events in the stadium stands. But it's a challenge to try to pick out which football team is which from that distance. Look for the varied colored jerseys. About midway up the roadway in the rear of Grandad's Bluff is a refreshment stand for quick sandwiches and soda.

From I–90 take Highway 53 south to State Street and go west to Riverside Park, where the La Crosse and Black Rivers join the Mississippi. At the north end of the park is **Riverside USA,** with an animated display focusing on the history of the Mississippi River. At the park, kids can try captaining a riverboat, the *Belle of La Crosse.* The pilothouse is a reproduction of what an actual vessel would look and sound like. Riverside USA is open daily during the summer from 10:00 A.M. to 5:00 P.M.

From the park take a ninety-minute cruise on the real thing, the **La Crosse Queen.** The 300-passenger stern-wheeler departs regularly for cruises along the river. Perching on the upper deck, leaning back in a chair, and admiring the sun's rays dancing across the water is a grand way to laze away a summer afternoon. For information or reservations, contact the *La Crosse Queen,* Box 1805, La Crosse 54602-1805 (for dinner cruises, 608–784–2893; for charter and group sales, 608–784–8523; www.greatriver.com/laxqueen/paddle .htm). The riverboat dock is located in Riverside Park, at the west end of State Street in downtown La Crosse.

Some years back, a friend and I tried a more rugged approach to the river. We took a small boat, loaded it with camping gear at a La Crosse dock, and aimed downstream for a week's adventure. Cruising past the 25-foot-tall, twenty-five-ton *Hiawatha* statue at the confluence of the La Crosse, Black, and Mississippi Rivers, we waved goodbye to comfort for a week. Of course, it was late autumn. The wind was fierce, the rain crept up under our ponchos, and the fish weren't biting. But that was all still ahead of us as we set off. Now, older and just a bit wiser, I'd still take such a jaunt out of town, but I'd probably do it in the summer aboard a houseboat.

Performing a Huck Finn routine on the Mississippi River is as easy as vacationing aboard a Mississippi River houseboat. **Fun 'n the Sun Houseboat Rentals** of La Crosse has three-day weekend, four-day midweek, and weeklong options for a family. Fun 'n the Sun is one of several companies in the area that put fully equipped boats on the river. All you need is the grub. If you get really hungry, go fishing! What we've liked about such river houseboating is the ability to go either upriver or downriver. (We became houseboating fans

La Crosse Queen

after a trip to Canada's New Brunswick when the kids were small.) Contact Fun 'n the Sun in Alma, 2221 State Highway 35; (888) 343–5670.

The city's nationally known fall festival, **Oktoberfest,** is held at the end of September. Capitalizing on the Germanic heritage of many of its current residents, the nine-day festival offers something for the entire family, including the Grand Maple Leaf Parade, authentic German entertainment, arts and crafts for sale, the Torchlight Parade, plenty of polka parties, beer tents, and grilled bratwurst (608–784–FEST).

Winter is a good time to come to the La Crosse area. There are numerous cross-country ski trails that range from beginner to advanced. Try pathways near the city in Hixon Forest, Blue Bird Springs, Goose Island, and Perrot State Park. For trail guides contact the La Crosse Convention and Visitors Bureau, 410 East Veterans Memorial Drive, La Crosse 54601 (800–658–9424; www .explorelacrosse.com).

Regardless of the season, however, La Crosse and its surrounding area have activities that are off the beaten path or off the wall, but not off the mark. Pen these suggestions in the old date book, starting with February and **Mardi Gras.** Just before Lent you can party before doing your penance—forty days' worth, according to the Roman Catholic religious calendar. The city's Mardi Gras weekend kicks off at the La Crosse Center, starting with a celebrity auction and masquerade ball. Dates vary from year to year, depending on when Lent falls. In that case, for details, contact La Crosse Mardi Gras, Box 1433, La Crosse 54602-1433 (608–782–3169; www.lacrossemardigras.com).

Reggae Sunsplash in May brings a bit of the Caribbean to Wisconsin, to dazzle the spring with lively music and Jamaican food at the Trempealeau Hotel. Call (608) 534–6898. **Catfish Days** celebrate one of the state's great-tasting fish.

Events are held at the Village Park in nearby West Salem. Softball tournaments, a crafts fair, a tractor pull, a parade, and music are on tap.

In July, **Riverfest** brings top-name entertainers to the city's Riverside Park. A Venetian parade on the Mississippi River lends an exotic touch. Call (608) 782–6000. August's **Art Fair on the Green** attracts artists from around the country, who exhibit their work on the campus of the University of Wisconsin–La Crosse. Call (800) 658–9424 or (608) 788–7439. A **Holiday Folk Fair** is held in November at the **La Crosse Center,** with wares showcased by more than 130 vendors. Items are geared specifically to the holidays. Call (608) 789–7410.

There's no need to miss any of those events because you don't know the time. Visit the **La Crosse Clock Company,** 125 South Second Street, (608) 782–8200. There are more than 1,000 timepieces on the shelves in the shop, which is across from the Radisson Hotel and the Civic Center in downtown La Crosse. The wide range of cuckoos, grandfather, mantel, and other clocks will keep you on schedule.

Downhill skiing is pretty good at **Mount La Crosse,** 2 miles south of the city on Highway 35. The hill has a 516-foot vertical drop and a run of 5,300 feet. It also offers cross-country skiing, instructions, and rentals. Call (608) 788–0044 (800–426–3665 if you're calling outside of Wisconsin) or www.mtlacrosse.com.

Here are more exceptional locales for winter thrills in the La Crosse area: **Bluebird Springs Recreation Area,** N2833 Smith Valley Road, (608) 781–

Milk Anyone?

Southern and southwestern Wisconsin have some of the state's prime dairy-herd acreage. It's a fact obvious to anyone driving past pasture after pasture with grazing Guernseys, Jerseys, and Holsteins. And always remember this advice: "Speak to a cow as you would a lady," said William D. Hoard, publisher of *Hoard's Dairyman* magazine and experimental farmer who settled in Fort Atkinson.

Encouraged by Hoard, the Wisconsin's dairy industry grew enormously. By 1899, 90 percent of the state's farms had dairy cattle. By the 1930s, the state could boast of having two million dairy cattle, which was 400,000 more than second-place New York. In the 1950s, dairying contributed 53 percent of the state's farm output. Today there are some 1.5 million dairy cows munching contentedly across the Wisconsin landscape.

Dairymen from around the county gathered in 1922 for the dedication of a bronze statue of Hoard, which stands outside the Wisconsin College of Agriculture's main building in Madison. "Cow College" or "Moo U" remains internationally known for its studies in dairy science.

2267, has 25 miles of groomed cross-country trails open during daylight hours. They are open April 15 through October 15. **Goose Island Park,** (608) 785–9770, near downtown La Crosse, also has excellent groomed paths. **Hixon Forest Nature Center,** 2702 Quarry Road, (608) 784–0303, presents about 5 miles of trail through heavy woods and along high ridges. The trails are always open, and the nature center is open Monday through Friday from 9:00 A.M. to 4:00 P.M. and 1:00 P.M. to 4:00 P.M. Saturday and Sunday; closed Novermer 1 to May 1 on Saturday and Sunday.

How about a winter sleigh ride? Try **Sunset Riding Stables,** W4803 Meyer Road, La Crosse 54601, (608) 788–6629 (by reservation only). The forty-five-minute ride through the snow is $5.00 per person with a minimum of ten people. Dress for the weather. After all, this is Wisconsin.

Approximately 100 miles of snowmobile trails crisscross La Crosse County, eventually hooking up with another 650 miles of trails in the surrounding region. Seven local snowmobile clubs ensure that the trails are groomed to what seem to be interstate highway specifications. To receive maps write or call the La Crosse CVB, 410 East Veterans Memorial Drive, Riverside Park 54601-1895, (608) 782–2366.

Other outdoor recreation opportunities are plentiful in the La Crosse area. Use the city as a jumping-off point for biking, hiking, canoeing, and other outdoor fun. In the spring we often tied in an excursion of some kind after daughter Kate won medals in her high school state champion track meets. The tourneys were held at the University of Wisconsin–La Crosse.

The **Black and La Crosse Rivers** are popular with paddlers, who also have discovered **Coon Creek,** the **Mississippi River,** and its backwaters. The latter might be difficult for beginning canoeists, due to the swift current and underwater obstructions. There are numerous rental and sales outlets throughout the region, supplying everything from anchors to life preservers. Check the La Crosse yellow pages for listings.

The **La Crosse River Marsh** on the west side of La Crosse is a marvelous example of a natural wetland, one used by schools and area universities for study. The marsh, which is included in the Mississippi River floodplain, covers 1,077 acres. Knowledgeable hikers can spot at least 100 different kinds of vegetation, including trees such as oak, cottonwood, and basswood, as well as the less obvious algae, moss, and fungi. On the animal side, there are twenty-four different species of mammals, 139 different species of breeding and migratory birds, nine species of reptiles, six species of amphibians, and fifty-three species of fish, plus hundreds of varied insects.

The La Crosse area is a cyclist's image of dying and going to heaven. The major state bike trails meander through the region to combine urban and rural rides geared to the interests of all ages. The **Great River State Trail** begins in Onalaska near La Crosse's far north side and rolls about 22 miles along the Mississippi River. Shuttle service is available by contacting the Center for Commerce and Tourism in Onalaska, 800 Oak Forest Drive (www.discover onalaska.com; 800–873–1901 or 608–781–9570), but twenty-four-hour notice is required. Rentals at $15 per day are available at the **Blue Heron Bicycle Works,** 114 2nd Avenue North in Onalaska, 608–783–RIDE (7433). Ken Miller's well-stocked cycle shop is about two blocks from the trail, and he can make repairs as necessary for visiting bikers. The shop is open from 10:00 A.M. to 6:00 P.M. Tuesday through Saturday, and 11:00 A.M. to 4:00 P.M. Sunday, but is closed Monday. Helmets come with the rental. Miller does not provide shuttle service, but can arrange for a local cab company to pick up riders who journey to nearby towns along the bike trail. Costs range from $20 to $25 for a vanload of cyclists. The **La Crosse River Bicycle Trail** is a 21.5-mile expedition paralleling the La Crosse River. The route cuts along farm pastures, streams, and maple groves. This trail connects with the Elroy-Sparta Trail and the **Great River State Trail.** There is plenty of camping along the routes, most of which are hard-surface crushed rock along old railroad beds.

West of La Crosse on Highway 16, about a mile or so north of I–94, is **West Salem,** home of pioneer author Hamlin Garland. The bushy-haired, Pulitzer prize–winning novelist was born here in 1860 and returned when he was an adult. He wrote dozens of short stories and novels about the farmers and other people who lived in the "coulee country" of La Crosse County. A *coulee* is a valley, usually with very steep sides. Among his best-known works were *Son of the Middle Border* and *Main-Traveled Roads.*

When Garland moved to Iowa late in his life, my poet father became friends with the old storyteller, who offered many good-humored suggestions on writing styles. Garland's West Salem house is located at 357 West Garland Street (608–786–1399) and is open 10:00 A.M. to 4:30 P.M. (Sunday 1:00 to 4:30 P.M.) Memorial Day to Labor Day. Admission is charged.

The West Salem Rustic Road, accessible from I–90 at the town's freeway exit, is the only one in the state featuring a residential area within a major stretch of its 2.5-mile route. The road edges past the home of Thomas Leonard, founder of West Salem; the village's main business district; Garland's homestead; the Octagon House (on the National Register of Historic Places) at the corner of Highways C and 16; and Swarthout Lakeside Park.

Lafayette County

The little community of **Belmont,** where today's Highway 126 bisects 151, can brag about its flirt with history in 1836. At the time, settlers were casting about for a capital of the Wisconsin Territory. Since the population was equally spread through what is now Iowa, the Dakotas, Wisconsin, and Minnesota, there was a lot of disagreement about the best locale. Governor Henry Dodge picked Belmont because of its centralized location and because it wasn't far from his own home. The choice received so much criticism that Dodge retreated and allowed the territorial representatives to suggest alternative locations. Subsequently, the capital was moved to Iowa for a time before coming back to Wisconsin. Madison eventually won the nod and continued as capital when Wisconsin was made a state.

The **First Capitol State Park and Museum** recalls that nineteenth-century controversy. Drive 3 miles north of Belmont on Highway G to the park, operated by the Lafayette County Historical Society (608–776–8340). The emotional air is calmer now, and the long-forgotten debate is far removed from the minds of picnickers and hikers on the trails.

Take a hike on the **Pecatonica Trail,** which follows a Milwaukee railroad line for almost 10 miles between Belmont and Calamine in Lafayette County. Look for the trail signs. The gravel-and-cinder-surfaced trail travels along the Bonner Branch of the Pecatonica River. Walkers and bikers are welcome during non-winter months. When the snow flies, snowmobilers and cross-country skiers can utilize the pathway. Bonner Branch is a swift moving little creek that swings back and forth under the trail, making it necessary to have twenty-four bridges on the stretch between the two towns. That totals 1,306 feet of planking. I've spotted quails, pheasants, squirrels, woodchucks, and the occasional deer on various strolls.

Speaking of capitols, the **Lafayette County Courthouse** in Darlington was built in 1905 through the generosity of local mining magnate Matthew Murphy. Financed through his will, the imposing limestone structure features a central rotunda and an elaborately painted dome. Marble walls and fancy woodwork round off the building.

Guests are free to wander the halls and study the graceful architectural style at their leisure. The county clerk requests, however, that visitors come during the week's regular working hours.

Lafayette County is geared for outdoors enthusiasts. **Blackhawk Memorial County Park** in Woodford annually hosts a black-powder shoot and Indian encampment in May, sponsored by the Yellowstone Flint and Cap Blackpowder Club. Adding variety to the program are tomahawk throwing and a candle shoot. Although we're black-powder shooters ourselves, using a smooth-bore Brown Bess musket patterned after the regulation British army piece of the Revolutionary War, I've never participated in the Blackhawk rendezvous. But the event is highly recommended by buckskinning friends who have enjoyed the reenactment.

Tell the kids the story behind the park, which is seemingly calm today when its hook-shaped Bloody Lake is smooth as glass in the afternoons. But this is the site of an 1832 battle in which outnumbered Sac and Fox Indians under Chief Blackhawk fought frontier militia and regular army troops. Later that year the Sac were slaughtered while trying to surrender to U.S. cavalry at Bad Axe in Vernon County along the Mississippi River. In 1990, Governor Tommy Thompson formally apologized to the descendants of the Sac Nation for what had happened those many years ago. It was the first time that any government representative tried to make amends to Native Americans for war crimes committed against their ancestors.

The oak- and willow-shaded park is hushed, except for the whoops of fishing fans pulling in whoppers. A boat ramp leads into the slow-moving east branch of the Pecatonica River, where bass, catfish, and trout are reported to lurk. Primitive camping is allowed, but there are no sewer, water, or electric hookups available. If you don't mind roughing it a bit, this park is great. It's not hard to find, tucked as it is along Sand Road and Lafayette County Highway Y near Woodford.

funfacts

Wisconsin covers 56,145 square miles (145,414 square kilometers). This figure includes 1,831 square miles (4,741 square kilometers) of inland water. Add to that figure the 9,355 square miles (24,229 square kilometers) of water from Lakes Michigan and Superior.

Just to the north, along Highway 78, is *Yellowstone Lake State Park* near *Blanchardville* (608–523–4427). The 445-acre lake is the focus of the park's activities. In the winter a 12-mile public snowmobile trail connects the park to Darlington. Each June the city hosts a 10-mile canoe race along the Pecatonica River with twenty categories for its hundreds of contestants. With odds like that, even landlubbing duffers like me who spend more time bumping into riverbanks than cruising merrily along have a chance to snare a trophy.

To help in this regard, Lafayette County's historic churches stand ready. In 1844, missionary Father Samuel Mazzuchelli built a neat wooden church in *New Diggings,* a lead mining town in the western section of the county. Serving the "badgers" in the neighborhood, hearty Mazzuchelli tromped through the woods to encourage his rough-and-tumble frontier flock to attend mass.

At the other end of the county, Lutheran pastors founded the East

Start at the Beginning

The *Point of Beginnings Heritage Area* has been designated by the state to preserve and promote history in Grant, Iowa, and Lafayette Counties. The name comes from the Point of Beginnings marker, a benchmark where government surveyor Lucius Lyon began the state's official survey in 1831.

For you geography buffs, the Point of Beginnings is where the fourth principal meridian crosses the Illinois/Wisconsin border, south of Hazel Green. Lucius's crew built a mound 6 feet tall and 6 feet square, hammering an oak post deep into its center. Every inch of the state has been surveyed from this mark. In the 1970s state surveyors dug up the original post and replaced it with a modern marker. The numbers in the center of the monument correspond to the land sections that come together at the Point of Beginnings.

For more information on Point of Beginnings, contact the trail offices at Box 608, Platteville 53818, (608) 723–4170; www.pointofbeginnings.org.

Wiota Lutheran Church in 1844. The church is still being used by descendants of Norwegian settlers who lived here in those days. The tidy, trim building is the oldest Norwegian Lutheran church in North America and is still used as a parish.

Like its neighboring counties, Lafayette County was born and weaned during those heady lead-rush days that extended from the late 1820s to the 1840s. The hub of the county's mining and commercial world was Shullsburg.

The county lies at the southern edge of the glacial movement that pancaked most of Wisconsin eons ago. Geologists call the vicinity west of town a "driftless area" because it was never smoothed under the towering plates of ice. The deep, dark valleys and moody ridgetops that were untouched by the ice are obvious while driving along Highway 11. Since the glaciers never dispersed or buried the lead deposits, early miners found fairly easy pickings.

The *Badger Mine Museum,* 279 Estey Street (608–965–4860; wicip.uwplatt .edu/lafayette/ci/shullsburg/mine.html), takes visitors into that era with an extensive display of old-time mining gear. The museum, on the site of the Badger Lot Diggings that began operations in 1827, is open daily Memorial Day through Labor Day from 10:00 A.M. to 4:00 P.M. Admission is charged.

The men who worked in the diggings labored twelve hours a day for the princely sum of $1.00. They were lowered by windlass 40 to 50 feet underground, where they crawled on hands and knees to the lead facings in the rock. Working by candlelight, these stocky Cornishmen could seldom stand completely upright, even though most of them were barely over 5 feet tall. Visitors have it easier now, although they are still 47 feet under the surface. You can stand up straight in parts of the mine traversed during the 0.25-mile tour.

The miners believed that a form of goblin, the Cornish Knockers, had followed them from tin mines in the Old Country and lived in the darkest recesses of the New World caverns.

Generally the Knockers would make their appropriate tap-tap sound to indicate a rich mineral vein. In exchange the miners had to leave a bit of their luncheon pasty as a thank you. If they didn't receive such a gift, the angry Knockers could cause mine roofs to collapse. Don't worry about that today—there haven't been any reports of Cornish Knockers in the Shullsburg vicinity since the Badger Lot Diggings closed in 1856.

Shullsburg itself is a community designed for strolling. Park anywhere and amble along winding streets with such lilting names as Hope, Charity, Friendship, and Justice. Originally the roads were mere paths followed by miners from their homes to the shafts and were named by the good Dominican friar, Father Mazzuchelli, on one of his Bible-thumping jaunts through town.

Monroe County

The earliest of the state's major bike paths, the famed *Elroy-Sparta Trail,* opened in 1966 and annually hosts more than 55,000 riders. Since the trail is on an old railroad bed, you'll even travel through three-century-old tunnels that save you the legwork you would have needed for steeper grades. The trail wanders for 32.5 miles across Monroe County into Juneau County. During the summer, all-you-can-eat pancake breakfasts are served in the Wilton Municipal Park. The breakfasts, put on by the Lions Club, run from Memorial Day weekend until Labor Day. Wilton is about the midway point on the ride. For information on bike rentals, auto shuttles, campgrounds, and other lodging and restaurant listings, contact the Elroy-Sparta State Trail, Box 297, Kendall 54638 (608–463–7109; www.elroy-sparta-trail.org). Highway 71 parallels the trail for almost the entire route, which makes it convenient for tired riders who need to be picked up.

Don't be surprised if you are driving through Angelo, just a hop and a jump north of Sparta, and a giant eagle appears to be taking wing from a parking lot. Look twice and you might see an elephant, a monster gorilla, a huge beaver, or some other bigger-than-life creature. There's no cause to worry, however, since the pack of critters is nothing more than completed products, made by F.A.S.T. Corp., headquartered in Sparta.

The acronym stands for *Fiberglass Animals, Shapes and Trademarks,* which makes the animals for displays around the world. They're often kept outside the plant until ready for shipping. As a result, F.A.S.T. president Jerry Vettrus is used to cars screeching to a halt in front of his place.

If you're so inclined, you can purchase something big for the backyard pool. How about a spouting whale or a leaping muskie? It'll probably cost about $2,000 for something under 20 feet tall. But wouldn't it be worth it?

Richland County

Richland Center hosts the **Wisconsin High School Rodeo Association Championships** each June at the Richland County fairgrounds on County Road AA on the city's north side. Kids from around the state compete in calf roping, bulldogging, bronc riding, barrel racing, and other bone-jarring events. Some of the youngsters eventually go on to college rodeo teams and then to the pro circuit. In addition to June Dairy Days, a Rodeo Parade also takes place the weekend of the Rodeo Championships. Call or stop by the chamber of commerce downtown office (608–647–6205), located in a 1937 Pullman railroad car. They'll also be able to tell you about the tractor pulls held at the county fairgrounds each July. Some of the heavy-equipment operators can haul 12,000 pounds or more over a set course on the dirt track.

Take Highway 40 north about 7 miles to **Rockbridge** and **Pier Natural Bridge Park,** site of one of the first white settlements in Richland County. There are scenic rock formations all along Highways 80, 60, 58, and 56, which spin around Rockbridge like spokes. The park's main feature is a long bridge of rock, at least 60 feet high and 80 feet wide.

If spelunking is your thing, the county's **Eagle Cave** is another of the state's larger underground caverns. The cave is just off Highway 60, west of Eagle Corners. But if claustrophobia hits and subsurface roaming is not to your liking, there are 26.5 miles of hiking trails above the cave site. Eagle Cave is open to the public Memorial Day to Labor Day, but the cave and grounds are used in the off-season by scout troops. For more details contact Eagle Cave, 16320 Cavern Lane,

Wisconsin Info

For Wisconsin travel information contact the Wisconsin Tourism Development Office, 201 West Washington Street, Madison 53707 (608–266–2161 or 800–372–2737 for Wisconsin and neighboring states; the national toll-free number is 800–432–8747), or use the Internet at www.travelwisconsin.com.

For information on the state's economy, history, or government, contact the Office of the Governor, State Capitol, Box 7863, Madison 53707.

Blue River 53518 (608–537–2988; www.eagle-cave.net). To keep the crowds coming, the Wisconsin Skyrocket Coon Dog Field Trials are held here each June.

Vernon County

About 38 miles north of Prairie du Chien on Highway 35, which is nicknamed the Great River Road, the Bad Axe River empties into the Mississippi. Here Black Hawk attempted to surrender his Sac and Fox followers to the white militia and Sioux warriors who had encamped at Fort Crawford. The troops, including Abraham Lincoln, ignored Black Hawk's white flag and chased the Native Americans into the river, where many drowned. The few survivors who made it across to the Iowa side were captured by the whites' Sioux allies on the far bank and sent back to the fort, where they were imprisoned.

The site is the saddest along this stretch of the Mississippi, especially when autumn mists rise slowly out of the hollows along the roadway. You can feel the heaviness in the air before the harsh sun drives the fog away.

This is Vernon County, which was originally called Bad Axe County, but in 1861 image-conscious residents asked the state legislature to change the name to the less negative "Vernon," a loose Anglicizing of *verdant,* meaning "green." The legislators obliged, recalling the incident with Black Hawk, no doubt.

The **Genoa National Fish Hatchery** (608–689–2605) raises both cold- and warm-water species of finny critters. Being avid fisherfolk, the Hintz clan likes to check out these kinds of places . . . just to be sure there will be plenty of stock for Wisconsin's lakes and streams hungry for our bait. Bass, walleye, trout, and sauger are among the two million fish produced annually and shipped to state and federal release points around the country. Now that's talking fish! The hatchery is 5 miles south of La Crosse. Visitors can tour the facility 8:00 A.M. to 3:30 P.M. Monday through Friday. Tours are free.

funfacts

Wisconsin became the thirtieth state on May 29, 1848.

While in the area we also like to park near **Lock and Dam No. 8** on Highway 35 (the Great River Road) and watch barges and boats navigate up and down the Mississippi River.

The eastern portion of Vernon County has a large population of Amish, some of whom work in a furniture factory on County Road D northeast of Westby. Their creations of bent hickory rockers and other pieces are excellent. With the slow-moving Amish wagons on the county's back roads, motorists must be very careful. The highways through the area are notorious for curves and loops. Of course, the scenery compensates for the required slower-paced driving.

Fishing Fun

We like to fish at the **Browntown–Cadiz Springs State Recreation Area,** where the living is easy and the crappies are jumping. The placid waters of Lakes Beckman and Zander—both within the recreation area boundaries—are divided by an earthen dike. Zander, the smallest of the two bodies of water, was used for raising bullfrogs commercially in the 1930s. Kids can catch largemouth bass and bluegills from several fishing piers overlooking the water.

Browntown–Cadiz sprawls over 723 acres of marsh and grassland. When I've walked quietly down to the end of the dike, I could get close enough to watch the Canada geese feeding in the sloughs. Be aware that hunting is allowed in the area during autumn, so don't go wandering off into the woods without brightly colored clothing. Better yet, stick to the picnic and fishing areas.

The recreation area is 7 miles west of Monroe on Highway 11. Get to the Allen Road exit, then go south a hilly 0.7 mile to Cadiz Springs Road, turn west, and drive 1.5 miles to the recreation area entrance. For details on the site, call the Department of Natural Resources in Monroe at (608) 966–3777 in the summer and (608) 325–4844 in the winter.

Trillium, a bed-and-breakfast in the heart of the Amish community, is a self-contained cottage where visitors can really get away from it all. For fresh-baked, homemade bread, owner Rosanne Boyett's touch is superb. Call (608) 625–4492.

The **Westby House** is another interesting bed-and-breakfast, located at 200 West State Street in **Westby** (608–634–4112; www.westbyhouse.com). The house is at the corner of Ramsland and State, only a block off Highway 14. The Victorian-style 1890s home has six rooms, done up with antiques and crafts made throughout the area. Rates range from $75 to $150. All of the rooms (two with private bath) have queen-size beds. Kids are welcome. If you can't stay for the night, the public dining room offers a wide-ranging menu and is open for lunch and dinner throughout the week. Reservations are always recommended.

Westby is also an outdoors town, with the **Snowflake Annual Ski Jumping Tournament** (www.explorewisconsin.com/communitypages/westby.html) in February. The event is held at the **Snowflake Ski Club** (north of town off Highway 27 on Vernon County Highway P). The 65-meter run's landing zone converts to a nine-hole, par-three golf course in the summer. I've never let the kids practice these dives off the roof of the house into a snowbank, but they got a thrill out of watching the airborne pros.

Wildcat Mountain State Park (608–337–4775) seems to appear out of nowhere, a mere twenty-minute ride west of Hillsboro on Highway 33. All of a sudden there it is, with deep gorges, pines, limestone cliffs, and racing waterways that show a dramatically rugged side of Wisconsin.

Good Old Days

For an old-time July 4, swing through Viroqua for the community's traditional Ice Cream Social on the lawn of the historic **Sherry-Butt Historic Civil War Museum,** 795 North Main Street (608–637–7336). An impressive nineteenth-century mansion, this fully restored home of a Civil War colonel and his family is furnished as it was in the late 1800s. The building is open from 1:00 to 5:00 P.M. Saturday and Sunday or by appointment from Memorial Day through mid-September. Devouring a heaping plate of strawberry shortcake is an integral part of the fun. Fireworks are held at dusk on the Vernon County Fairgrounds (608–637–2575). For more details, check www.viroqua-wisconsin.com.

Hillsboro itself is a quaint village that boasts its own museum, an 1860s log cabin on the northeast side of town. The little house is open on Sunday from 1:00 to 4:00 P.M. early June to Labor Day. By calling the city clerk at (608) 489–2521 or (608) 489–3192, you can probably get inside on other days. Half the building looks like an old post office, and the other half contains typical pioneer furnishings.

If fishing is one of your favorite pastimes, be sure to travel in western Vernon County, for it borders the great Mississippi River. Stoddard is located in the northwest corner of the county, where ice fishing is a popular sport for those who don't mind braving the freezing temperatures and howling winds of Wisconsin winters. The village of Genoa draws people from more than 200 miles away, offering some of the best Mississippi catfish, bullheads, and other creatures of the Old Maid. De Soto Harbors, in the southwest corner of the county, is the historic area of the final defeat of the famed Indian chief Black Hawk. Blackhawk Memorial Park, where you can find your fill of camping and fishing, is just north of the village.

The Czechs and Bohemians celebrate their heritage in mid-June with an annual town festival. Polka-dancing fans come from miles around to flit around the dance pavilions. The active exercise is a requirement to get rid of pounds gained from nibbling rich Bohemian foods at the concession stands.

County seat Viroqua annually hosts the county fair on grounds on the north edge of town. Some of the best harness racing in the state can be seen at the September event. Drivers and breeders don't mind bragging when inquisitive visitors come around to see the stables and the animals.

There's a lot of competition in dairy classes as well. Watching the judging will help you learn the difference between a Holstein and a Guernsey. There's a lot of difference between one breed and an-udder.

Later in the month, usually on the last Saturday in September, nearby Viola (just 13 miles east of Viroqua on Highway 56) features a yearly horse and colt show. Get there by 9:30 A.M. to watch the pony- and horse-pulling contests. No, the spectators don't pull the horses. The teams are hitched to weighted sleds that are to be pulled a certain distance. The horse show usually begins at 9:00 A.M. and runs throughout the day. There's an afternoon parade, a dance at night, a tractor pull, midway rides, and exhibits by the Future Farmers of America and the 4-H. It's all real down-home.

The descendants of Norwegians, Czechs, and Bohemians make up a strong percentage of the Vernon County population. In fact, one of the largest clusters of Norwegians outside the Old Country lives in the stretch along Highway 14 between La Crosse and Westby. *Norskedalen,* on County Road P at Coon Valley, is a refurbished pioneer homesite and a 350-acre arboretum along with nature trails.

The arboretum is a project of the University of Wisconsin–La Crosse to give students a firsthand look at the most up-to-date horticultural techniques. Tours are conducted by appointment, but drop-by visitors are always encouraged. Admission is $5.00 for adults, $2.00 for students kindergarten age through twelve, and $12.00 for families. The Norwegian homestead's summer hours (April 15 to October 31) are Monday through Friday, 8:30 A.M. to 5:00 P.M., Saturday from 10:00 A.M. to 5:00 P.M., and Sunday from noon to 4:00 P.M. During the winter, it's closed Saturdays, but otherwise open daylight hours. Tours start at 10:00 A.M. with the last tour beginning at 4:00 P.M. Call (608) 452–3424.

The on-site visitor center is open year-round. From April 15 to October 31, the visitor center is open 9:00 A.M. to 5:00 P.M. Monday through Friday, 10:00 A.M. to 5:00 P.M. Saturday, and noon to 5:00 P.M. Sunday. From November 1 to April 14, the visitor center is open 10:00 A.M. to 4:00 P.M. Monday through Friday, closed Saturday, and open noon to 4:00 P.M. Sunday.

Places to Stay in Western Wisconsin

DARLINGTON

Towne Motel,
245 West Harriet Street,
(608) 776–2661
Inexpensive

LA CROSSE

Days Inn Hotel,
101 Sky Harbour Drive,
(608) 783–1000
Inexpensive

Radisson Hotel,
200 Harborview Plaza,
(608) 784–6680
Moderate

Wilson Schoolhouse Inn,
W5718 Highway 14-61,
(608) 787–1982
Moderate

LANCASTER

Martha's Hot Mustard Bed & Breakfast,
7867 University Farm Road,
(608) 723–4711
Moderate

NEW GLARUS

Chalet Landhaus Inn,
Highway 69,
(608) 527–5234 or
(800) 944–1716
Moderate

New Glarus Hotel,
100 Sixth Avenue,
(608) 527–5244 or
(800) 727–9477
Moderate

Swiss Aire Motel,
1200 Highway 69,
(608) 527–2138 or
(800) 798–4391
Inexpensive

WESTBY

Old Towne Motel,
U.S. Highway 14/61 and
State Highway 27 South,
(608) 634–2111 or
(800) 605–0276
Moderate

Westby House,
200 West State Street,
(608) 634–4112
Moderate

Places to Eat in Western Wisconsin

DARLINGTON

Darlington Golf and Country Club,
17098 Country Club Road,
(608) 776–3377
Best overview of any 18th hole this side of the Mississippi River. You want meat? You get steak in the club's well-appointed dining room, where service is attentive and no one minds talking golf. In fact, you better have at least one good "birdie" story to tell at the bar. Guests welcome. Inexpensive to moderate.

Towne House Restaurant,
2322 Main Street,
(608) 776–3373
For home-style cooking, with all the basic comfort foods, the Towne House offers goodies that would make grandma proud. Fish, meats, and soups are all lovingly prepared, with generous portions for the hungry. Lunch and dinner times are popular with the locals so plan accordingly. Inexpensive to moderate, depending how hungry you are.

DESOTO

Great River Roadhouse,
9660 Highway 35,
(608) 648–2045
Homemade pizza, ribs, chicken, and pasta keeps the locals coming back time and again. Carryouts are available for the fish fry on Friday if motorists want to eat on the run or do a carry-back to the nearest motel or campsite. Open daily, with one of the best views of the Mississippi River in the upper Midwest. The restaurant is about 0.5 mile north of DeSoto, facing the river. Very casual, inexpensive.

FENNIMORE

Eagle Creek Inn,
1096 Lincoln Avenue,
(608) 822–3782
Formerly the Silent Woman Restaurant, noted for its signage with a headless colonial lady out front, the Eagle Creek has kept the supper club look with its comfortable interior and polished tables for those special occasions

that call for being pampered with good food and friendly service. Soups are great, as are the steaks. Drop by for lunch or dinner. Inexpensive to moderate.

Frederick Family Restaurant,
430 Lincoln Avenue,
(608) 822–3782
Food is certainly not merely relative here at the Frederick Family Restaurant, but it's downright delicious, especially after a long day exploring the neighborhood. Nothing fancy, just hearty fare appreciated by townsfolk who know a good meal when it's placed in front of 'em. Steaks, chops, seafood, salads, and soups. It's all there. Open for breakfast, lunch, and dinner. Inexpensive to moderate.

LA CROSSE

Freighthouse Restaurant,
107 Vine Street,
(608) 784–6211
The Freighthouse is the self-proclaimed premier steak and seafood restaurant in La Crosse, but for good reason. Aged prime beef is one of the most popular items on the large menu. The Freighthouse has also won a *Wine Spectator* award for its extensive wine selection and has made the *La Crosse Tribune's* "reader's choice" list. A comfortably blazing fireplace makes for great lounging in the winter. Open daily for dinner. Moderate to expensive.

**Three Rivers Lodge,
Radisson Hotel,**
200 Harborview Plaza,
(608) 784–6680
This is a contemporary-style
hotel restaurant that goes
beyond the usual with its
upscale feel. Lots of stone
and hardwoods give a natural feel to the decor. Come
hungry in the morning for its
breakfast buttermilk griddle-
cakes, banana-almond
French toast, and prime rib
hash with poached eggs.
Open daily, so try the lunch
and dinners as well. Steaks,
seafood, and all the trimmings contribute to making
the Radisson a popular stay-
over. Reservations are suggested for nighttime dining.
Moderate to expensive.

LANCASTER

Doolittle's Pub & Eatery,
135 South Jefferson Street,
(608) 723–7676
Hang on to your hat from
9:00 P.M. to 1:00 A.M. on
Wednesdays when Doolittle's
rocks with such wild, live
bands as Mr. Obvious and
even crazier. Music also
other nights, but call for
times and dates. So get on
down every night with burgers, beers, and fries. This is a
happening evening place so
put on your dancing clogs
and be ready to hit the floor.
Inexpensive.

MONROE

Gillett's Restaurant,
1713 Eleventh Street,
(608) 328–4373
Open daily, year-round,
Gillett's has a marvelous reputation, known for its breakfast with servings starting at

6:00 A.M. for people who like
to get up and go. You can
get some of the best grits
north of the Mason-Dixon
Line, as well as no-calorie
(ha! We wish!) cinna-ring
donuts and Southern-style
biscuits and gravy. A diverse
menu is presented at lunch
and dinner, with dishes
including chopped steak
burgers and a whopper
called a "triple feature," a
bacon, turkey, and ham
sandwich on Texas toast.
Inexpensive to moderate.

NEW GLARUS

**Flannery's Wilhelm Tell
Restaurant,**
534 First Street,
(608) 527–5244
Many guests feel like yodeling after they eat at
Flannery's, dining on Old
World delicacies such as
schnitzels, cheese fondue,
and locally-made Swiss-style
sausages. But you can go
American as well, with suc-
culent prime rib, hefty steaks,
and seafood. For the dis-
cerning, nightly specials are
available. Be aware, how-
ever, that groups and busses
are welcome here, so the
dining room might be
crowded. Call ahead. Open
at 4:00 P.M. Tuesday through
Saturday. Moderate.

**New Glarus Hotel
Restaurant,**
100 6th Avenue,
(608) 527–5244, (800)
727–9477,
www.newglarushotel.com
The New Glarus Hotel
Restaurant is located in the
heart of New Glarus. It's
owned and operated by
Hans Lenzlinger for more

than thirty years and is
famous for its Swiss food
and hospitality. Some of the
specialties are beef, cheese,
and chocolate fondues. Go
for the wienerschnitzel and
sauerbraten. And don't miss
the buffet dinners on Friday
and Saturday nights. Wake
up weekend-early and hit the
Sunday brunch, which starts
promptly at 10:30 A.M. Polka
bands get everyone hand-
clapping and cavorting
Swiss-style each Friday and
Saturday, making the hotel
restaurant a favorite place
both for locals and visitors.
For a special touch, the
restaurant serves local New
Glarus beers, in addition to
imported Swiss beer and
Swiss wines. Open daily.
Moderate to expensive.

ONALASKA

Lakeview Restaurant,
N5135 Highway 35,
(608) 781–0150
This is the perfect place for
a relaxing meal after a day
of biking on the Great River
State Trail and canoeing in
nearby Perrot State Park
after, naturally, a soothing
bath o'suds. Sit back, have
a brewski or other beverage,
and order a haunch (well,
okay, a steak cut) of buffalo
(the restaurant specialty) or
at least a buffalo burger. The
place is easy to find, only a
mile or so north of Ona-
laska. *Wisconsin Trails* magazine readers rate the Lakeview as having the best fish
fry and best hamburger in
this part of the state, as well
as being the best restaurant.
Who's to argue? Inexpensive
to moderate.

PENDARVIS

Redwood Restaurant,
615 Dodge Street,
(608) 987–2242
This is a family-style restaurant with accommodations for groups (that means large families as well), which features pasties, pies, and mmm-good daily specials. Go for the soup and sandwiches for a light lunch. Inexpensive and, oh, so good.

PLATTEVILLE

Steve's Pizza Palace,
15 South Fourth Street,
(608) 348–3136
Pizza is king here at Steve's, where they can whip up a cheese, sausage, and mushroom (load up on the anchovies!) lickety-split. When it comes to this Italian soul food, even the spirits of long-gone Cornish miners who used to live in these parts rise up and sniff the aroma of pasta sauce and hot peppers . . . or green. Go for it. And take-out too. Inexpensive.

The Timbers Supper Club,
670 Elm Street,
(608) 348–2406
Look for the monster electronic theatre pipe organ suspended in its dark wooden rafters. But then concentrate on the extensive menu, one that includes everything from steaks to vegetarian marvels. What's also great about the Timbers is that it is so convenient, located directly across the street from the Super 8 Motel at the intersection of Highways 80/81/151 and barely one mile from the University of Wisconsin-Platteville. And it's perfect for travelers seeking a comfortable dining experience after a long day on the road. Moderate prices, too.

PRAIRIE DU CHIEN

Culver's,
1915 South Marquette Road,
(608) 320–5360
This is the perfect roadside drive-through pitstop when long-haul traveling between Wisconsin and just beyond the Mississippi River. Stop, load up with a fish sandwich or burgers, plus hot fudge malts, and then hit the road again. Makes the miles fly by. Open daily. Inexpensive.

Jeffer's Black Angus,
Highway 18,
(608) 326–2222
Don't drop by the Black Angus unless you are thinking meat. Think porterhouse, dream big! Twenty juicy ounces of chowdown marvel! Yet for the delicate souls, there's the Angus Ladies Special, eight ounces of fine aged beef tenderloin fresh off the open grill. Mmm, delectable. For the offbeat, try the chicken livers sautéed with bacon and onions, exactly what my sainted grandma used to have every Sunday morning at home, along with a heap of scrambled eggs. Then there's plenty o' pasta, a net full of fish dishes, and lots more to burnish the palette. Open daily at 5:00 P.M. Moderate to expensive.

The Main Entrance,
215 West Blackhawk Avenue,
(608) 326–4030
Every Thursday at 9:00 P.M., the bar presents an open mic acoustic jam, hosted by Jon "Ramblin'" Burlingam. Guests are invited to bring an instrument and join the show. Who knows what blues groups might show up next. Maybe Mama's Worry, the Velcro Jones Band, Karl with a K, or Lisa and Mississippi on Tuesday, Wednesday, or Friday. Go for the beer–sip Peroni Gran Riserva or a smooth Pilsner Urquell. Snack only. Inexpensive.

SPRING GREEN

Round Barn Restaurant & Lodge,
E4830 Highways 14 and 60,
(608) 648–2045
The Round Barn actually was a barn before becoming a restaurant, serving traditional Midwestern fare. In 2004 John and Mary Pat Kaul purchased what was then the Round Barn Lodge & Restaurant and converted the eatery into an Italian-themed restaurant called the Pasta Barn. Eyeball, then eat, the Italian-style baked cod, one of the restaurant's signature dishes. It's a fillet lightly seasoned with sweet basil, oregano, and bread crumbs, topped with a mild house cheese and alfredo sauce, baked and served with fettuccine alfredo. There are plenty of pizza dishes too. Serves breakfast, lunch, and dinner daily. Moderate.

**Spring Green General
Store and Cafe,**
137 South Albany Street,
(608) 588–7070
The Mostly Mostly Mondays
Poetry Society meets every
Monday, naturally, at the
store and eatery. On Fridays
and Saturdays, you might be
able to take in a short play or
a reading. Bob Fest (Sunday
of Memorial Day weekend),
visitors can celebrate the life
of singer Bob Dylan. As with
other special occasions,
there is a menu match and
plenty of micro brews. Don't
miss breakfast with its oat-
meal or five-grain cereal, dol-
loped with strawberry jam or
butter and brown sugar or
raisins, plus omelets to die
for. Then there's lunch, with
chili of both the hearty and
vegetarian kind, as well as
quiche, bean burritos, and
sweet chicken salad. A full
menu is served until 5:30 P.M.
Inexpensive.

SELECTED CHAMBERS OF COMMERCE

**La Crosse Convention and
Visitors Bureau,**
410 Veterans Memorial Drive,
La Crosse 54601, (800) 658–9424

**New Glarus Tourism Bureau and
Chamber of Commerce,**
418 Railroad Street, New Glarus 53574-
0713, (608) 527–2095

Platteville Chamber of Commerce,
275 Highway 151 West, (608) 348–8888

**Prairie du Chien Chamber of
Commerce and Tourism Council,**
211 South Main Street, Prairie du Chien
53821-0326, (800) 732–1673, or (608)
326-8555

Central Wisconsin

Central Wisconsin is a rare mixture of tourism fun, urban bustle, political muscle, and natural beauty. It seems as if the best of what the state has to offer has come together here in a potpourri of sights and color.

There's the hustle and bustle of Dane County and Madison, the state capital, combined with the rural "outcountry" of Wisconsin's river heartland.

Columbia County

About 4 miles south of Arlington on Highway 51 is the **University of Wisconsin Agricultural Research Station,** an outdoor lab run by the University of Wisconsin. Researchers work on crop, livestock, and soil studies, and no one minds if you stop by for a quick visit. The farm on Hopkins Road (608–846–3761) is open all year from 8:00 A.M. to 4:30 P.M. Monday through Friday. If you need a goose to get you to Arlington, there are plenty to be had at the Goose Pond, so take Highway K west from town to Goose Pond Road.

Spring and fall migrations cover the marshland and nearby cornfields with great gaggles of geese. I've always wondered about how many pillows and quilts we could fill with all those fluttering feathers.

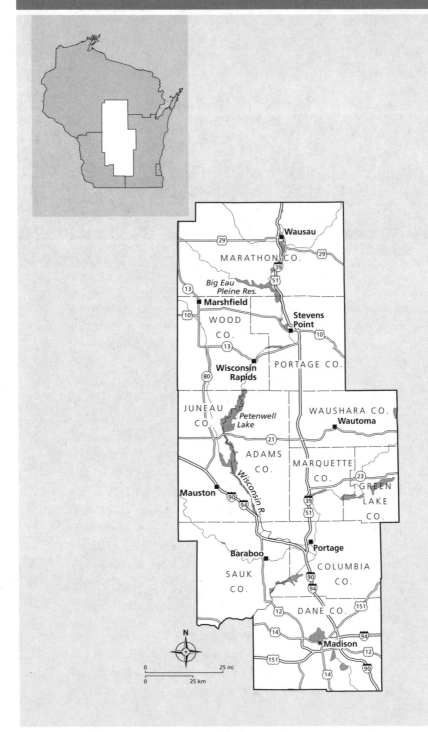

Four miles north of Arlington is the *MacKenzie Environmental Center* at Poynette, 1 mile east of town on Highway CS. The state Department of Natural Resources manages the center, which offers displays of native Wisconsin animals and has an interlocking network of excellent hiking trails. The center is open daily from 8:00 A.M. to 4:00 P.M. (the grounds are open until dark) and is closed on winter holidays and weekends November 1 through April 15. Call (608) 635–8110 if you need more specifics.

Folks in *Portage,* the Columbia County seat, say this is where "the North begins." A trading post was established here in 1792, and entrepreneurs formed transport companies to aid commercial travel between the Fox and Wisconsin Rivers. Oxen would tow empty barges across the connecting mud-flats for $10. Fifty cents per one hundred pounds of merchandise was the going price for loaded vessels. A canal eventually was dug, linking the rivers and open-ing with much fanfare in 1851.

Portage is home of the *Old Indian Agency House,* built in 1832 for agent John Kinzie and his wife, Juliet, a prolific writer. One of her works, *Waubun,* was a detailed account of her family's trip to Fort Winnebago that told as well

CENTRAL WISCONSIN'S TOP HITS

Art Fair off the Square	Mid-Continent Railway Museum
Capital Brewery and Beer Garden	Mission Coffee House/Supreme Bean
Cave of the Mounds	Museum of Norman Rockwell Art
Christopher Columbus Museum	National Watermelon Seed Spitting Contest
Circus World Museum	
Devil's Lake State Park	Old Indian Agency House
Geology Museum	Rib Mountain
Hoofbeat Ridge	Song of Norway Festival
Law Park	State Historical Museum
Leopold Memorial Reserve	Wisconsin Veterans Museum
MacKenzie Environmental Center	Wollersheim Winery
Merrimac ferryboat	

about general pioneer life and their frontier home. Their granddaughter, Juliette Gordon Low, founded the Girl Scouts of the U.S.A.

The Kinzie house has been restored in the style of 1833 and is open for tours May 15 to October 15 (608–742–6362). Admission is $5.00 for adults, $4.00 for seniors and AAA members, and $3.00 for students (seven to eighteen). Hours throughout the season are 10:00 A.M. to 4:00 P.M. Monday through Saturday, and Sunday 11:00 A.M. to 4:00 P.M.

The house is opposite the site of the old fort, facing the canal built near the portage between the two rivers. The Fort Winnebago Surgeon's Quarters is the only remaining building in what was once an expansive complex of barracks, offices, and stores. Several well-known military men served at Fort Winnebago during its heyday. Their ranks included Jefferson Davis, then a young lieutenant, who went on to become president of the Confederacy during the Civil War.

Admission prices and tour hours for the surgeon's quarters are the same as at the Old Indian Agency House. The surgeon's quarters overlooks the site where French explorers Louis Joliet and Father Jacques Marquette beached their canoes in 1673 on the Fox River banks. Displays in the rough-looking building include period medical books, desks built by soldiers, an operating table, and the fort's records.

Anyone interested in building restorations should study the design of the place. Shaved pine logs squared off by axes form the outer walls. Tamarack poles make up the floor and ceiling joists. Much of the original plank flooring is still in place. The interior was plastered over handmade lathwork. The restorers left a portion uncovered so visitors can see the skill that went into making the building inhabitable.

AUTHORS' FAVORITES

Circus World Museum,
Baraboo

Devil's Lake State Park,
Baraboo

International Crane Foundation,
Baraboo

Madison's lakes

Madison museums

Mid-Continent Railway Museum,
North Freedom

Wisconsin Chamber Orchestra
Concerts on the Square, Madison

Wisconsin Dells water slides

Wisconsin State Capitol,
Madison

TOP ANNUAL EVENTS

Wollersheim Winery Open House,
early March, Prairie du Sac

World Dairy Expo,
October, Madison

Midwest Horse Fair,
mid-April, Madison

Fall Polka Fest,
early November, Wisconsin Dells

Art Fair off the Square,
mid-July, Madison

Capitol Christmas Pageant,
mid-December, Madison

Mad-City Ski Team,
summer, Madison

Pardeeville, about 8 miles east of Portage on Highway 33 and 2 miles south on Highway 22, annually hosts the *National Watermelon Seed Spitting Contest* on the second Sunday in September. Admission is free, but come early. Competition in twelve different categories is always tough. Hope for a strong wind.

Across the river from Portage is the *Leopold Memorial Reserve* (608–393–7352), covering 1,300 acres of "sand country" loved by the famed naturalist Aldo Leopold. If you plan on visiting, read an excellent book on the outdoorsman's life by Curt Meine, entitled *Aldo Leopold: His Life and Work* (University of Wisconsin Press, 1988). In the 1930s and 1940s, Leopold wrote much of his famous *Sand County Almanac* in "The Shack," a converted chicken coop that he used to get away from the rush and bustle of urban life. The spartan retreat is still on the reserve property, the nucleus of eighty acres that had been part of Leopold's river-bottom farm. Tours are by appointment only. A $10 donation is requested from non-members.

Columbus is proud to be named after the great Italian explorer, and it celebrated in grand style the 1992 anniversary of Columbus's landing in the New World. A sprawling *Christopher Columbus Museum* is packed with artifacts and memorabilia from the 1893 World's Columbian Exposition, which marked the 400th anniversary of the navigator's arrival in America.

The museum is on the top floor of the Columbus Antique Mall. The mall's 82,000 square feet, 200 dealers, and 400 booths make it the largest antiques sales outlet in Wisconsin. "You name it, we have it. If it isn't here, you won't find it anywhere," claim the sales clerks. Owner Dan Amato purchased the three-story, tan brick former canning plant and opened the mall in 1983. Collecting the Columbus material started out as a hobby and then grew out of control. The mall and museum are open 8:15 A.M. to 4:00 P.M. daily except Thanksgiving, Christmas, and Easter. There's a $2.00 (18 and older) admission charge to the museum.

The building, at 239 Whitney Street (920–623–1992), is on the west side of the Crawfish River adjacent to the Columbus Water & Light Company.

Dane County

The greater **Madison** area has been making a hit with visitors since noted nineteenth-century newspaper publisher Horace Greeley wrote, "Madison has the most magnificent site of any inland town I ever saw." That was in 1855, ten years after the community received the nod as capital of the state. Several generations later, the magic was still there. The old *Life* magazine took a closer look and proclaimed that the city's image best represented the "good life in America."

In 1978, the National Municipal League tagged Madison as an All-American City. Other studies have said that Madison is one of the most livable cities in the country. Of course, all the tourist and chamber of commerce promotions proudly toot their collective horns over the praise. But is it true? We think so. Besides, Madison's beaten paths are really a bit offbeat anyway, which makes everything in this town a delightful lark. Mad City is fine-tuned to the needs of citizens.

We like to think **Madison's lakes** make the city something special. Mendota, Monona, Wingra, and Waubesa are within the city limits, comprising some 18,000 acres of watery surface on which to splash, puddle, paddle, or fish. Two sections of town are linked by an isthmus between Monona on the south and Mendota on the north, with the Capitol complex smack in the center. You can get a free map of the lakes at bait shops in town.

Speaking of free, the Capital City Ski Team presents delightfully nerve-racking water-skiing shows at 7:00 P.M. Thursday and Sunday, Memorial Day through Labor Day, at **Law Park** on Lake Monona, 0.5 mile southeast from Capitol Concourse. Get there early, because the regulars stake out their grassy patch well before show time, bringing well-stocked coolers, Frisbees, and blankets. Don't forget mosquito repellent for July nights. The buzzers aren't as big as their North Woods cousins, but they can be as aggravating as lobbyists outside the assembly chambers at state budget time.

How can you beat a town that has 150 parks within the city limits, comprising some 3,600 acres of recreation land? In addition, Madison has one of the best places

thegiftoffood

The Wisconsin Restaurant Association offers a booklet of gift certificates to member restaurants around the state. Contact the organization at 2801 Fish Hatchery Road, Madison 53713, (800) 589-3211. The certificates can be ordered in any denomination and are valid at any of the restaurants listed. There is a $1.00 per certificate charge for shipping and handling.

OTHER ATTRACTIONS WORTH SEEING

Arlington Experimental Farm

Dane County Farmers Market on the Square, Madison

Fort Winnebago Surgeon's Quarters, Portage

Henry Vilas Zoological Society, Madison

Pioneer Log Village and Museum, Reedsburg

Sauk County Historical Museum, Baraboo

Tower Hills State Park, Spring Green

University of Wisconsin Arboretum, Madison

Wisconsin River ferryboat, Merrimac

in the world to view a sunset: on the Memorial Union Terrace of the University of Wisconsin, overlooking Lake Mendota.

We have totaled up some other statistics for you, thanks to friends at *Isthmus* magazine who put out an "annual manual," as well as other knowledgeable Madison insiders: The city has 89 tennis courts, 22 touch-football teams, 16 bathing beaches (13 staffed with lifeguards), 6 million volumes in the community's various libraries, 965 softball teams, 27 fine arts and performing theaters in addition to the 2,200-seat complex in the downtown Civic Center, 10 boat-launching sites ($2.00/day), and 5,016 parking meters. The excellent bus system is one of the best in the state for ease of transportation.

Biking is a relaxed way to see the city. According to confirmed pedalers who work for the Madison police department, there are three bikes to every car in the city, with some 98 miles of posted bike trails—perhaps that's because of the city's youthful makeup. Out of the total population of about 208,054 residents, about 42,000 are university students, with two-thirds of the city's population—when school is in session—thirty-five years of age or younger.

Bring your own bike to town or rent one at the ***Budget Bicycle Center & Bicycle Rental,*** 1230 Regent Street (608–251–8413), just 5 blocks from the U.W. Arboretum and near the Lake Mendota bike path.

One of the better trails is the loop around Lake Monona through Law Park, B. B. Clarke Park, and the fifty-one acres of the Olbrich Botanical Gardens. Give yourself at least a half day for that jaunt. Other good trails cover the scenic lakeshore from the university's Helen C. White Library to the apple trees at Picnic Point, Madison's best-known locale for smooching, proposing marriage, and munching Oscar Mayer ring bologna on Ritz crackers (not necessarily in that order).

firstkindergarten

The first kindergarten in the United States was opened in 1856 by Mrs. Carl Schurz in Watertown. Mrs. Schurz was a pupil of Friedrich Frobel, a German educator considered the founder of the kindergarten movement in Europe. Frobel started his first kindergarten in 1837.

Walking is a good way to see Madison up close, too. Start in *Capitol Square,* more popularly called the Concourse. The *Wisconsin Chamber Orchestra* puts on free classical concerts there the last Wednesday of each June, every Wednesday in July, and the first Wednesday in August. On the first Saturday in June, kicking off the state's Dairy Month, you can milk a Holstein or a Guernsey cow on the Concourse. The bovines belong to the university, brought to the Capitol steps from the school farms on Campus Drive, a mile west of the Concourse. (Madison has the honor of being the country's only major city with a working farm almost downtown.)

Another agricultural tie is the farmers' market, which sets up camp on the Concourse 6:00 A.M. to 2:00 P.M. each Saturday. May through autumn, you can squeeze melons to your heart's content. (In November and December, the market moves indoors to the Civic Center.)

We make a practice out of hitting the Madison Art Fair on the weekend after July 4, a show that fills the Concourse with really respectable fine arts. What's most fun is watching the entertainers who ramble through the crowds. The Morris Dancers, who put on a traditional act dating to medieval England, are regulars, prancing around in their tattered clothes bedecked with ribbons. They expect donations after their routines, so be prepared to drop some change into the tin cups and old hats they pass around. Then there are the fire-eaters and jugglers, the balancing acts, the poetry readers, and the legislators shaking hands. Entertainers all.

Over the past few years, more restaurants have begun to provide varieties of food, getting away from the ordinary brat and hot dog review. The *Essen Haus un Trinken Halle,* 514 East Wilson Street (608–255–4674), presents a German beer garden complete with polka bands. The *White Horse Inn,* 202 North Henry Street (608–255–9933), sets a fabled Sunday brunch.

On the same weekend, the *Art Fair off the Square* in Olin Terrace Park, 2 blocks southeast of the Concourse, features tons of items in the crafts vein. This alternative art fair also leans toward unconventional art, the more unusual the better—so turn your mind loose.

The *Taste of Madison,* on the Sunday of Labor Day weekend, brings fifty of the city's best restaurants to the Capitol Concourse. It's always fun to watch the waiters' race, an institution at the event. Dignitaries "love" the Gelatin Jump, into which they can leap for charity fund-raising.

Speaking of racing, enter the **Mad City Marathon** at the end of May. Whether crawling, walking, or running, the leg-stretching event is fun and great exercise for families and folks of any age. The loop extends around the city, starting on the south side of Lake Monona, then winds through downtown and neighborhoods to the north, through maple Grove (wave to the governor, who comes out to stand on the front porch of the executive mansion), and back down to Lake Wingra.

Take advantage of the free tours in the imposing Wisconsin Capitol building itself, built between 1907 and 1917. Kids like to find as many carved badgers as possible hidden in cornices, over stairwells, and elsewhere.

The outside dome is topped by a gold-leafed statue officially known as *Wisconsin,* artist Daniel Chester French's rendition of what he thought the image of the state should be. No, it isn't a dairy cow, but a toga-draped woman of indeterminate age who has a badger on her head! The best place to view this dauntless lady, other than by helicopter, is from the eighth-floor Top of the Park restaurant at the Inn on the Park Hotel, 22 South Carroll Street (608–257–8811). The restaurant windows are across the street from the Capitol Concourse to the west. The food is worth the view, but the place is a bit pricey.

But let's get back to the Capitol, an occasional old haunt when I was a reporter with the old *Milwaukee Sentinel.* In those days, I was dedicated to chasing politicians and bureaucrats through the labyrinth of hallways in pursuit of truth, justice, and a front-page byline. I learned that some of the byways in the building were more interesting than the politicos. A favorite place was, and still is, the **Grand Army of the Republic Memorial Hall** (608–267–1799), honoring the 83,400 Wisconsonites who served in the Union army during the Civil War.

The state sent fifty-three infantry regiments, four cavalry units, and one battalion of heavy artillery into the conflict's smoke and fire, as part of the famed Iron Brigade. Of the total, 11,000 of the men never returned, dying of wounds or disease. Their regimental battle flags are on display in the fourth-floor hall, along with other memorabilia.

The displays are open to the public 9:00 A.M. to 4:30 P.M. Monday through Saturday and also noon to 4:00 P.M. Sundays from Memorial Day to Labor Day.

After strolling around the Concourse, hit State Street. In Madison that's the avenue to see and be seen on. It's lined with oddball shops where you can purchase 1930s ball gowns or mountaineering gear, scuba equipment, fish sandwiches, books, and crystals. The street is home to the **Madison Civic Center and Gallery,** a couple of theaters, hot singles bars, and the city's trendier restaurants. We won't discuss the last because they tend to come and go. But you'll generally do all right at any of them. Don't simply look at ground level, either. Many of the eateries are on second floors, with banks of windows overlooking the parade below. *Ella's Deli,* a Madison institution for more than a generation, is located at 2902 Washington Street (608–241–5291). Ella's is an old-fashioned kosher deli with all the corned beef and bagel trimmings. Try their decadent hot-fudge sundaes.

The eclectic crowd on the street is a mixture of bustling government workers, intent university students, high school kids trying to look cool, bearded street musicians, tourists, and middle-class shoppers.

Williamson Street, better known as Willy Street, is Madison's hip avenue running along the Lake Monona shoreline, with its range of services from a tattoo parlor to a community health clinic. At the mouth of Willy Street is the Gateway building, a strip mall of ten stores making a neat welcome to the street. The merchants and residents in the neighborhood sponsor a great street fair in mid-September.

Nearby is *Willy St. Co-op* (1221 Williamson, 608–251–6776), for getting last-minute coffee in bulk, fresh avocados, or health foods. *The Pink Poodle,* 5918 Odana Road (608–276–7467), is a shop of another type. The upscale designer shop offers resale fashions, antiques and collectibles, as well as jewelry and handbags.

For pampering of another sort, the *Mansion Hill Inn* is Madison's ultimate in style. The building on 424 North Pinckney Street was constructed in 1858 by the tradesman who built Madison's second capitol building. It went through a succession of owners and housed students during its declining years. The place was purchased by Randy Alexander, a young rehabilitation specialist who had resurrected other fading Madison homes and buildings. He returned the mansion to its former elegance, a veritable posh palace. Alexander brought in his army of craftworkers, who spent a year patching, plastering, and painting the place. The antiques-filled rooms are comfortable and cozy, especially when you're com-

funfacts

The state flag was adopted in 1913 and bears the state seal. The name, *Wisconsin,* and year it became a state, 1848, were added to the design in 1981. The state seal, which was adopted in 1881, includes a sailor and miner supporting a shield with symbols of agriculture, mining, navigation, and manufacturing. The United States coat of arms, signifying Wisconsin's allegiance to the Union, also is included. The badger above the shield represents Wisconsin's nickname as the Badger State.

ing in from a fog-bound, late-winter day. Each bathroom has been snazzed up by Kohler Corporation (Wisconsin-made!) bath devices that bubble, whirl, and refresh the most battered bodies.

Other pluses: A valet parks your car; another serves coffee by the downstairs fireplace. Mansion Hill has become the "in place" for executives and visiting government types who appreciate such little touches.

Honeymooners enjoy the Mansion as well. They probably don't pay much attention, but the telephones have computer modem hookups and teleconference connections. Call (608) 255–3999 for reservations.

Other must-see places in Madison:

The *Credit Union National Association,* 5810 Mineral Point Road (608–231–4000), has an interesting museum that traces the history of economics and coinage, leading to the formation of credit unions. The complex at the corner of Mineral Point and Rosa Roads is also home to the World Council of Credit Unions, with sixty million members. The museum is open during weekly business hours.

funfacts

Ninety-seven of every one hundred Wisconsinites were born in the United States. More than half the residents are of German descent. About 5 percent are African-American. Other major population groups are Polish, Irish, Italian, and English. Hmong and Laotians from Southeast Asia present a sizable new ethnic face to the state, especially in the Stevens Point and Milwaukee areas.

The *Chazen Museum of Art* (formerly the *Elvehjem),* 800 University Avenue (608–263–2246), is one of the better places in town. But you have to check the traveling exhibits as well as the 10,000 pieces in the permanent collection. The gallery is open 9:00 A.M. to 5:00 P.M. Tuesday through Friday and 11:00 A.M. to 5:00 P.M. Saturday and Sunday. Closed Monday.

Visiting the *Wisconsin Historical Museum* is like exploring my grandmother's attic; I never know what I'll find. Subsequently the place is one of my favorites in Mad City. Even as it has grown familiar, I've always learned something new on each visit. Three floors of permanent exhibits hold objects of state interest (and mine, too) from the prehistoric past to contemporary times. Two galleries have regularly changing displays. One recent exhibit focused on Wisconsin during the dawn of the atomic age. The museum has a lot of quirky items, including a button from the vest of Revolutionary War hero John Paul Jones. The museum is located near the State Capitol at 30 North Carroll Street, (608) 264–6555 or visit www.wisconsinhistory.org/museum. Open 9:00 A.M. to 4:00 P.M. Tuesday through Saturday; closed Sunday and Monday.

Another great museum that is a really hard place to get away from—pun intended—is the **Geology Museum,** at 1215 West Dayton Street. This university facility has a walk-through cave that is spooky enough to be fun for kids and educational enough to be satisfying for serious-minded grown-ups. The main eye-opening display in the museum is the towering skeleton of a mastodon, a critter that roamed Wisconsin during the last Ice Age, 10,000 years ago. Call (608) 262–1412 for more details. The Geology Museum is open 8:30 A.M. to 4:30 P.M. Monday through Friday and 9:00 A.M. to 1:00 P.M. on Saturday. Admission is free.

Amid the bustle of grown-up stuff to see and do in Madison, don't forget the littlest tykes. You might even walk past the **Madison Children's Museum** if you weren't aware of its location on bustling State Street (at 100 State, to be exact). This is definitely a necessary kid-oriented off-the-beaten-path stop. The museum is a hands-on child-friendly place. Everyone is encouraged to try out a scientific experiment or get involved in some kind of craft. Eye-level exhibits (for those squirts among us) are aimed at toddlers to grade schoolers. Displays and activities change regularly. For details on current admission prices, call (608) 256–6445. The museum is open Tuesday through Friday 9:00 A.M. to 4:00 P.M., Saturday 9:00 A.M. to 5:00 P.M., and Sunday noon to 5:00 P.M. From Memorial Day through Labor Day, it's also open Monday 9:00 A.M. to 4:00 P.M.

There is one more Madison museum that does not yet get all the nods it deserves. The **Wisconsin Veterans Museum** is part patriotism, part poignancy, and all pride. The museum is located on Madison's Capitol Square at 30 West Mifflin Street, (608) 267–1799. Hours are Monday through Saturday (year-round) 9:00 A.M. to 4:30 P.M. and Sunday (April through September) noon to 4 P.M. The museum has 10,000 square feet of displays on the state's citizen-soldiers. The exhibits range from the Civil War to contemporary times. Lifelike dioramas depict historic military events in which Wisconsin troops participated. A computerized Wisconsin Civil War database helps visitors track relatives and other persons who were in service during the war. One diorama has Union troops charging through a cornfield. These, as well as all the other lifelike characters, have faces modeled after real people. It's almost disconcerting.

I was dismayed on one visit, however, when a family came through the museum and paused to look at the Vietnam display. Suspended from the ceiling in a simulated rescue flight was a full-size helicopter. The chopper hovered over some grunts in a firefight. One soldier leaned out the open side door of the helicopter, machine gun at ready. The mother pointed up at the figure and exclaimed to her wide-eyed kids, "Look, there's Rambo!" All I could think was a mental "ouch" on behalf of all the men and women who served

Fun on the Farm

The Wisconsin Department of Agriculture can provide details on county fairs and agricultural tourism (farm tours, cheese plant visits, and so on). Contact the ag folks at 2811 Agriculture Drive, Madison 53707, (608) 224–5131 (phone), or (608) 224–5111 (fax). The department's e-mail is williams@wheel.datcp.state.wi.us.

For custom-designed tours of rural areas, contact Fred H. Capell of Educational Travel Centre/Value Holidays. He'll line up just about anything you need that moos, bleats, baas, whinnies, grunts, or snorts. The tour offices are located at 438 North Frances Street, Madison, (608) 277–7722. E-mail: fcapell@execpc.com.

in the military during that troubled time. Yet I strongly suggest a visit to this museum, one you might ordinarily pass up. There's valor here.

The **Madison Museum of Contemporary Art** (formerly the Madison Art Center) closed its galleries temporarily in the spring of 2004 during construction of a new display facility within the Overture Center for the Arts. The museum continues to offer numerous off-site exhibits during the construction period, which will run through autumn of 2005. The new facility is scheduled to open in early 2006 as part of the Overture Center for the Arts. A rooftop cafe and outdoor sculpture terrace with indoor/outdoor eating space are included in the design. The facility is located at 227 State Street; (608) 257–0158.

The multi-floored museum will continue to feature modern and contemporary painting, sculpture, photography, works on paper, video, and multimedia work by area, regional, and internationally known artists.

Don't you dare miss **Babcock Hall** at the University of Wisconsin-Madison. "Ice cream, ice cream, we all scream for ice cream" is the anthem at Babcock, the university's dairy science building, on 1605 Linden Drive.

From the Capitol Concourse, drive west on University Avenue and take the campus exit near the university greenhouses (which look like greenhouses) to Linden, the first left at the four-way stop. Babcock will be immediately on the left by the Stock Pavilion, an export center for horse shows and other agricultural events.

The university's own contented cows and friendly Dane County farmers provide the base product for the whole, 2 percent, and skim milk, buttermilk, cheese, and yogurt produced there. Yet ice cream is the best-seller in the Babcock Hall retail store, the Memorial Union, and Union South. Cones and sundaes are available in the two union buildings, while quarts and gallons can be purchased in Babcock Hall. The university's dorm food service also offers the dairy goods for the cafeteria lines.

Helpful Madison Contacts

Greater Madison Convention and Visitors Bureau, 615 East Washington Avenue, Madison 53703 (608–255–2537 or 25–LAKES or www.visitMadison.com). A twenty-four-hour answering service can take messages or record a request for an information packet. Just leave a name and address.

Isthmus *magazine* (free on newsstands; $35 annual subscription fee), 101 King Street, Madison 53703 (608–251–5627). The magazine does the best job reporting on entertainment and events on a weekly basis, coming out on Thursday.

Parks Department, Madison Municipal Building, Suite 120, 215 Martin Luther King Jr. Boulevard, Madison 53701–2987 (608–266–4711).

The ice cream is 12 percent butterfat, rather than the industry standard of only 10 percent, according to the plant directors. Pure cane sugar instead of corn sweeteners is used. With Babcock ice cream, you'll never get just a cone full of air, as with some other commercial preparations.

Warner Park is where Madisonites watch baseball like it oughta be played. The park is home of the Madison Mallards, the city's summer collegiate baseball team, where eager young players smack base hits and snag flies. The promotion-minded team offers regular ticket discounts and game-night giveaways. Families get in for a $20 four-pack (four tickets, four sodas, four hot dogs) on Wednesday night. The Mallards also offer a fireworks show every Saturday evening. The team, made up of college all-stars, plays from June through August against state rivals such as the La Crosse Loggers, Wausau's Wisconsin Woodchucks, and the Eau Claire Express. There's hardly a better way to spend a hot summer evening. Be aware that promotions change each season. Call the Mallards at (608) 246–4277.

Guests often wind up on the radio waves during the *Whadya Know* show hosted by Madisonite storyteller/comic Michael Feldman. This internationally syndicated program on **Wisconsin Public Radio** (608–263–7903) features the irreverently hilarious Feldman, who regularly pulls people into his goofy on-air quizzes. Hiding in the back rows doesn't work for the bashful. Feldman often crawls over rows of seats to get at folks. It's all in good fun, and it's a good way to win a prize. The program is broadcast on Saturday morning starting at 10:00 A.M. from the Monona Terrace Convention Hall. In addition to its airing on stations around the United States, *Whadya Know* can be heard in Berlin, Stockholm, Helsinki, and Geneva.

Middleton, Madison's closest western suburb, is home of the **Capital Brewery and Beer Garden,** on 7734 Terrace (608–836–7100), one of the area's most popular breweries. Weather permitting, the beer garden here is a great place to loll away a summer Saturday afternoon. This microbrewery makes a smooth GartenBrau in light, dark, and seasonal draughts. Tours are Friday at 3:30 P.M. and Saturday at 1:30 and 3:30 P.M. Brewmaster Kirby Nelson pours mean brews while he chats about malts and barleys.

Middleton is also home of **Clasen's European Bakery,** 7610 Donna Drive (608–831–2032), probably one of the state's best bakeries. The company is owned by Ernest and Rolf Clasen, who immigrated from Gerolstein, Germany, in the late 1950s. Both are *konditors,* officially recognized pastry chefs. They emphatically state they are *not* just bakers. For a time, the brothers made only candy.

When the price of sugar skyrocketed in the 1960s, they moved into tortes and coffee cakes, although a major portion of their business remains manufacturing chocolate that is shipped out by the semitrailer truckload and in fifty-pound wafers. But, oh, those baked items. In the rear self-service room, banks of refrigeration units house towering cream cakes. Trays are laden with breads and cookies. Just remembering a recent stop adds pounds where they shouldn't be. Shop hours are 7:00 A.M. to 5:30 P.M. Monday through Friday and 7:30 A.M. to 5:00 P.M. Saturday

The **Old Middleton Centre** offers a variety of gift shops and boutiques. The outdoor gazebo in the center of the complex, located at 750 Hubbard Avenue, is a good place to relax and rest your feet after shopping. The Centre is 3 blocks northeast of the Capital Brewery. From Terrace Avenue East, take the first left (Hubbard), then go 2 blocks, and the shops will be on your left.

Mounds of History

Wisconsin has a wealth of Indian mounds. Among those that are really off the beaten path is a site on land owned by Bryce Tollackson, a retired farmer who lived west of Madison. Tollackson donated the site to the Archaeological Conservancy in the mid-1990s. The elder Hintz, accompanied by son Steve, interviewed Tollackson for a story in *American Archaeology.* The Tollackson site consists of thirteen large effigies, one of the most complete clusters of undamaged prehistoric burial units in the state. The largest is 4 feet high and at least 80 feet long. But it's tough to find the eagle, bear, and other shapes. Brush, trees, and winter snow cover and/or obstruct the view today, whereas about 1,000 years ago they were easily seen.

Tollackson wanted to protect his "graves," as he calls them, so he contacted the conservancy. He worked with University of Wisconsin–La Crosse archaeologist Jim Theler to plot the forty-acre site containing the mounds. For an interesting historical twist, more than a century ago, a state surveyor had found but mistakenly mapped the locale. Those notes were forgotten until 1993, when a Mississippi Valley Archaeology Center student stumbled across the mounds on a survey tour of the area.

The Centre is considered one of the best places in the Madison area for pur-chasing smaller imported gift items such as plates and crystal.

For eating in Middleton, try **Captain Bill's,** 2701 Century Harbor Road (608–831–7327). Captain Bill's offers a casual, rustic, Key West atmosphere and is located on beautiful Lake Mendota. Enjoy fresh seafood, steaks, chicken, pasta, or sandwiches while admiring the brilliant reds and purples of the sun-set illuminating the sky. The restaurant is open every evening at 4:30 P.M.

Cave of the Mounds (www.caveofthemounds.com) is only 20 miles west of Madison on Highways 18 and 151 in **Blue Mounds.** The caves have the usual selection of stalagmites, stalactites, and pools that make a great several-hour stopover for anyone with a carful of kids. The history of the place is the most interesting, however. The farm where the caves were discovered dates from 1828 and is one of the oldest in Dane County. In December 1987 Cave of the Mounds was designated a National Natural Landmark by the Department of the Interior. Tickets to Cave of the Mounds cost $12.00 for visitors thirteen and older, $11.00 for seniors sixty-five and older, and $6.00 for children four to twelve. Three and under are free. Hours are 9:00 A.M. to 4:00 P.M. from November 15 to March 15

Cave of the Mounds

and 9:00 A.M. to 7:00 P.M. from Memorial Day to Labor Day. It's best to call ahead for weekday visits dur-ing the winter. Tours take about one hour and are kicked off by a video show. A self-guided nature trail over seven acres of the farm is also avail-able. Although there's a restaurant on the premises, the cave owners don't mind if guests bring picnic lunches. They've provided a pleasantly shaded grove for snacking. They also have a great rock and mineral gift shop. For more details contact Cave of the Mounds at (608) 437–3038.

"Velkommen" is the greeting in Mount Horeb, one of several Nor-wegian communities at the western edge of Dane County. Although the town was originally settled by English, Irish, and German settlers in 1861, three-quarters of the popu-lation was Scandinavian by 1870.

Downhill Delights

Wisconsin doesn't have the Rockies for downhill ski thrills, but it does have thirty-three great sites that are guaranteed to pump the adrenaline. I've never been one much for careening down a cliffside on two skinny sticks, but I must admit that I enjoy a winter weekend at Whitecap or Mount Ashwabay in northern Wisconsin, Rib Mountain in the center, or in southern Wisconsin's Tyrol Basin and Alpine Valley. These aren't bunny slopes, folks; they offer grandiose vertical drops. Most of the state's ski centers have snowmaking equipment in case Ma Nature takes a holiday.

For a listing of slopes, call the Wisconsin Division of Tourism (800–432–8747) for its latest *Fall/Winter Event & Recreation Guide*.

Since there is one-quarter Larson in our blood, we occasionally like to stop and find out the latest on the Norskie front. The folks there annually put on a six-week midsummer program called the **Song of Norway Festival,** which culminates in the presentation of the musical comedy *Song of Norway.*

The play is loosely based on the life of Norwegian composer Edvard Grieg. The show is usually offered the last Saturday in June and each Saturday in July. For times and ticket prices, contact the Mount Horeb Chamber of Commerce, P.O. Box 84, 100 South First Street, Mount Horeb 53572.

You'll know this is the right town by the giant trolls lurking outside **Open House Imports,** 308 East Main Street, one of several excellent import and gift shops. The trolls are statues, of course, yet when our kids were younger they were never quite sure. Since trolls turn to stone in the daylight, they had a sneaking suspicion that there might have once been such live creatures.

Even if you're not a mustard lover, the **Mount Horeb Mustard Museum** at 100 West Main Street is a must-see. In 1986 owner Barry Levenson had a brainstorm to open such a facility while meandering through supermarket aisles. He decided to amass the world's largest collection of mustard. So, in 1991 he quit his job as an assistant attorney general for Wisconsin and opened the museum a year later. His dream came true. He is now the proud owner of about 4,000 mustards from all over the world, making it the world's largest collection of the condiment. He has been featured on *Oprah, The John Walsh Show,* and HGTV's *The Good Life.*

Samples are available before purchasing. The museum hours are daily from 10:00 A.M. to 5:00 P.M. Its phone is (800) 438–6878. National Mustard Day is held there the first Saturday in August. There's no need to pass the mustard—plenty is within reach.

Other attractions in the Mount Horeb area include the **Tyrol Ski Basin, Blue Mounds State Park,** and **Little Norway,** a Norwegian pioneer homesite and church.

The only Wisconsin winery on the National Register of Historic Places is the *Wollersheim Winery,* on Highway 188, 0.25 mile south of Highway 60. Just across the Wisconsin River is the village of Prairie du Sac. The original vineyards were planted in the 1840s by Count Agoston Haraszthy, a Hungarian whose dreams exceeded the reality of Wisconsin's harsh winters. The noble became discouraged after several years of cold, so he eventually sold out, moved to California to help establish the wine industry there, and subsequently made his fortune. The new owner was Peter Kehl, whose family were vintners since 1533 in Germany's Rhineland.

Kehl built most of the complex's existing buildings, operating the winery until a killing frost in 1899 effectively destroyed the crop. After a generation of vacancy, the grounds were purchased in 1972 by Bob and JoAnn Wollersheim. They replanted the slopes with such hearty hybrids as Millot, De Chaunac, and Foch for red wines and Aurora and Seyval Blanc for white wines.

The Wollersheim's wine maker, Phillipe Coquard, whose family is also in the wine business in the Beaujolais region of France, is especially proud of the ruby nouveau produced each autumn. This young wine has beaten out competitors from Oregon, California, New York, and other wine-growing states in major competitions.

Public Transportation

Wisconsin's towns are served by a number of motor-coach companies. One of the best is Wisconsin Coach Lines, 1520 Arcadian Avenue, Waukesha 53186 (262–542–8861; www.wisconsincoach.com). There is no need to drive an auto to O'Hare International Airport in Chicago. Milwaukee and other communities in southeastern Wisconsin are served by United Limo motor coaches, which whisk passengers to the proper terminal. This certainly beats worrying about long-term parking or rental-car return when flying in or out of the Windy City. Call (800) 833–5555 for ticket prices and information.

On the national scene there's always Greyhound. For fare and schedule details, call (800) 231–2222. There also are charter firms in many major cities. Look in the local yellow pages for specifics.

Badger Coach Lines provides fast, frequent service between Milwaukee and Madison's downtown, as well as to the University of Wisconsin campus. Call (414) 276–7490 for fares, departures, and arrivals. The route runs along I–94.

Most large cities also have excellent bus transportation along their streets. This is generally an inexpensive, eye-opening way to look over a town from the ground level. A local bus can get you into the most off-the-beaten-path locales, in addition to hitting all the high points. Even if you aren't familiar with bus riding, hop on board. Such a ride is generally cheaper than a cab, and you'll see plenty more.

In 1990 the Wollersheims purchased the old Stone Mill Winery in Cedarburg (Ozaukee County). Renamed the Cedar Creek Winery, that facility also has started winning its share of awards.

Winery tours are offered every hour from 10:15 A.M. to 4:15 P.M. daily, followed by a wine tasting, of course. Throughout the year, the Wollersheims do more than just show off their kegs and casks of award-winning wine.

As great promoters they sponsor numerous programs, ranging from a spring folk festival to grape-growing seminars, wine-making instructions, and a harvest festival that features a grape-stomping contest. For specific dates contact the Wollersheims at their winery (608–643–6515).

If you come to the area in winter, bald eagles can occasionally be seen swooping high over the snow-covered cornfields. The huge birds dive for fish on the Wisconsin River, with the best opportunities for spotting the eagles being in the vicinity of the Prairie du Sac dam.

The **Wisconsin Folk Museum** is housed in a renovated 1880s hardware store. Its displays focus on the ethnic heritages and other forces that shaped the history of southwestern Dane County. The museum is located at 100 South Second Street in downtown Mount Horeb, twenty minutes west of Madison.

One of the main attractions is the award winning "Ethnic Evolution and Contribution in Southwestern Dane County" exhibit. Brian Bigler, museum president, explains that the exhibit relates the stories of the seven predominate ethnic groups in the area. Also featured are exhibits covering pre-settlement days to the twenty-first century. Call (608) 437–4742 for more information. The museum is a nonprofit organization that gratefully accepts donations.

One of the most interesting displays is a large hand-whittled American flag, dating from the 1930s. The stars on the flag's blue field are carved from a single block of wood. The stripes are whittled chains, some of which are 5 feet long. It's quite a sight.

Mazomanie is located along Reeve Road off Highway 14. The town name was taken from the Sauk Indian term loosely translated as "iron horse" or "iron that walks," referring to the old-time trains that rumbled through here during the pioneer era. Take Reeve Road on the west end of town to **Hoofbeat Ridge,** an accredited American Camping Association horseback-riding camp that offers numerous weekend and special events in addition to its regular camp and riding-lesson schedules. The camp has been operated by the Bennett family (founders John and Betty Bennett had eleven kids!) and assorted in-laws since 1963. It's one of the largest horse camps in Wisconsin, with strict adherence to safety and promoting the understanding of what horses are all about. Both western and English styles of riding are taught. All our kids have attended several years of summer camp at Hoofbeat and subsequently have become competent, careful riders. What makes Hoofbeat special are the adult riding weekends, family camp-outs, riding shows, dressage presentations, and similar programs beyond the regularly scheduled riding classes and summer camp. Remember, this is a casual place, one for blue jeans and boots, but highly professional in its approach to teaching folks how to ride properly and well. For details contact Director Ted Marthe, Hoofbeat Ridge Camp, 5304 Reeve Road, Mazomanie 53560 (608–767–2593). Store hours are 9:00 A.M. to 5:00 P.M. Monday through Wednesday, 9:00 A.M. to 6:00 P.M. Thursday through Saturday, and 11:00 A.M. to 5:00 P.M. Sunday.

To the southeast of Madison on Highway 18 is the small community of Cambridge, home to several pottery works. **Rowe Pottery,** with its factory at 404 England Street, has a broad selection of pottery in gray and blue hues. Rowe's company store is located at 217 Main Street (608–423–3935). Store hours are 9:00 A.M. to 5:00 P.M. Monday through Wednesday, 9:00 A.M. to 6:00 P.M. Thursday through Saturday, and 11:00 A.M. to 5:00 P.M. Sunday.

This farming community is at the western edge of Wisconsin's major tobacco-growing area. Along the highway are farms with their distinctive open-sided barns, used for drying the tobacco leaves. This Wisconsin product is generally used for cigar wrappings.

Famed artist Georgia O'Keeffe is remembered around her home community of **Sun Prairie,** a rural community about 7 miles northeast of Madison. She was born on a farm 3.5 miles southeast of town on November 15, 1887. A red roadside plaque now marks the spot. When she was fourteen, she moved away with her family to Virginia and went on to pursue her meteoric career in the American Southwest. An autographed copy of one of her catalogs and one of her works are displayed at the **Sun Prairie Library and Museum** on Main Street. A meeting room in the library, where the town council meets, was dedicated to O'Keeffe in 1987, the year after her death.

The dramatic power of the Ice Age is readily evident throughout this part of the state, especially in the Devil's Lake area and the Baraboo Range. This stretch of jagged limestone cliffs, moraine deposits, and deep valleys lies about 3 miles south of Baraboo and 20 miles south of the Wisconsin Dells. Wisconsin Highways 159, 123, 113, and 33 enter the area of gorges, hills, crests, flatlands, and river bottoms. Access to the state roads is easy via Interstates 90/94, with interchanges some 12 miles east and north of Devil's Lake. Highway 12 cuts straight south from the Dells to the Wisconsin River, crossing at Sauk City and on into Madison.

That highway must have more roadhouses per mile than any other stretch in the state. A roadhouse, as you know, might have a wild and woolly history comprised of equal parts bathtub gin, flappers, and who knows what else.

Wisconsin roadhouses these days are calmer, of course, but you can drop by for a shot and a beer, a sandwich, and some great local conversation tossed in for good measure. The Missouri Tavern, Ma Schmitty's, Charlie Brown's, the Springfield Inn, and others along Highway 12, between Highway 19 and Madison, have long been great old diamonds in the rough. But give 'em a try —you'll generally like what you find. They are especially cozy on a blizzardy Wisconsin afternoon, before the plows arrive to beat back the drifts creeping in across the fields.

Marathon County

The sprawling paper factories of **Wausau** pale in significance when compared to **Rib Mountain,** the billion-year-old hunk of rock that towers above the city on its west side. The mountain, complete with a state park campground, mountain biking, and ski runs, was not crunched by the glaciers that flattened the rest of Wisconsin 10,000 years ago. The mountain is 1,940 feet high, the second-highest peak in the state, providing plenty of recreational opportunities for the activity-minded. Just to the south of Rib Mountain is the county's **Nine-Mile Recreation Area** on Red Bud Road off County Highway North, a labyrinth of back roads and logging paths that are available for cross-country skiing and more biking.

For a more urbane experience, Wausau's Artrageous Weekend in September takes over the downtown pedestrian mall, where artists and craftworkers display their wares. In addition to wandering musicians, jugglers, and other street performers, there is a children's hands-on area where they paint and learn to make pottery.

Just south of Wausau on Highway S is the 20,000-acre **George W. Meade Wildlife Area** (715–421–7800), one of the best picnic areas in the state. It's also a good location for deer and duck watching.

Maybe it's because Stevens Point is a college town, where folks like to sit around and chat over a brew, but there are two great coffeehouses in town. I always like to hang out in one or the other for a sip o' brew whenever I'm there. Even though my cup of choice is tea, I still can be accommodated at either the **Mission Coffee House** or the **Supreme Bean.** The Mission, 1319 Strongs Avenue (715–342–1002), also has a full line of espresso drinks for those who like high-octane java. Sandwiches, bagels, pastries, and soup round out the menu. This is a great place, even for families. Poetry readings, board games, and folky-type music fill in the hours. If there is a show, they are open late. Otherwise the Mission is open 7:00 A.M. to 8:00 P.M. Monday through Friday, 9:00 A.M. to 8:00 P.M. Saturday, and 9:00 A.M. to 5:00 P.M. Sunday.

The Supreme Bean has cinnamon rolls to die for . . . well, don't be rash, because if you did bite the Big One, you'd miss the fresh baked scones. Choices, choices. Cappuccino, lattes, and mochas, as well as the usual espressos and straight coffees, are served. What I like about the Supreme Bean is the smoke-free, kick-back ambience. You'll find the place at 1100 Main Street (715–344–0077).

Sauk County

According to archaeologists, the ancient Wisconsin River cut an 800-foot-deep trench through this vicinity in the eons before the Ice Age. When the latest push by glaciers moved southward in several waves (70,000 to 10,000 years ago), ice from the so-called Green Bay glacial lobe spread its cold fingers around the hills that make up today's rocky Baraboo Range. Both ends of the river gorge were plugged with ice, which created the Devil's Lake basin. Eventually, the ice melted and dumped millions of tons of debris into the riverbed, pushing the river itself about 9 miles to the east, where it is today.

mightyflowage

The mighty Wisconsin River rises in the Lac Vieux Desert on the Wisconsin-Michigan border and flows south 430 miles through central Wisconsin. The tannin-colored waters rush past Portage and then turn west. The Wisconsin empties into the Mississippi River about 2 miles below Prairie du Chien. Near the Wisconsin Dells, it forms Lake Delton, while cutting through sandstone rock to a depth of about 150 feet.

Subsequently softened by expansive stands of oak and birch groves, the resulting landscape, with all its bumps and dips, is considered some of the most beautiful scenery in the state. The centerpiece is the 5,100-acre ***Devil's Lake State Park,*** which attracts more than 1.5 million visitors a year.

The park offers 450 campsites, hiking trails, swimming, fishing, and sailing. Since the place is so expansive, you can generally rummage around to your heart's content without rubbing shoulders with anyone else.

The busiest days, however, are those bustling June, July, and August weekends, when the campgrounds are generally booked and the lake banks seem knee-deep in kids with plastic fishing rods.

But don't let that keep you away at other times. Midweek and off-season visits leave plenty of room to ramble. Since the state park is central to the tourist attractions in the Dells, the Madison scene, and other getaways in the vicinity, it makes for a good jumping-off point if your family is in the camping mood.

The second major physical feature of central Wisconsin is the mighty Wisconsin River, which bisects the state. It's the longest river in Wisconsin, easily earning the same name. The waterway runs some 430 miles from the lake district in northeastern Wisconsin to the Mississippi River at Prairie du Chien. At Portage, the Wisconsin connects to the Fox River, which eventually links up with Lake Michigan.

These days, the tannin-colored river is a favorite for canoeists and anglers. In early years the river was a major route for the massive lumber rafts floated downstream to the sawmills. Today, sunbathers, looking like bratwurst on a grill as they loll about during hot summer afternoons, enjoy the seclusion of dunes and sandbars along the riverbanks.

Over the past few years, several of the more remote stretches of beach frontage have been taken over by nudists, many of them college students from the University of Wisconsin in nearby Madison. More than one canoeing party has been surprised by tanned (or brightly sunburned pink) folks in the buff who wave friendly greetings. For decorum's sake, we won't tell you the exact sandbars . . . but . . . if you put your canoe in the river at the Highway 14 crossing, across from Helena and Tower Hill campground. . . .

A more staid way to make the river crossing is via the **Merrimac ferry-boat.** Best of all, it's free! Since the Wisconsin Department of Transportation gained control of passage over the Wisconsin River in 1933, motorists, hikers, and bikers have been getting a free ride. The first ferry was operating at the same site as early as 1844. Currently, the new *Colsac III* runs twenty-four hours a day between April 15 and December 1, depending on winter ice conditions. *Colsac* stands for Columbia and Sauk Counties, linked by the ferry. The seven-minute ride accommodates fifteen cars or trucks each run; the ferry makes some 40,000 trips a season while carrying 195,000 vehicles. The crossing is reached via Highway 113 between Okee on the south shore and Merrimac on the north. The Wisconsin River is 0.5 mile wide at this point, but the crossing saves a 9-mile drive west or a 12-mile drive east to the closest bridges.

Impress your kids by telling them that an underwater cable links the boat to shore, with the vessel's monster diesel engine pulling the boat and its load back and forth. The tykes will think you're a veritable maritime encyclopedia.

Rest rooms and privately run refreshment stands are conveniently located on each shore. Yet a warning is necessary. Don't get boxed between other waiting cars if the kids have to make a last-minute panic pit stop prior to boarding. It's difficult to pull out of line to retrieve a pokey youngster still in the facilities. The child may have to pick up the next ride over if you get carried away in the flow of traffic onto the ferry deck.

Tragic Land

Hiking the Black Hawk Unit of the Lower Wisconsin State Riverway is a challenge. You scamper up steep slopes, trudge across sun-drenched meadows, plunge through mosquito-dense forests, carefully avoid deer droppings, and generally have a wonderful time. It wasn't so swell more than one hundred years ago, when a small band of Sac and Fox warriors under Black Hawk held off an overwhelmingly superior force of U.S. militia on this site. In 1832 the Native Americans were trying to flee across the nearby Wisconsin River where they hoped the whites would leave them alone. But the troops caught up with the band on the ridges overlooking the river. While Black Hawk's few able-bodied warriors fought back with bows and arrows, their starving women, children, and elders fled down the hill and crossed the river. One soldier and several dozen Native Americans died in the fierce fighting.

The centrally located **Wisconsin Dells,** touching Juneau, Adams, Sauk, and Columbia Counties, is the epitome of what outsiders consider summer fun in Wisconsin. Visitors are drawn from around the Midwest to see the fudge shops, arcades, wax museums, shooting galleries, souvenir shops, and hamburger joints that line the streets of the Dells and the adjacent town of Lake Delton. Tourism is nothing new in the Dells neighborhood. Before the turn of the twentieth century, thousands of visitors flocked here to cruise the upper and lower sections of the Wisconsin River and marvel at the scenery. That remains the best part of a vacation in the region. There's little that can beat a river ride upstream on a warm summer day, with the chance to put your feet up on a rail and to admire the passing river bluffs.

It seems as if every high promontory has a Native American maiden leaping to her death because her lover died in battle or some other legend. The Dells also has such a cliff.

A sunset cruise is a great way to see the Dells. Trips run from 7:45 to 9:15 P.M. from the Dells landing downtown.

I've always thought the Upper Dells were more scenic than the section below the town. But you can make that choice for yourself. An exciting way to see the flowage is a ride on the Ducks, surplus World War II amphibious vehicles that bump and leap over set trails, splash through the Wisconsin River, and rumble along pathways near the town streets—much to the delight of riders. Keep your camera bags and purses off the floor because the splashing water often swirls along the base of the vehicle and out the back. Several companies offer rides.

The crown prince of the Wisconsin Dells was probably the late Tommy Bartlett, the impresario of a water, sky, and thrill show that has been a staple of Dells entertainment for three decades. Bartlett, who looked like Santa Claus on vacation, had packaged a great program of divers, splashers, fliers, and clowns for a show that runs several times daily throughout the season. It's a rain-or-shine proposition, so dress accordingly. Ask for the reserved seats, which are actually comfortable lawn chairs.

Attached to his water-show park is **Robot World,** Bartlett's vision of a futuristic home operated by mechanical people. It's a worthwhile stop, with just the right tongue-in-cheek combination of hokeyness and fun. The lower level of the building is a hands-on science hall, where kids and adults can conduct all sorts of interesting physics experiments. You can often find Bartlett down there, having a good time along with his visitors. This place is a boon on a rainy day if you are traveling with youngsters. They'll have plenty to do. But get there early—other parents often have the same idea.

Some other rewarding stops in the neighborhood are the **Haunted Mansion, Timba Vati Wildlife Park,** and the **Wax World of Stars.** The interior features glitzy Hollywood sets. An excellent attraction for photography fans is **Bennett House,** which reopened in June 2000 as a Wisconsin state historic site. This was the home of noted photographer Henry Hamilton Bennett, a nineteenth-century photographer who concentrated on the rocky Dells landscape for his scenes. You can compare his photos of early Dells tourism to today's lifestyles. There isn't that much difference, other than clothing and hair arrangements. Admission is charged.

But its waterparks now have secured the Dells on the vacation map. In 1980, the appropriately-named Waterman family opened the first slides at its **Noah's Ark** complex (608–254–6351; www.noahsarkwaterpark.com), which remains one of the largest in the country at seventy acres of fun and games. It wasn't long before other properties jumped on the waterwagon. The **Kalahari** touts itself as the largest indoor waterpark in the country, with its 125,000 square feet of splash areas. Watch out for the FlowRider surfing simulator, which pushes 50,000 gallons of water per minute into ocean-like waves. Call 877–253–5466 or visit www.kalahariresort.com/waterparks.

At **Great Wolf Lodge,** 1,000 gallons of water roar down from a tipped bucket high on a scaffolding overhead to drench happy kids and adults alike. For details on the Wolf's Howlin' Tornado 53-foot vertical drop into a pool, call 800–559–WOLF (9653) or visit www.dells.greatwolflodge.com. The **Wilderness Waterpark Resort** brags of its combined 350,000 square feet of indoor and outdoor pools and slides. The fun here includes water blasters and depth charges on the Surge, the five-person raft ride on the Fantastic Voyage, and the four-story Ransack Ridge with its water firing cannons. For more on the Wilderness, check in at 800–867–9453 or www.wildernessresort.com.

For comprehensive listings of prices, accommodations, and attractions, contact the Wisconsin Dells Visitor & Convention Bureau, 701 Superior Street, Wisconsin Dells 53965 (608–254–8088); in Wisconsin call toll-free, (800) 223–3557.

Our favorite place in Sauk County is **Baraboo,** old home of the Ringling Brothers Circus. Wisconsin is known as "the Mother of the Circus" because more than one hundred shows were organized here from pre–Civil War days to the 1980s. Baraboo is subsequently "the High Seat of Circusdom" in Wisconsin. The town is gung-ho show biz all the way, calling itself "the Circus City of the Nation."

August Ringling, father of the famed circus family, operated harness shops in Baraboo after moving there from Prairie du Chien in the mid-1800s. The Ringling boys loved entertainment life and began their Greatest Show on Earth (it wasn't quite that yet) in 1884. They winter-quartered along the Baraboo River (some folks still claim that an elephant or two was buried along the banks). Their cousins, the Gollmars, also operated a circus out of Baraboo, and numerous city residents were employed in wagon and harness making for the shows. Entertainers built homes in town, with practice barns and halls in their backyards. The friezes around the Courthouse Annex depict this delightful history.

The showpiece of Baraboo is the refurbished **Circus World Museum,** site of the old Ringling headquarters. In 1987 the CWM received a Phoenix Award from the Society of American Travel Writers for its preservation efforts. The museum's buildings and tents house the world's largest collection of rebuilt circus wagons and show off an extensive display of memorabilia, in addition to housing a vast research collection of posters, photos, route books, diaries, and

Bridge to the Past

For an out-of-the-way place to hike, the elder Hintz recommends **Natural Bridge State Park,** a 560-acre site 16 miles south of Baraboo on U.S. Highway 12 and 10 miles farther on County Highway C. The most interesting feature of the park is a sandstone arch with an opening 25 feet high and 35 feet wide. Located in the state's "driftless area" not smushed by glaciers, the "natural bridge" was created by weather erosion of the soft sandstone.

It is estimated that 10,000 to 12,000 years ago, humans were living in the area. They used the rock shelters near the bridge as a retreat from storms, enemies, and wild animals. The site has been extensively researched, with remains of ancient fires and rubble showing that people wandered this region at least 500 generations ago. This fact certainly shows that we are nothing more than another tiny blip on history's forward march. Will anyone notice our remains (decayed shopping malls and an abundance of Styrofoam) in another 500 generations?

similar artifacts. Wagons from the museum are shown each July in the Great Circus Parade in Milwaukee, hauled there by steam train. Being a circus nut myself, I've been coming to the CWM since the early 1960s, when the place opened. A selection of my own circus photos has even been displayed there. They were taken while I was a correspondent for *Amusement Business* magazine, a national entertainment publication.

off-roadgetaway

The **Dell Creek Wildlife Area** is a favorite hiking spot for getaway strolls far from the maddening crowd. The area spreads out over 2,125 acres of state-owned land in Sauk and Juneau Counties. The main entrance is 7 miles northeast of Reedsburg on County Highway H. You can see ruffed grouse, wild turkeys, rabbits, and plenty of deer. This is an adventure because there are no marked trails in the wildlife area, but take the meandering deer paths and old logging roads. Nearby is Tower Hill State Park, (608) 588-2116, if you need more information.

Driving around town, you'll see the **Al Ringling Theater,** the harness shop owned by the Ringlings' father, and numerous houses in which circus performers lived. Live performances, including loading and unloading a circus train, are part of the show back on the grounds. Kids love getting their photos taken in the gorilla wagon near the front entrance. I've seen more than one teacher or guide glad to "lock up" a few wild tykes, even if only for a few minutes. The museum, operated by the State Historical Society, is located at 550 Water Street (608–356–8341).

Five miles north of Baraboo, just off Highway 12 on Shady Lane Road, is the **International Crane Foundation,** where you can see several species of cranes from around the world. The conservation group that runs the center is always happy to have visitors. The center is open from 9:00 A.M. to 5:00 P.M. April 15 to October 31. Tours start at 10:00 A.M.; and 1:00 and 3:00 P.M. Memorial Day through Labor Day. Self-guided tours are also available. Call first (608–356–9462) because of the mating and hatching season. During that time the curators often have to perform crane mating dances to get the big birds in the appropriate frame of mind. Now *that* makes for quite a sight, although the ritual is closed to the public. Call for current admission prices.

North Freedom is home of the **Mid-Continent Railway Museum,** operated by volunteers who love oil cans, iron, steam, and old trains. There are some 300 members of the Mid-Continent Railway Historical Society, which has restored dozens of ancient engines and railcars, offering rides on a regular basis in the summer and autumn.

The D&R No. 9, built in 1884, is one of the country's oldest operating locomotives, repaired by society members in a huge car barn on their property. The "clubhouse" is a depot built in 1894, which houses exhibitions of equip-

D&R No. 9 at the Mid-Continent Railway Museum

ment and railroad mementos. I've always enjoyed the autumn color tours that the club sponsors on weekends when the leaves are reaching their maximum rainbow effect. Occasionally, at a particularly scenic curve, the train stops to allow photographers to get off and take pictures from near the tracks. The train will back up and make a steamy, roaring run past the clicking shutters to magnificent effect. And, yes, the train does return to pick everyone up.

The winter snow run during the third week in February is also great for photographs, but dress warmly. The coaches are heated by woodstoves, just as they were in the old days. Those closest to the stove almost bake while the poor riders in the rear can get *preeeettty* frosty by the time the jaunt is completed. When getting off the train for those extra-special winter-weather photos of a steam locomotive in action, be sure to wear appropriate foot coverings, because snow along the tracks can be quite deep.

During the summer the fifty-minute tour travels over its own rail bed between the hills and valleys of the Baraboo Range from North Freedom to Quartzite Lake, stopping at the iron mining town of La Rue. Now a ghost town, the once bustling community was served by the railroad in 1903.

Trains usually begin rolling toward mid-May, keeping up the action through Labor Day and some weekends through mid-October. Rides are scheduled for 10:30 A.M. and 12:30, 2:00, and 3:30 P.M. daily during the season. The museum is open from 9:30 A.M. until 5:00 P.M. Admission prices for adults are $12.00, children three to twelve pay $7.00, and senior citizens pay $11.00.

Every few summers, some historical society members live on the grounds, sleeping in the private rail coaches for the ultimate in luxury. The care that they have put into repairing the venerable gear is worth a stop, since much of the rolling stock has been featured in commercials and movies. It's like watching someone you know appear in a starring role. Equipment from the museum has been featured in the Swedish film *The Emigrants* and in the movie *Gaily, Gaily,* among numerous others.

North Freedom is reached by taking I–90 to the Baraboo exit and going through Baraboo on Highway 33 to Highway 136, where you can then follow the signs on County Road PF to the depot staging area. The complex is 6 miles west of Baraboo and 50 miles northwest of the Wisconsin Dells. For information on the Mid-Continent Railway Historical Society, contact the organization at Walnut Street, North Freedom 53951 (608–522–4261).

Every traveler needs a bit of history to jump-start such an adventure here. The best place to begin is at Reedsburg's ***Pioneer Village,*** featuring a number of restored log cabin structures and pioneer homes gathered from a 30-mile radius of town. Pioneer Village sits in a fifty-two-acre park east of Reedsburg on Highway 33. One of the most interesting is the Kruse cabin with its unusual puncheon floor made of black locust stakes pounded into the earth. At the Willow Creek Church, if ears are attuned properly, a gentle breeze seems to pick up faint strains of nineteenth-century Lutheran hymns.

The Norman Rockwell Exhibit at the ***Voyageur Inn,*** 200 Viking Drive, showcases about 4,000 postcards, original magazine covers, calendars, and similar items on original paper stock painted by the famed illustrator between 1911 and 1976. The artwork, collected by Darlyn Merath, adorns the hallways around the Inn.

Wood County

Wisconsin Rapids has been a papermaking hub since the 1830s. ***Stora Enso,*** 510 High Street (715–422–3111), offers tours of its plant and self-guided walks in nearby forestland owned by the firm.

Wisconsin's only drive-through dairy store is located in ***Marshfield.*** The Weber family, and assorted in-laws, has been prominent in Wood County's dairy industry for more than ninety years. The retail outlet is just west of Marshfield on Fourteenth Street, about 0.75 mile from Central Avenue. The ***Weber's Farm Store*** produces, processes, and retails its own milk from its 265-head herd, which grazes contentedly on 600 nearby acres. Talk about fresh. The milk is ready for sale within hours after milking. You can get whole milk, reduced-fat milk, low-fat milk, skim milk, and chocolate reduced-fat milk (How do they get the cows to do that?). Ice cream, eggs, butter, heavy whipping cream, cheese curds, and fresh cheese also are offered. And the family has excellent lean ground beef from its own beef cattle. Store hours are 8:30 A.M. to 7:00 P.M. Monday through Friday and 8:30 A.M. to 5:00 P.M. Saturday. Call (715) 384–5639.

The region around Wisconsin Rapids is known as the state's Cranberry Country, with its many bogs filled each autumn with brilliant red berries destined for the holiday table or for juice. There are several bogs open to visitors during the season, with others available for a look-see from adjacent roads.

But first, some details. The state produces around 50 percent of the country's cranberries, with about 240 growers in twenty counties continuing an agricultural tradition that started in the nineteenth century. In fact, some bogs have been good producers for more than a century. Cranberries need a marshy area with acidic soil, with abundant water and sand. Those requirements fit Wood County's environment to a "T"—or is it a "C" for "cranberry"?

The cranberry is a low-growing vine that blossoms in late June or early July, with green berries visible by August. After the berries mature, they are floated to the surface of the flooded bogs and dislodged from the plant by mechanical harvesters. The berries are then corralled by booms, lifted into waiting trucks at the edge of the bog via mechanical elevator belts, and then taken to a processing facility.

Now that you know the methodology, you can watch all this taking place along the roads wending their way around "The Rapids." Follow County Z west from the city's south side and south to where it connects with Highway 73. Take 73 west to Nekoosa and pick up 173 to D, then north to 54 and back east to town. If all that sounds confusing, don't worry. Pick up a map that outlines the **Cranberry Highway** tour from the Wisconsin Rapids Area Convention & Visitors Bureau, 2507 Eighth Street South, (715) 422–4650 or (800) 554–4484, www.visitrapids.com.

One of the best places to stop to observe the picking is at **Glacial Lake Cranberries,** 2480 County Road D, (715) 887–4161, www.CranberryLink.com. Minibus tours depart from company offices at 9:00 and 11:00 A.M. and at 1:00 and 3:00 P.M. Monday through Friday during the harvest. Depending on the year's conditions, the best viewings are in the month of October, from October 1 on, so it is always wise to call ahead. A small store on-site peddles almost anything anybody would ever want with a cranberry theme.

The bogs are important environmentally, as well. These expansive water reservoirs are homes to loons, great blue herons, sandhill cranes, black terns, Canada geese, and other waterfowl. The surrounding forests and open fields dotted with lilies, blazing stars, and blue flag iris are perfect for birdwatchers seeking a peek at wild turkeys.

While motoring along Wood County's Cranberry Highway, be sure to visit the **Sandhill State Wildlife Area** off County X, just west of **Babcock.** Take the marvelous 14-mile Trumpeter Trail, which loops through the preserve, providing opportunities to see all sorts of wild critters. Bison, red fox, and ruffed grouse are on the list. Three observation towers are accessible off the trail: One is near the bison herd, the second is atop North Bluff, and the third overlooks Gallegher Marsh.

Hiking and cross-country skiing are also allowed within the wildlife area. Unfortunately, many of the popular naturalist programs once held at the skills center at the entrance to Sandhill have been cut back due to Wisconsin's budget crunch. But the remaining rangers there are always glad to answer questions. Call (715) 884–2437.

The **Wood County Park System** is also one of the best in the state, offering five major parks (three of which have campgrounds), a 400-acre all-terrain vehicle area, and 38,000 acres of public forestland. Fishing on the placid Nepco Lake can be serious or simply kickback; just bring plenty of bait. Outing details can be provided at the Wood County Park & Forestry Department, located in the courthouse in Wisconsin Rapids, (715) 421–8422.

All this outdoor business is sure to work up an appetite, so before jaunting out on the road, stop first for breakfast at Wisconsin Rapids' **Little Pink Restaurant,** 910 Dura Beauty Lane, (715) 421–1210. Helen and Melvin Poncroch have been running the eatery since the 1950s, starting by serving the area's sawmill workers. Warning! this is not a fast food place, and it's only open from 6:00 A.M. to 2:00 P.M. on weekdays. Yet the fresh, homemade bread is out of this world. Mrs. Poncroch has the experience, baking up to forty-two loaves a day when the mills were in full operation. If you can't make it to breakfast for her hand-crafted jams and warm toast, be sure to visit for lunch and indulge in a heaping hot beef sandwich platter. She promises never to run out.

Or try **Herschleb's Restaurant,** an old-time drive-in at 640 North Sixteenth Street, (715) 423–1760. Look for the giant ice cream cone in the parking lot at the corner of Baker and Sixteenth. The place opened as a dairy in 1939 and is still owned by family members who know the value of down-home chicken soup, potato pancakes, and real cherries in the ice cream. Herschleb's annually makes 20,000 gallons of "ice dream" (yes, it's that good!). Getting into the swing of things during the cranberry harvest, folks here produce their ever-popular cranberry supreme, cranberry splash, cranberry truffle, Alice in Cranberryland, and related tasty varieties of the cold, sweet stuff.

Places to Stay in Central Wisconsin

MADISON

Annie's Garden Bed & Breakfast,
2117 Sheridan Drive,
(608) 244–2224
Inexpensive

Arbor House, an Environmental Inn,
3402 Monroe Street,
(608) 238–2981
www.arborhouse.com
Moderate to expensive.

Canterbury's Booksellers Inn,
315 West Gorham,
(608) 258–8899
www.madisoncanterbury.com
Moderate to expensive.

Collins House Bed & Breakfast,
704 East Gorham,
(608) 255–4230
Moderate

Hilton Madison,
9 East Wilson Street,
(608) 255–5100
Moderate to expensive.

Mansion Hill Inn,
424 North Pinckney Street,
(608) 255–3999 or
(800) 798–9070
Moderate to expensive.

The Edgewater Hotel,
666 Wisconsin Avenue,
(800) 922–5512
www.theedgewater.com
Moderate to expensive.

STEVENS POINT AND AREA

Americinn,
1501 American Drive, Plover,
(715) 342–1244
Inexpensive to moderate.

Holiday Inn,
U.S. Highways 39/51,
exit 161, (800) 922–7880
Inexpensive to moderate.

A Victorian Swan on Water,
1716 Water Street,
(715) 345–0595
Moderate

WISCONSIN DELLS

Aloha Beach,
1370 East Hiawatha Drive,
(608) 253–4741
Moderate

Caribbean Club Resort,
1093 Canyon Road,
(608) 254–4777 or
(800) 800–6981
Moderate

Copa Cabana,
611 Wisconsin Dells Parkway,
(800) 364–COPA
Moderate

Polynesian Resort,
857 North Frontage Road,
(800) 27–ALOHA
Moderate

WISCONSIN RAPIDS

Hotel Mead,
451 East Grand Avenue,
(715) 423–1500 or
(800) 843–6323
Moderate

Places to Eat in Central Wisconsin

BARABOO

Kristina's Family Cafe,
5067 Pine Street
(Highway 12),
(608) 355–9213
This is a place where smart critics say you get more for the dollar. Kristina's is small and often crowded, but the food is worth rubbing elbows for. Excellent waitstaff makes sure the coffee cup is full and that dessert is ready when you are. Nothing fancy but worth the drop-by. Open daily. Inexpensive.

Log Cabin Family Restaurant,
1215 8th Street,
(608) 356–8245
Open daily for breakfast (available any time), lunch, and dinner, the rustic Log Cabin is cozy enough to make Abe Lincoln feel comfortable. One of its best items on the menu is the homemade Italian sausage soup. You name it, and the Log Cabin probably has it. This is scratch cooking at its best. The restaurant also squeezes more than 1,000 pounds of oranges each week to make sure guests get fresh, fresh, really fresh juice. The staff also does the same with its grapefruit for a refreshingly tart breakfast juice and with lemons for lip-

smacking lemonade. Yet the most dangerous items on the menu are the 200 to 300 award-winning pies made each week. Take one home. Ask for apple. Nah, make that lemon. Oh, go for the pumpkin. What the heck— take one of each. Inexpensive to moderate.

EDGERTON

Mario's Italian Restaurant,
201 West Fulton Street, (608) 884–9488
Pizzas, pastas, plus American-style dishes, are the highpoint at Mario's, which serves up its mostly Italian fare with flair. Area families have found this to be their home away from home, whenever a meatball craving strikes. A wide array of dishes load up the menu, one fit for a legion of centurions. Go for the tomato sauces, which happy patrons agree are out-of-this-world. Inexpensive to moderate.

MADISON

Chocolate Shoppe Ice Cream Company,
466 State Street, (608) 255–5454
Chocolate Shoppe Ice Cream Company is family-owned, starting in 1962 in Madison and now distributing quality products throughout Wisconsin. The National Ice Cream and Yogurt Retailers Association has given the company's strawberry ice cream a national first place award, plus a second place in the "best coffee-based flavor" for the espresso almond fudge. Can't go wrong there, especially with the high butter fat content! Take any flavor and then any sundae topping, pile it up with real whipped cream, cashews, or pecans. Don't forget the cherry topping. Open daily. Inexpensive.

Ella's Deli & Ice Cream Parlor,
2902 East Washington Avenue, (608) 241–5291
Ella's has some of the best matzo ball soup this side of heaven. The combination of a hearty broth and a huge matzo makes the perfect comfort food. In addition to the traditional sandwiches (mmm, the chopped liver), vegetarian products are also available. The restaurant originally started as a kosher grocery in the early 1960s on Madison's downtown State Street. Owner Ella Hirschfeld then found that a restaurant made good sense and subsequently opened at a couple of locations, eventually moving to the current site on the west side of town. You can't miss the place—look for the carousel out front, which operates in the summer. Open daily. Inexpensive.

Essen Haus German Restaurant,
2902 East Washington Avenue, (608) 241–5291
The Essen Haus is Madison's best, albeit the only real, German restaurant and *trinken halle.* Live oompah music or the 10-cent jukebox gets feet tapping. Adding to the German touch, the staff is dressed in dirndles (for the women) and lederhosen (for the men). Seventeen German biers are on tap, plus another 200 imports making for lots of *gemuetlichkeit,* or friendly good times. Open daily, with breakfast served on Saturday and Sunday. Moderate.

Great Dane Pub & Brewing Company,
123 East Doty Street, (608) 284–0000
What better place to have a brew pub than in a building with two antique looks: The Victorian cream brick half was erected in 1883, while the Queen Anne pressed brick side, originally built in the 1850s, was remodeled to its present appearance in 1901. The entire interior was remodeled in 1994, presenting a lot of woods, comfortable chairs, and spacious tables where a lot of noon business deals are done. Don't miss the Friday night walleye fry or Saturday night prime rib specials. A late night menu is available until 1:00 A.M. On the lounge side, there's billiards, beer, and cigars with free live music on Thursday, Friday, Saturday, and Sunday nights. Open daily. Moderate.

Irish Waters,
702 North Whitney Way, (608) 233–3398
On St. Patrick's Day, the Irish Waters becomes Dublin Town for the lost Celts of Madison, with plenty of partying. But

now, you don't always have to wear green here. During the rest of the year, the restaurant serves up burgers, hefty salads, steaks, and seafood. Lamb stew is served every Wednesday. The Molly McGuire Tenderloin, a six-ounce Black Angus center cut, is one of the most mouth-watering menu items. Open daily for lunch and dinner. Inexpensive to moderate.

Milio's,
454 West Johnson Street
(locations also at 2145 Regent Street, 540 University Street, and 6234 University Street),
(608) 251–8444
Super subs get interesting names at Milio's, ranging from the Texas Longhorn (shaved roast beef) to the Godfather (ham and Italian cheese). Other sandwiches are the usual stock-in-trade for the college crowd, with turkey, chicken, and combos on just about everything. The motto here is "Eat Well, Eat at Milio's." Freshly baked bread, especially the wheat rolls, are dangerously delicious. Open daily. Inexpensive.

MAZOMANIE
The Old Feed Mill,
114 Cramer Street,
(608) 795–4909
The restaurant is located in a refurbished mill that dates back to 1857, now serving lunch and dinner Tuesday through Sunday. Its signature dinner items include turkey and broccoli pie and pot roast served with veg-

etables, garlic mashed potatoes, and a rich pan gravy. Its Miller's Meat Loaf, made with Italian sausage, is topped with onion rings and served with a high pile of thick, mashed potatoes. The hickory smoked pork is just as flavorful. Moderate to expensive.

MOUNT HOREB
Blue Sky Cafe,
114 East Main Street,
(608) 437–6100
Located in the heart of Mount Horeb, the self-proclaimed Troll Capital of the World to capitalize on its Scandinavian heritage, the cafe serves up breakfast, lunch, and dinner daily for the locals and visitors who appreciate good sandwiches, soups, and salads. Drop in after a day of walking the streets for a bit of shopping, visiting the nearby Mustard Museum, or hiking/biking in the rolling hills outside of town. Inexpensive.

PORTAGE
A&W Portage,
717 East Wisconsin Avenue,
(608) 742–5759
Best root beer in town. What more can we say about A&W, except that its burgers, chili dogs, and fries are great on a hot summer night after a long day of driving. In late August the facility hosts its Nostalgic Night where poodle-skirted carhops serve the customers, a DJ spins classic songs, and everyone can swing along with hula hoops and participate in a root beer chugging contest.

Often collectors come in their 1950s and 1960s hot rods and customized cars and the crowd "ooohs" and "aaahs" at the chrome, giant fins, and paint jobs. Open daily year-round. Inexpensive.

Gramma's Corner Cafe,
100 East Cook Street,
(608) 742–1468
Gramma's is a family-style restaurant, noted for its full menu of homemade foods and strong, strong, strong coffee. Be aware that there are smoking and non-smoking areas. On Friday, the restaurant stays open until 8:00 P.M. (one hour beyond its regular daily closing) to accommodate the flock of locals enjoying the all-you-can-eat evening fish fry. Waitstaff is friendly, experienced, and will tell ya like it is concerning the specials. So ask. Inexpensive.

Levee Restaurant,
N6794 U.S. Highway 51,
(608) 742–2772
Breakfast is served all day in this traditional old-style cafe, with its countertop with stools and kickback atmosphere around the tables. In business for more than 50 years, the folks here know what their patrons love: home cookin'. You have to try the biscuits and gravy in the morning and a hot beef sandwich or liver and onions for heartier fare. The restaurant is open from 5:00 A.M. to 2:00 P.M. Monday through Saturday. Follow your nose. The perfume of perfect cooking will lead you here, only 1 mile south of town. Inexpensive.

REEDSBURG

Greenwood's Cafe,
116 South Walnut Street,
(608) 524-6203
The tables here usually have plenty of local good ol' boys sitting around, chatting up the days' political, sports, and gossip scene over their toast and coffee. You can get breakast and lunch here daily, but the cafe does offer a great Friday fish fry dinner, closing at 8:00 P.M. instead of the usual 3:00 P.M. It opens at 6:00 A.M. for the early birds. Inexpensive.

Longley's Family Restaurant,
1599 Main Street,
(608) 524-6497
This family restaurant is within 1 mile of the Reedsburg airport, making it easy for the corporate and private pilots who use the facility to drop by for that last cuppa coffee before takeoff. Daily specials are posted on the windows. Open early for that breakfast crowd. Inexpensive.

STEVENS POINT AND AREA

Aldo's Italian Restaurant,
2300 Strongs Avenue,
(715) 341-9494
This is the place to find when craving a thin crust pizza. Satisfied patrons emphasize that Aldo's has some of the best in the state, replete with plenty of toppings. Keep an eye open for their regular "half price" sales. Their hot beef, mushroom, and cheese sandwiches also rate positively for the discerning clien-

tele. You can also get other typical Italian dishes such as lasagna, as well as chicken, salads, and soups. Open daily. Inexpensive.

Belts Soft Serve,
2140 Division Street,
(715) 344-0049
Locally famous, Belts Soft Serve is a favorite of pupils from nearby Pacelli High School, as well as from kids at the University of Wisconsin-Stevens Point who flock here on weekends. When the shop reopens after a winter hibernation at 11:00 A.M. on one of the first Fridays in early May, many eager young customers have already been lining up since pre-dawn to sample the first scoop of the season. From 2,000 to 3,000 customers regularly turn out for each opening day, purchasing cookie dough flurries, brownies, and apple crisp. Daily during the summer season. Inexpensive.

Blueberry Muffin Restaurant,
2801 Stanley Street,
(715) 341-1993
Cheeseburgers served on hoagie rolls may surprise some customers, but the juicy burger taste remains great. Folks have been known to drive up for miles around just for the coffee served by an attentive waitstaff. Open daily for breakfast, lunch, and dinner on weekdays, but be aware that the restaurant closes at 3:00 P.M. Saturday and Sunday. Be sure to purchase lots of muffins. Inexpensive.

Ella's Restaurant,
616 Division Street,
(715) 341-1871
Some reviewers consider Ella's as their "hands-down" best place to meet friends and have a great meal, or a simple beverage and snack. The adulation is for good reason, considering the wide variety of soups, sandwiches, and entrees offered here, as well as the spacious seating, which allows plenty of mental room for conversation. Open daily. Inexpensive.

WISCONSIN DELLS

Big Country Colossal Buffet,
1541 Wisconsin Dells Parkway,
(608) 254-2450
Open daily, the Big Country Colossal Buffet offers a breakfast, lunch, or dinner spread year-round. A feeding here can keep a patron going until dinner. Although they serve dinner and lunch, I've only attended the breakfast session. For breakfast, guests can select donuts, pancakes, pastries, and hot and cold cereals, as well as yogurt and fruit. Kids can always find something to chow down. Other meals offer the usual soups, salads, and entrees. It's nothing fancy at the steam tables, so if bulk is craved, this is the right place to visit. Even at the height of the summer tourist season in the Dells, there is usually little or no wait. Coupons for meals can regularly be found at area lodgings. Inexpensive.

The Del-Bar,
800 Wisconsin Dells Parkway,
(608) 253–1861
This is one of the Wisconsin Dells' top supper clubs, presenting prime steaks, walleye, chicken, lamb chops, and roast duck among its treats. An impressive appetizer list includes escargot, shrimp, sashimi, and wonderful platters of onion rings. Jim and Alice Wimmer opened their restaurant in 1943, specializing in steaks. Still family-owned, the building's prairie-style architecture was designed by James Dresser, a student of noted architect Frank Lloyd Wright. The Del-Bar opens nightly at 4:30 P.M. Moderate to expensive.

The House of Embers,
935 Dells Parkway,
(608) 253–6411
The House of Embers Restaurant was launched in 1957 and still serves its special ribs, layered with a secret sauce safeguarded through several generations of the Obois family. Australian veal cutlets sauteed with shallots and mushrooms get a double kick when flambéed with brandy. On the seafood side, there are lobster tails, shrimp, and walleye pike. Homemade cinnamon rolls are always included in the bread dish. A comfortable fireplace in the dining room makes for a snug feel when the weather turns cool. Open daily at 4:30 A.M. Moderate to expensive.

Monk's Bar & Grill,
220 Broadway,
(608) 254–2955
Monk's makes eating a freshly ground hamburger almost a religious experience. With all the trimmings, a burger here is plump, juicy, and ready to munch. But you can also go with a monster chef's salad, as well, with its turkey breast and ham slathered with onions, green peppers, black olives, tomatoes, and a mix of American/Monterey Jack cheese, plus garden greens and served in a crisp tortilla shell. Located in a building dating back to the 1880s, the restaurant is open daily. Since 1947, the good, cheap eats at Monk's have been drawing a crowd for lunch and dinner. Inexpensive.

Paul Bunyan Meals,
411 Highway 13,
(608) 254–8717
A staple of the Wisconsin Dells since the 1950s, an all-you-can-eat breakfast is served from 7:00 A.M. until noon daily from late April through the middle of October. The price is set for flapjacks flowing with a special syrup, plus sausage links and ham, scrambled eggs, fried potatoes, buttermilk donuts, orange juice, and coffee. Bunyan, that famous logger of folk tales, would love the spread of prime rib, seafood, and pasta served at dinner, which starts at noon. However, vegetarian and dietary specialties can be requested. A Friday "fish blast" includes all-you-can-eat cod, pasta, chicken, and potato pancakes. To find your way here, look for the towering signage outside with an image of Ol' Paul. Inside are logging artifacts, stuffed animals, and other North Woods memorabilia. Inexpensive.

SELECTED CHAMBERS OF COMMERCE

**Madison Convention and
Visitors Bureau,**
615 East Washington Avenue,
Madison 53703, (608) 255–2537 or
(800) 373–6376,
gmcvb@visitmadison.com,
www.visitmadison.com

Sauk-Prairie Chamber of Commerce,
421 Water Street, Suite 103,
Prairie de Sac 53578,
(608) 643–4168 or (800) 68–EAGLE

Spring Green Chamber of Commerce,
150 East Jefferson Street,
Spring Green 53588
(800) 588–2054

**Stevens Point Area Convention
and Visitors Bureau,**
340 Division Street North,
Stevens Point 54481,
(715) 344–2556 or (800) 236–INFO,
info@spacvb.com; www.spacvb.com

**Wausau Area Convention and Visitors
Council,**
Box 6190, Wausau 54402-6190,
(715) 845–6231 or (800) 236–9728

**Wisconsin Rapids Chamber
of Commerce,**
1120 Lincoln Street,
Wisconsin Rapids 54494,
(715) 423–1830

Northern Wisconsin

There is a hoary joke they tell in the far reaches of Wisconsin whenever an Alberta Hook weather system swings down from Canada across Lake Superior to slam a wintry punch at the state. Amid the hail, frozen rain, and snow, the lament goes up, "I'm gonna put a snow shovel on my shoulder and walk south, stopping when the first person says, 'What's that you're carrying?'"

The northern rim of the state is considered a frosty snow-belt, with snowfall often hitting upwards of 100 inches a year, while southern Wisconsin along Lake Michigan often barely reaches 40 inches. As an example of snow conditions on the Wisconsin "tundra," Bayfield County's Iron River recorded 32.75 inches in January 1988, concluding a three-month fall of 64.5 inches, making it one of the heaviest on record. But such weather delights outdoor enthusiasts who know how to prepare for it.

Some folks do abandon Wisconsin, thinking that less frosty winters will be a panacea to wintertime woes. Most people along the upper rim of the Badger State, however, take their seasons in stride. What are a few nasty February days when considering long summers in the pine woods, the excitement of snowmobiling and skiing in the winter, with the fresh explosion of spring wildflowers and the hazy crimson woods

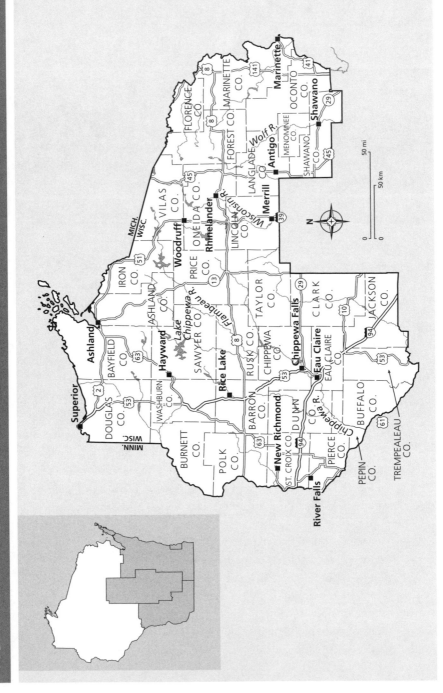

of autumn? These delights of Wisconsin ensure that its residents remain hardy and open to life around them.

And there are plenty of nooks and crannies that need exploring in northern Wisconsin.

Ashland County

The city of **Ashland** calls itself the Garland City of the Inland Seas. That's a pretty hefty title, but since the community celebrated its centennial in 1987, we should allow them some imagery excess. Stepping back further into history, French trappers and traders stopped by here regularly as early as 1659. Where the French used canoes to skirt the shoreline because the timber was so thick on shore, today's travelers can easily drive to **Kreher Park and Beach** or **Prentice Park and Campground** and gaze on the wind-ruffled waters of Chequamegon Bay. Payment is by the honor system.

A century ago, passenger and freight trains made Ashland a major transportation hub in the North Woods. With the demise of passenger trains, Ashland's Soo Line station crumbled. The wreck was a challenge to developer Mike Ryan, a former airline traffic manager who dabbled in refurbishing old buildings. At first, renovating the depot was a task that made him wonder about this avocation. Then he looked beyond the piles of rubble and the gaping hole in the roof and decided it wasn't so bad after all. After taking about sixty truckloads of trash and wreckage from the shell, Ryan saved the depot

NORTHERN WISCONSIN'S TOP HITS

Amnicon Falls State Park	HighGround Veterans Memorial Park
Apostle Islands Cruise Service	Ice Age Interpretive Center
Bad River Chippewa Reservation	Lumberjack World Championships
Big Top Chautauqua	National Fresh Water Fishing Hall of Fame
Chequamegon National Forest	
Copper Culture State Park	Nicolet National Forest
Crex Meadows Wildlife Area	Peshtigo Fire Museum
Dave's Falls	SS *Meteor*
The Hideout	Timm's Hill
High Falls Dam	Wisconsin Concrete Park

from being razed. He turned it into a warren of restaurants, dance floors, and pub rooms with railroad themes. The place opened to the public in 1988, after long hours of hauling debris and rebuilding the interior of the structure.

Ryan kept the best of the old. The carved graffiti in the woodwork along the trackside windows still carries travelers' mute testimony from the turn of the twentieth century. Names, dates, and even short poems are etched into the oak.

But alas, on April 1, 2000, the Depot burned down in a spectacular display of flame and smoke. The incident was not much of an April Fool's joke on the staff and management. But they picked up what could be salvaged from the smoking ruins and moved about seven blocks to the west. There they opened a new restaurant, *L. C. Wilmot's Deep Water Grille and the South Shore Brewery* (808 West Main Street, 715–682–4200).

The restaurant has branched out to offer such exotic items as shrimp jambalaya ($14.99), white fish ($13.99), and chocolate lava ($4.50). The brewery, which had been located in the late, lamented Depot, was moved lock, stock, and yeast to the upscale new property in historic downtown Ashland. It offers twenty-four types of brews, from ales to lagers to pilsners and more. Just as with the Depot, L. C. Wilmot's is a great local watering hole.

Anchoring the other end of the boardwalk at 101 West Lake Shore Drive is the *Hotel Chequamegon* (715–682–9095), modeled after a landmark hotel that was destroyed by fire in 1955. But the modern hotel could have stepped from the pages of history, opening in 1987 about 100 yards from the original site. The hotel's interior decorating scheme is Victorian, with plenty of woodwork, antiques, and ferns. Each of the hotel's suites is named after a local community and decorated with photographs, paintings, and other artifacts donated by residents. Sixty-five rooms are available, which range in price from $105 to $170 in the summer and $72 to $115 in the winter.

Nice touches include handmade soap in the bathrooms, fresh flowers everywhere, and box lunches that can be prepared for hikers.

The hotel's Fifield Room offers gourmet and regional specialties such as planked whitefish. Its lineup of fresh pasta beats anything this side of the Tiber River. I enjoyed the Superior trout on the one opportunity I had to eat there. A group of us stayed at the hotel for a night while snowmobiling in the area, taking over part of the dining room. Although the fare was fancy, no one minded our casual attire.

For standard food, and plenty of it, you can't beat the buffet at the *Breakwater Café* (715–682–8388), across Highway 2 from the Lake Superior shore. I've learned to trust where professional eaters such as truckers and mechanics congregate; the Bradley certainly lives up to that adage. There's plenty of parking around the cozy building, a testimony to accommodating the needs of long-haulers who frequent the restaurant.

Northland College (715–682–1699) in Ashland is an independent, coed college that focuses on environmental and Native American studies and outdoor education in addition to other liberal arts. It also led the fight to establish Earth Day, a national remembrance of the need to be respectful of the natural world around us. With this emphasis, the school has an expansive reputation for its conferences and programs on environmental studies. Simply wandering around the campus, perhaps pausing in the ivy-covered Sigurd Olson Environmental Institute, is a respite from the rush of a typical busy day. You'll see more than one canoe mounted atop a car as students head out for a field class.

The *Bad River Chippewa Reservation* at the northern tip of the county annually hosts a powwow the third weekend in August, attracting tribes from around the upper Midwest. The reservation also has a furniture-building school, producing everything from picnic tables to desks, and factory making kits for log homes . . . sort of a giant Lincoln Log set. Both businesses are

TOP ANNUAL EVENTS

Snowshoe Weekend, Bayfield, early February, (800) 447–4094 or (715) 779–3335

Victorian Tea & Entertainment at Fairlawn Mansion, Superior, mid–March, (715) 394–5712

Journeys Marathon, Eagle River, early May, (715) 479–6400

Folk Festival, Ashland, early May, (715) 682–1289

Apostle Islands Lighthouse Celebration, September, (800) 779–4487; www.lighthousecelebration.com

Christmas in Torpy Park, Minocqua, early November, (800) 446–6784 or (715) 356–5266

open to visitors on Tuesday, Thursday, and Friday and are located on Highway 2, the major roadway between Ashland and Bayfield (Bayfield County).

Across the street from the tribal offices is the headquarters of the Great Lakes Fisheries and Game Commission, which monitors the Chippewas' hunting and fishing activities guaranteed under treaty rights. Ponds to the rear of the building contain walleyes for stocking lakes around Ashland County.

One of the best places to commune with nature in northern Wisconsin is in the pines of the ***Chequamegon National Forest.*** The 848,000 acres of woodlands make up one of the 155 national forests in the United States. Chequamegon (pronounced *Sho-wah-ma-gon*) derives its name from the Chippewa term, "place of shallow water," a reference to the nearby placid Chequamegon Bay of rugged Lake Superior. This sprawling forest was replanted in 1933 from overcut and burned land, the result of heavy timber harvesting by private individuals and the government in the 1800s.

funfacts

Wisconsin has two national forests, both established in 1933. Their total area covers three million acres. The Chequamegon National Forest lies in north-central Wisconsin. Nicolet National Forest is in northeastern Wisconsin. The Chequa-megon has 170 lakes within its borders, while the Nicolet has 260 lakes.

Every year, thousands of adventurous types hike, bike, and fish in one of the sections of the forest. The Glidden District is located in Ashland County, and other tracts are in Price and Taylor Counties. Dan went into the Glidden area on his first deep-woods camping trip when he was about seven years old, bouncing over the more rugged back trails via a four-wheel-drive vehicle. I was working on features for an adventure driving guide at the time. When we got to our Day Lake campsite, we tested our best rod-and-reel techniques but wound up eating beans and canned stew instead of the walleye that were supposed to go into our skillet that night. But, of course, it must have been the "other guy" who caught the biggie.

So the next day we packed the poles and hit the backwoods roads crisscrossed by numerous rivers, among them the Moose, Torch, and Chippewa. Dingdong Creek, Hell Hole Creek, Dead Horse Slough, and Rocky Run Rapids are the names of smaller streams in the area. Supposedly there was good fishing, according to the locals. But with our already bruised egos, we decided not to embarrass ourselves anymore, so we headed out of the woods. It was time, however—already late October with the temperature hovering around 20 to 30 degrees Fahrenheit.

A good day's jaunt through the Chequamegon, one that includes some fishing and hiking, is along the ***North Country Trail.*** The tour is a 60-mile link that meanders through the Glidden, Hayward, and Washburn districts of the forest.

The route begins on Forest Road 390, about 2 miles west of Mellen, and ends up at County Highway A near Ruth Lake, 5 miles south of Iron River. One of the best stops on the trail is off Forest Road 199 at St. Peter's Dome, a huge outcrop of bald rock from which you can spot Lake Superior about 22 miles to the northeast. It is a steep climb up the back slope of the Dome, fighting your way through the brush. Once on top, you'll find

pedalpower

The Chippewa River State Trail is a 20-mile multiuse recreational pathway system linking trails in the city of Eau Claire to the Red Cedar Trail near Dunnville. The eastern 5 miles are blacktopped and open to in-line skaters as well as bikers and hikers. Snowmobilers can use the trails in the winter. The trails meander along the scenic Chippewa River, passing prairies, farms, and woodlands.

the view worth the struggle. Bring hiking boots if you plan to do much crawling through the underbrush and over the boulders. There is a trail of sorts to the back of the dome, but it is overhung with thorny berry bushes.

The town of **Glidden** is the Black Bear Capital of the World, located just outside the forest entrance on Highway 13. The folks here offer a reward to anyone bringing in a bigger bruin (dead, they expect) than the 665-pounder on exhibit in a glass case on the main street overlooking the rest of the city. The bear was nailed in the nearby woods by a hunter who weighed it on the local mill's truck scale because no one else, not even the local butcher, had a scale big enough to do justice to the brute.

Here's a hint for keeping those walking floor rugs out of your camp at night. If you don't take precautions, you could have a real problem on your hands. *Keep all food hanging high in trees or inside locked car trunks. Be sure everything is out of reach of scratching claws.* Chequamegon's bears have been known to demolish coolers and food lockers in their foraging. And they are not playful teddies on a picnic.

For detailed information about events in Ashland County, call Ashland City Hall, (715) 682–7071. For more information on northern Wisconsin in general, call the Northern Great Lakes Visitor Center, (715) 685–9983.

Barron County

The **Rutabaga Festival** in **Cumberland** elevates this lowly veggie to unimagined heights. Held the fourth weekend in August, the festival features a 130-unit parade, the Rutabaga Walk & Run, an arts and crafts show, a hot pepper–eating contest, a Rutabaga Queen contest, and the Rutabaga Olympics. In the latter, rutabagas are tossed, turned, and tumbled in a variety of family-themed events

OTHER ATTRACTIONS WORTH SEEING

Amsterdam Sloughs Wildlife Area,
northwest of Siren

Crystal Cave,
west of Spring Valley

Fire House & Police Museum,
Superior

Fruit of the Woods Wine Cellar,
Three Lakes

Gaslight Square, Minocqua

Irvine Park, Chippewa Falls

**Lac du Flambeau Chippewa Museum
& Cultural Center**

Lac Du Flambeau Tribal Bingo

Scott Worldwide,
Marinette

guaranteed for a laugh and a lot of fun. Cumberland is easy to find, located as it is on Highway 48, west of Rice Lake. The city chose the rutabaga as its prime image maker because of the numbers of farmers in the area who grow the crop. But when not munching rutabagas, you can hike the Ice Age, Tuscobia, Old Indian, and Old Swamp Trails, which cut through or near the city. The well-marked pathways make Barron County an outdoor lover's paradise.

Hikers also love the Blue Hills of eastern Barron County, noted for their rugged, smoky appearance. The scenery is especially delightful in spring and autumn, when the fog hangs heavily around the valleys and deep gullies that score the region. Some of the ridges there are as high as 20,000 feet. While the area's rough edges were smoothed down by glacial action eons ago, there are still plenty of opportunities for a leg-stretching meander.

Bayfield County

Bayfield County is the largest of all the Wisconsin counties, yet it doesn't have a stoplight. Honest.

Almost 10 percent of the freshwater in the world is around the *Apostle Islands,* according to environmentalists. The sprinkling of islands dotting Lake Superior off the coast of Bayfield County were left there by the glaciers.

The ice drifts left behind huge mounds of rubble on their retreat northward eons ago. An early missionary who couldn't quite add gave the archipelago its name. Actually there are twenty-two islands, ranging in size from the three-acre Gull Island to the 22 square miles of Madeline Island. Long Island is only 10 feet above the waterline. The entire area is federally protected as part of the Apostle Islands National Lakeshore.

Camping is possible on seventeen of the islands. Interpretive programs include lighthouse tours on Raspberry Island; campfire programs at night on South Twin, Rocky, and Stockton Islands; and a tour of a commercial fishing camp on Manitou Island. For cruises around the islands, if you don't own your own sailboat, take the **Apostle Islands Cruise Service** tours (715–779–3925 or 800–323–7619), which operate out of Bayfield. The line offers various excursions, including sunset voyages and a Sunday brunch voyage.

In the winter of 1988, I snowmobiled across the frozen 2.6-mile lake strait to Madeline Island in the predawn hours. It was a time when even the late stars seemed frozen against the sky. The ice bridge linking the island to the mainland is a travel-at-your-own-risk proposition, but generally quite safe in the minus 20 degrees of a January predawn. Cars and trucks even take the route regularly in the winter. When the thaw comes and the summer finally arrives, the **Madeline Island Ferry Line** (715–747–2051) beats swimming.

The island has a nifty museum located 1 block from the ferry dock. The facility is operated by the Wisconsin Historical Society and is packed with artifacts dating from the earliest Native Americans to the white settlers. A Native American burial ground is 0.5 mile from the dock as you drive around the marina. Several of the tombstones date back 200 years. For details about the island, contact the Madeline Island Chamber of Commerce, Box 274, La Point 54850 (715–747–2801).

Another visitor information center is run by the National Park Service, located in the old **Bayfield Courthouse**, 415 Washington Avenue. The building is open seven days a week May through October and Monday through Friday November through April. For specific information on the islands, including the interpretive programs, contact the Apostle Islands National Lakeshore, 415 Washington Avenue, Bayfield 54814 (715–779–3397; www.nps.gov/apis/).

The area is dotted with wrecks, remains of vessels caught in the headwinds that howl around Bayfield County, a thumb that juts into Lake Superior's belly.

Snowmobiling Adventure

Snowmobiling clubs help maintain the state's winter trail system, which consists of some 25,000 miles of top-quality runs that link every corner of Wisconsin. The Sno-Drifters, Black River Rock Dodgers, Northwoods Riders Snowmobile Club, Medford Stump Jumpers, Jump River Runners, Pine Creek Riders, Moonlite Sno-Kats, Westboro Sno-Dusters, and Interwald Wanderers are among the many organizations that ensure quality riding and safety. In the North Woods the entire family finds snowmobiling a prime winter adventure.

For a free statewide trail map, call the Wisconsin Department of Tourism (800) 432–8747.

bikinginthewoods

One of the best North Woods bike trails is the Hiawatha State Park Trail near Tomahawk. The 6.6-mile stretch of crushed rock was built by Lincoln County and takes riders through dense pine stands and rolling hill country. Watch for deer and other wildlife. A good place to start is on Somo Avenue near Tomahawk's Sara Park, where you can leave your car. Then follow the trail signs. The "Hiawatha" tag is derived from a passenger train that once brought travelers here in the 1940s. Call Lincoln County Forestry Land & Parks for more details, (715) 536–0327.

Bayfield is a pleasant resort community, with the usual collection of antiques shops, small restaurants, and motels/hotels. One of the best rainbows we ever saw arched over the marina there after a brief summer storm a few years ago.

The little park at the corner of Rittenhouse Avenue and Front Street was freshly washed by the rain. The sailboats were bobbing quietly on the smooth water; only the clinking and tinkling of chains on metal masts could be heard. The sun was dipping low behind us, with just enough light to pop that brilliant rainbow out from the dark clouds scudding over the eastern background.

The *Old Rittenhouse Inn* (715–779–5111; www.rittenhouseinn.com) is a restored Victorian mansion dating from the 1890s, now a bed-and-breakfast with rates ranging from $99 to $299 per night. The dining room is open to the public, offering the most elegant meals in the north country. The Rittenhouse hosts special programs throughout the year, ranging from concerts to Christmas displays.

The *C-Side Inn* (715–373–5794) is about 5 miles west of Washburn on Highway C, along the eastern edge of Bayfield County's northern hunk of the Chequamegon. It's a perfect stop for snowmobilers and skiers. A huge pot of homemade chicken soup is always bubbling in the kitchen, to go along with the homemade bread served with slabs of peanut butter and strawberry jam. The food is stick-to-your-ribs fare, just the thing needed when rumbling through the forest's snowbound *Valhalla Recreation Area.* If you prefer fancier fare, have steak, eggs, toast, and hash browns.

The *Bad River Lodge and Casino,* 10 miles west of Ashland along U.S. Highway 2 in the reservation village of Odanah, brings a bit of Las Vegas glitter and Reno glamor to the North Woods. A

funfacts

There are ten metropolitan areas within the state. La Crosse draws many of its workers from across the Mississippi River in Minnesota. Minneapolis–St. Paul and Duluth–Superior also extend their metroplexes into the Badger State.

Braving the Storm

You've never seen a storm until you've seen one on Lake Superior. Remember the *Edmund Fitzgerald,* the superfreighter that sank with all hands two decades ago? It's that kind of weather that curls the toes and runs the surf so high around the Apostle Islands that you'd think even Noah would have had a hard time surviving. Elder Hintz was caught far out on Michigan Island in such a storm, stranded for four days after a hiking excursion. Luckily I was able to stay with two National Park Service volunteers who were manning the lighthouse and visitor services there for the summer. We hunkered low, with no electricity (using gas lanterns/candles) and almost no water (no wells on the island). The waves crashed high up the island cliffs, rain lashed the pines, and wind—what a wind—seemed powerful enough to flatten the 100-foot light-house that was built in 1886. There are 143 steps leading up from the lighthouse keeper's dock to the cliff top. The waves made it up those steps faster than I could run.

When a Park Service boat finally showed up with extra supplies, I had to be ferried out aboard a rubber raft because the surf was still lashing over the pier. The runabout couldn't dock because of the high water, so the operation was a rescue mission worthy of Demi Moore in the movie *GI Jane.* Worth it? You bet.

fifty-room lodge adjacent to the casino offers Jacuzzi suites, wheelchair-accessible rooms, and other amenities. If it is your first visit, the management ponies up $5.00 in casino tokens for stopping by and joining the facility's Casino Club. Call (715) 682–6102 or (800) 795–7121 for the details. Slots and blackjack tables keep the action jumping in the main hall. But in case things slow down, drop in at the all-you-can-eat buffet in the casino's restaurant. While gambling may not be everyone's thing, stop anyway to see how it's being done in the forestland.

The **Big Top Chautauqua** in Washburn brings alive the spirit and fun of the old-time traveling tent shows of the nineteenth century. Performances are held from early July through Labor Day in a breezy park overlooking Lake Superior. For a schedule contact Warren Nelson, Box 455, Washburn 54891 (715–373–5552).

The **Stockyard H&L Cattle Co.** sprawls over 500 acres of undulating hills, pine groves, and fields near **Mondovi.** If you want horses, this is the place to find them. Within the Stockyard H&L is **Lazy L Tack & Trailers,** one of the best western-themed tack shops in this part of the state, with sad-dles, bits, cinches, horseshoes, and other accoutrements necessary for any equine-related fun—such as jeans, jackets, hats, and shirts. For serious rid-ers, owners John and Susan Loomis offer team penning, barrel racing, and horse shows. But there are also wagon rides and a Labor Day weekend event for the slower paced. The farm is adjacent to the Buffalo State Trail for bicy-cling during non-snow months and for snowmobiling when it chills. Contact the Loomises at W394 U.S. Highway 10, Mondovi 54755 (715–926–5309).

The *Crex Meadows Wildlife Area* is 0.5 mile north of the village of Grantsburg in west-central Burnett County. While off the beaten path, the "paths" into the wildlife area are actually all-weather, hard-surface roads. The site is only ninety minutes east of the Twin Cities via I–35. County Trunk F marks the western and northern borders, with County Trunk D making up the south portion. Grantsburg itself is easy to find—just take State Highways 70 and 18. You'll find a wildlife area project headquarters at the southwest corner of the property, east of the junctions of Trunks D and F.

The marshes here were formed when glacial Lake Grantsburg retreated. The place was well utilized by the Fox, Dakota, and Ojibwe nations for cranberry and wild-rice gathering, as well as for hunting.

Today this is bird-watchers' paradise. Swing out your scopes for glimpses of all types of ducks: mallards, ring-necks, green-winged teal, and other species. On the grass prairie you can find grouse and some prairie chickens. Sandhill cranes and Canada geese abound. If you wonder about the 300 acres of plantings in the center of the wildlife area, don't worry. There's a reason. The corn is left standing for the migratory birds.

Clark County

One of the most poignant retreats in Wisconsin is the *HighGround Veterans Memorial Park,* about 4 miles west of Neillsville on Highway 10 (715–743–4224; www.thehighground.org). Overlooking a deep valley, High-Ground was dedicated in 1988 as the state's official memorial to its Vietnam vets. It's a powerful place, where emotional reunions constantly occur among men and women who survived that ugly conflict.

A statue there features several wounded soldiers and a nurse. Under the nurse's cape hang 1,215 dog tags, each with the name of a Wisconsinite who died during the war. The wind causes the tags to tinkle gently, a sound that no one forgets.

Regular ceremonies are held at the park, which is constantly being expanded. Memorials to World War II and Korean veterans also are on the site.

Northern Wisconsin **97**

Douglas County

The city of **Superior** is the largest community in northern Wisconsin. Founded as a mining center, it is now a commercial hub for the North Woods counties. Hugging the south rim of Lake Superior, it is linked to Duluth, Minnesota, by the Richard I. Bong Memorial Bridge. The gracefully curving structure is named after the World War II flying ace born in nearby Poplar, a fifteen-minute drive east of town. In the late 1980s Superior was used as a setting for a film starring Jessica Lange. The location scouts came to town several times seeking picturesque sites draped with birch trees. The advance crews fell in love with the entire community and convinced the director to expand his shooting operation around the vicinity.

The **SS Meteor,** the world's last remaining whaleback freighter, is anchored at the Superior docks off Barker's Island. You can climb its decks and investigate the pilothouse and galley. The old ore vessel gets its name from the odd-appearing whale shape that provided extra stability in rolling waters. The ship was launched in 1896.

The museum (715–392–5742 during the season) is open from 9:00 A.M. to 5:00 P.M. Monday through Saturday and 11:00 A.M. to 5:00 P.M. Sunday from mid-May through Labor Day. From September through mid-October, hours and days vary, so it is best to call to confirm. Free parking is available. Tickets for the SS *Meteor* are $5.00 for adults and $3.50 for seniors and students.

For a peek into Superior's Victorian-era past, the **Fairlawn Mansion and Museum** provides a wonderful look at the city's history. The forty-two-room house was constructed in 1890 and was also used as a children's home for four decades. The mansion with its assortment of period furniture and accessories is open from 9:00 A.M. to 5:00 P.M. Monday through Saturday and from 11:00 A.M. to 5:00 P.M. Sunday for much of the year. Tours are held on the hour; the last tour is at 4:00 P.M. Admission to Fairlawn is $7.00 for adults, $5.50 for seniors and students up to age eighteen. Kids under six are free.

There's always a hot time in Superior, at least during the summer, when the **Old Firehouse and Police Museum** is open from 10:00 A.M. to 5:00 P.M. Monday through Saturday and from noon to 5:00 P.M. Sunday. The old brick building, restored to its original yellow paint job, can't be missed at the junction of Twenty-third Avenue East and Fourth Street (Highways 2 and 53). Admission is $4.00 for adults and $3.00 for seniors and students. Among the artifacts on display is a 1906 steam pumper.

For the latest details on any hour, day, or price changes for these facilities, contact Superior Public Museums (715–394–5712; www.superiorpublic museums.org).

Douglas County's **Amnicon Falls State Park** is one of the state's most photogenic waterfalls, crying for a calendar cover shot. The 800-acre park is located on Highway 2, about 10 miles east of Superior (715–398–3000). The Amnicon River divides around an island in the center of the park, with a covered bridge linking the banks. Good photo vantage points are from the bridge or from either shore.

One of the best trout flowages in the county is the Brule River, which passes through Douglas County from Solon Springs into Lake Superior. Presidents Grant and Cleveland enjoyed fly casting on the river, and Silent Cal Coolidge had his summer White House at a resort there for several years. Cal never talked much about his secret fishing holes, but local bait-shop owners will tell you everything you need to know about the entire stretch of river. Part of the waterway meanders through the rugged Brule River Forest.

Forest County

Larry the Logroller is Wabeno's famous attraction. The statue of a timber cutter stands 21 feet 9 inches tall, symbolizing the area's main industry as well as providing a mascot for the town's high school sports teams. The statue is next to the Wabeno High School band shell in town. Straight-backed Larry looks a little stiff, as if he has been chopping wood too long, but he's a good backdrop for a family portrait.

Laona is in the heart of the **Nicolet National Forest,** where many local loggers still work—cutting out about 200,000 cords of hardwood per year. The wood is sent to mills in the Fox River Valley to the south. The Nicolet Forest encompasses about 651,000 acres, within which are the headwaters for the Wolf, Pine, Popple, Oconto, and Peshtigo Rivers. The Nicolet was named after Jean Nicolet, the French explorer who "discovered" Wisconsin in 1634.

While in the Nicolet Forest, look for the MacArthur Pine, named for the famed general. The tree is one of the oldest in the nation, standing 148 feet high and with a circumference of 17 feet. The tree was old when Nicolet and his voyageurs were first finding their way to the southlands some 300 years ago. To find the tree, turn north onto Highway 139 just as you leave the village of Cavour to the west. (Cavour is 8 miles north of Laona on Highway 8.) Continue to Forest Road 2166 near Newald and turn west to Forest Road 2167. Make a sharp turn north and you'll spot the pine towering above its neighbors.

Laona has been putting on a **Community Soup** annually for the past sixty-plus years, the first Sunday of every August. Townsfolk donate the ingredients for the homemade vegetable soup, made in large cast-iron pots over an open fire. The only requirement for eating is that you bring your own bowl and spoon.

Some of the fun is coming to the city park to watch the preparations, which begin about 6:00 A.M. The soup is simmered until noon, when serving starts. The recipe includes some secret ingredients, but generally it contains fresh onions, carrots, celery, potatoes, beans, and whatever else might be in the garden.

The soup-serving tradition started years ago when neighbors got together for a friendly outing. The attendance grew so large that the Laona Lions Club took over operations a few years ago to help coordinate the event.

Laona is also home to the *Camp Five Lumberjack Train*, a steam train that operates Monday through Saturday from June to late August. Camp Five is a typical turn-of-the-twentieth-century lumber camp, with an environmental hike nearby and a country store on the grounds at the junction of Highways 8 and 32 (715–674–3414 in summer or 800–774–3414; www.camp5museum.org). The train ride through the woods is fun, giving kids the chance to see a working locomotive up close. Tickets are $16.00 for adults, $10.00 for teens ages thirteen to seventeen, $6.00 for children four to twelve, and free for tykes three and younger. A family package costs $45.00.

Forest County has another interesting Rustic Road that extends through the woodlands for 7.4 miles off Highway 70. It meanders across Brule Creek along Fishel Road to Cary Dam Road to Lake View Drive, concluding in the hamlet of Alvin on Highway 55. The village is about 2 miles south of the Michigan border.

Travel Games

Roger Jasinski, manager of the state's natural resources department for the Turtle-Flambeau Flowage in Iron County, and Melanie Eklof put together a fun "young person's vacation guidebook" that is packed with trivia and games for kids. One of the best is unscrambling the names of northern Wisconsin wildlife.

Try these on the tykes: 1) obbatc, 2) skatrmu, 3) esoum, 4) reshw, 5) tiewhaltide eerd, 6) punkihcm, 7) oxedrf, 8) wuckchodo, 9) love, and 10) raveeb. Okay, so you want answers? It's not going to be that easy. You figure 'em out, too! But okay, here's a sample to get you started: 5) white-tailed deer. That's enough for now. Get busy.

The flowage, by the way, once consisted of the Flambeau and Turtle Rivers, Beaver Creek, and sixteen lakes. A dam was built in 1926 where the rivers met, flooding the lakes and the surrounding land. This formed one large lake called the Turtle-Flambeau Flowage. The dam was built to save water that could be used to generate electricity at other dams farther downstream. The flowage has subsequently become one of the state's major aquatic waterfowl breeding and migratory grounds. Bring a canoe, waders, cameras, and binoculars.

Iron County

The **Frontier Bar** on Highway 2 near Saxon is a loud, happy place. It's the jumping-off point on the Iron Horse Snowmobile Trail for a 20-mile run northward through the Bad River Indian Reservation in next-door Ashland County. Tucked off the highway, about 7 miles south of Lake Superior, the Frontier is the place to hang out, tell a few lies, and eat chili—not necessarily in that order. Owned by John and Kay Innes, longtime North Woods residents from nearby Cedar, the Frontier outdoes fast-food joints with its hefty burgers. If you are the last of the big spenders, add some cheese for only a dime. In the wintertime Innes serves up a "snowshoe," schnapps with brandy.

funfacts

Wisconsin has forty-seven state parks, ten state forests, and twenty-four state trails. For information on the park system, contact the Bureau of Parks and Recreation, Department of Natural Resources, Box 7921, Madison 53707 (608–266–2181).

Mercer is proud of its title, "the Loon Capital." The large birds have a distinctive, haunting call that echoes over the lakes and forests of Wisconsin. They are such a part of the North Woods world that Mercer dedicated a large statue to the fowl on Highway 51 at the southern outskirts of town. The 16-foot-high bird is in a little park adjacent to the town's information center. The big bird weighs 2,000 pounds and contains a speaker with a tape recording explaining all the loon calls and facts about the bird's habitat. There is a serious reason for the Mercer display as well. It is a reminder that the lakes in Iron County provide one of the few prime breeding grounds for the large waterbird.

Langlade County

The roar of white water is music to the ears of outdoors fans in Langlade, Marinette, Menominee, and Oconto Counties, where canoeing, kayaking, or rafting are more than just Huck Finn adventures. Using rubber rafts, the rides can be slow, easy drifting or furious careening along the Wolf, Peshtigo, or Menominee Rivers. The routes twist and turn through the pine woods, with action paced by the height of the water during each season. Commercial raft operators usually hit the water from Memorial Day through Labor Day on the Menominee and from mid-April to late October on the Peshtigo and Wolf. The Menominee is dam controlled, which determines the amount of high water, so it's always good to call an outfitter before arrival to check on water levels.

Wisconsin's Rustic Roads

For a really "back roads" look at Wisconsin, sample the state's *Rustic Roads.* These designated stretches of getaway lanes and byways retain the charm of a less complicated era. There are fifty-six such designated roadways in the state, ranging from 2.5 miles to 10 miles in length. Most are paved, but some are gravel. These roads aren't built for the heavy metals set, and the speed limit hovers around 45 mph. Subsequently, be aware of slow-moving vehicles. For a comprehensive pamphlet describing the roads and their locales, contact Rustic Roads, Wisconsin Department of Transportation, Box 7913, Madison 53707 (608–266–0649; www.dot.wisconsin.gov/travel/scenic/contact.htm). Get one now. State budget cuts may mean that the fliers won't be available in the future.

Gear is simple. Use tennis shoes or rubber-soled shoes because rafts have soft bottoms that can get slippery when racing the rapids. Regular riders often use wet suits when the weather turns chilly. Windbreakers are important in early spring. There's no sense in being uncomfortable. Rafts hold from two to four persons, with trips ranging from one to five hours.

Newcomers to the rafting scene will enjoy a mild ride on Langlade County's Wolf River, which alternates between rugged boulders with gentle waves to bedrock that churns the water into a hearty froth. There are plenty of fast chutes for stomach-tingling action.

The higher stretch of the river between Hollister and Langlade offers long stretches of smooth water. In the lower section of the Wolf, the water picks up speed through Boy Scout Rapids. This is not a place for beginners, edging as it does into a rocky funnel that is strewn with boulders. A narrow channel follows, where rocks are close enough to shave a preteen. The run then slides back onto smooth water.

Quality outfitters include Jesse's *Wolf River Lodge* at W2119 Taylor Road, north of Langlade (715–882–2182) and Shotgun Eddy's Rafting on Highway 55 just south of Langlade in Menominee County (715–882–4461; www.shotgun eddy.com).

Lincoln County

For good reason, *Merrill* is called the "City of Parks." The town has nine major parks within its boundaries, making it the picnic capital of the north country. Green grass, brilliant flowers, huge shade trees, playgrounds, and shelters seem to pop up around every corner. For an excursion outside of town, *Council Grounds State Park* is located on Highway 107 only a few miles

northwest of Merrill. Traditionally a gathering spot for Chippewa Indians, the area became the hub of the North Woods logging industry. Between the 1870s and early 1900s, hundreds of lumberjacks chopped and sawed the towering pines that once ruled the forestlands. Some 600 million board-feet of timber were eventually floated downstream on the Wisconsin River from Merrill's immediate vicinity during the boom days. Council Grounds park now is much quieter and trees have been replanted, so you barely can tell that this land-scape once had the appearance of a crew cut. The park has some excellent swimming areas (keep an eye on the kids because there are no lifeguards), plus boating and cross-country skiing in season. There is also a breathtaking (literally) exercise trail that weaves in and out of the trees, so get in shape.

Marinette County

Few people outside Wisconsin know much about **Peshtigo.** In 1871, a raging forest fire destroyed much of Marinette County's drought-stricken timber, taking the town with it on October 8. The fire swept through the community on the same day as the Great Chicago Fire, which pushed the incident onto the back pages of the nation's newspapers. Yet the Wisconsin incident was more horri-fying. Between 600 and 800 people died in the Wisconsin fire, more than five times the number who perished in Chicago.

The Peshtigo River meanders past the Badger Paper Mill, one of the mainstays of the town's economy. The river itself saved hundreds of people, who survived the nineteenth-century fire by leaping into the steaming water. The inferno is remembered in the **Peshtigo Fire Museum** (715–582–3244), which is highlighted by a huge painting depicting that fateful day and the role of the river as a lifesaver. The museum is in an old church that replaced one burned in the forest fire. Its display cases are carefully filled with melted coins, broken dishes, and other artifacts donated by area residents. A mound near the museum is a common grave for 350 unidentified victims of the fire. The museum is 1 block north of Highway 41 on Oconto Avenue. Turn at Ellis Street and you'll see the building.

The town is laid out much as it was before the fire: along the east and west sides of the river. Streets are wide and lined with maples and oaks. Gone are the huge pines that ranged all the way from Green Bay toward the Michigan border.

Things are generally quiet now on the Peshtigo, but there's a 5-mile stretch of water called Roaring Rapids that puts a rafter's heart in his or her mouth. The river rolls through the thick forest, cutting like a hot knife through butter into Five-Foot Falls, which has a vertical drop of bedrock and only one way to go—straight ahead with a yell and all the pumping adrenaline you can muster.

The chute whops rafts into a sheet of smooth water near the left bank, but rowers have to watch out for upcoming boulders. Horse Race Rapids, where the narrow chute cuts through steep cliffs, is the longest ride on the river. High waves are kicked up over the rocks, and it takes lots of extra muscle and steering expertise to battle through without being swamped. That 30 or so yards of heart-murmur slides into several tight corners and drops over submerged rocks into a quiet pool where you can get your head back on straight again, according to experienced rafters.

The Menominee River, which forms the border between the state of Michigan and Marinette County, is a good rafting locale, according to friends who take the white-water route quite often. They suggest putting in at *Little Quinness Falls Dam* for a 2-mile run through heavy woods and into a short stretch of rapids. The first drop, according to ace rafter John Shepard, is about 7 feet on a "pour-over" called Mishicot Falls. There's a tricky backwash at the base of the waterfall, he warns.

The county is noted for its waterfalls, the bane of the lumberjacks but a boon to photographers. The loggers hated coming to the narrow rapids that

Read All about It!

For the latest in what to see and do in any of the state's communities, turn to the local newspapers. Their entertainment sections, usually published by dailies on Wednesday and/or Friday, are excellent resources. If you are in a college town, pick up one of the school newspapers. The Marquette University *Tribune,* the University of Wisconsin-Milwaukee *Post,* the Wisconsin *Badger,* and others contain a wealth of information on concerts, sports events, gallery openings, lectures, films, and other activities.

The state also has several ethnic newspapers, most of which are published in the Milwaukee area. Each offers news and calendar information pertaining to its heritage, whether African-American, Jewish, Italian, or Irish.

Wisconsin Trails, a monthly four-color publication highlighting the state's scenery and attractions, has been a swell resource for the state's visitors for more than thirty-five years. Copies are available in most libraries. For more details or subscription information, contact the publication at P.O. Box 317, 1131 Mills Street, Black Earth 53515 (608–767–8000 or 800–236–8088).

Key Magazine, a free publication distributed in Milwaukee area hotels, provides more valuable details on the entertainment scene. If you don't find a copy in your room, ask at the front desk or contact Beth Ewing or Roger Stafford at the publication's offices at (414) 242–2077.

So, as you can see, there are no excuses for sitting in your hotel room because you have no idea of what is going on! Get out there and do something!

Hungry Hiking

Hungry after a day of hiking in the woods? Try these healthy snacks for late nights around the campfire: Brush halved pears with melted butter and place the pieces on a square of heavy-duty foil. Fill the center of the pears with chopped nuts and raisins. Dot the centers with some more butter. Seal the package and place on medium coals for about ten minutes. Then dig in.

Now try this one: Core several apples and fill each cavity with a teaspoon of raisins. Top them off with sugar and cinnamon and dot with butter. Seal each apple in a square of foil and place on medium coals for about forty-five minutes or until the apples are tender. You also can substitute marshmallows, cloves, or other goodies for the raisins. Be creative.

could often cause jams, lost time, and deaths. Nobody enjoyed ramming the timber over the waterfalls. Today's visitor doesn't have to be concerned about those problems. Finding the best picture angle is enough.

The county's most picturesque falls are just off the meandering Parkway Road in the western stretch of the county. Some of the roughest falls in this area have been channeled or partially tamed over the past generations by artificial dams. To get to **High Falls Dam,** take High Falls Road off Parkway Road. The dam creates the 1,700-acre High Falls Flowage. Just to the north of the dam about a mile or so is **Twin Bridge Park,** which provides another good spot to see the High Falls Flowage. The park is also off Parkway Road. You need to be careful at Veteran's Falls (just off Parkway Road in **Veterans' Memorial Park** on the Thunder River) because of the steep slopes dropping down to the falls themselves. Be sure to wear hiking boots or other strong shoes. A picturesque little wooden bridge angling high over the rapids is a perfect setting for autumn camping and picnicking.

To see the Caldron Falls Dam, take Boat Landing 8 Road off Parkway. The dam creates the 1,200-acre **Caldron Falls Flowage,** where a boat launch is available. McClintock Falls is located in **McClintock Park** off Parkway Road. The falls is actually a series of rapids and white water with several bridges leapfrogging from bank to bank. This is one of the nicest picnic areas in Marinette County. Strong Falls is in **Goodman Park,** on the Peshtigo River off Parkway Road. Many hiking trails wander through the dense forest and brushland in the park itself. The park planners provided log shelters in the area, handy refuges in case of rain.

Other waterfalls in the county also are easily reached off the beaten path. To see **Twelve Foot Falls,** scene of several television commercials, take Lily Lake Road south off Highway 8 to Twelve Foot Falls Road. Several magnificent drops make up the waterway. Each has its own name: Horseshoe Falls, Eighteen Foot Falls, Eight Foot Falls, and Bull Falls. We like Horseshoe best because of the surrounding framework of trees.

The list continues, a fact making waterfall lovers gleeful. For Long Slide Falls, drive along Morgan Park Road to the east off Highway 141. A small sign marks the direction, so be alert or you might miss the turnoff. Park your car and take the short walking trail to the falls themselves. A county park with camping, swimming, and picnicking is up the road to the east. Piers Gorge is a white-water rapids area along the Menominee River in the far northern section of the county. To get to the viewing area, take Highway 8 when it branches to the east off Highway 141, just before the Michigan-Wisconsin border. On the northeast side of the county's border with Michigan is Pemenee Falls, which is a really wild stretch of the Menominee. You'll find the spot just to the left as you enter Michigan on County Highway Z.

Dave's Falls is my personal favorite, located south of Amberg on the Pike River. There's a county park there with a neat wooden bridge arching high over the water. A nineteenth-century folk song tells the sad lament of how a logger named Dave died while breaking up a jam on the river in that location. Ever since that accident, the falls has carried his name.

If you're looking to spend a little time in the **Crivitz** area, be sure to check out **Twin Bridge Resort and Supper Club.** The vacation cottages are carpeted and have fully equipped kitchens, automatic gas heat, and bathrooms with showers. Public dining and cocktails are available and breakfast is served on the weekend. Aluminum boats are accessible for lake fishing, sandy beaches await the swimmers and sunbathers, a golf course is nearby, and there are miles of leafy forest trails for hikers. Twin Bridge can also be enjoyed in the winter months. It is a winter playland for cross-country and downhill skiers, and there is easy access to more than 100 miles of well-marked groomed snowmobile trails. Anglers can ice fish for musky, northern, walleye, bass, or trout. For information on Twin Bridge, N9661 Parkway Road, call (715) 757–3651 or write Twin Bridge Resort, N9661 Parkway Road, Crivitz 54114.

With all this water in Marinette County, remember that one-third of all the best trout streams in the state are located here.

Menominee County

One of the country's largest and most complete logging museums, the **Menominee Camp Logging Museum** is located on Highway 47 and County VV, on the Wolf River at Grignon Rapids in **Keshena.** Unless you knew it was there, however, you might miss the facility. The camp (715–799–3757) is on the 230,000 acres of the **Menominee Indian Reservation** about 168 miles north of Milwaukee. Native American guides take visitors through the seven log buildings that have been rebuilt in the heavy forest. A cook shack is complete with table settings and a well-stocked kitchen. The blacksmith shop, woodworker's building, and bunkhouse are outfitted as well with the appropriate nineteenth-century details. The camp is open 9:00 A.M. to 3:00 P.M. daily Tuesday through Saturday, May 1 to October 15. Admission is $10.00 for adults, $7.00 for seniors, and $6.00 for children ages ten to sixteen.

The museum is one of several economic-development packages in Menominee County aimed at making the tribe more self-sufficient. Other industries include a sawmill, bingo parlor, and a rafting outfitter to guide travelers on the 59-mile stretch of the Wolf River that meanders through tribal lands.

Oconto County

Southwest from Peshtigo is **Oconto**, on the sun-dappled shore of Green Bay. Camping for recreational vehicles is available at the **North Shore Recreation Area** on the edge of the bay, just a few minutes' walk to the banks. You can fish from land or use waders to get a few steps closer to the chinook and trout that swim in the murky waters offshore.

As with Peshtigo, Oconto's neighbor just to the north, a forest fire almost destroyed the town in 1871. A rain came just at the right time, as the flames were creeping to within a few blocks of some of the stately mansions that still can be seen along Park Avenue and its side streets. Edward Scofield, Wisconsin's governor from 1897 to 1901, lived in Oconto for a time. His home at 610 Main Street was built in 1868, next door to the Bond house, whose occupants ran a pickle factory. These magnificent old houses were among the dozens saved by that lucky downpour.

About 2 miles west of Oconto is **Copper Culture State Park** (920–492–5836), where artifacts have been found from a clan of prehistoric people. Apparently these ancient craftworkers mined the copper from nearby deposits, made tools and other items from the precious metal, and traded with groups as far away as the Gulf of Mexico.

Oneida County

The hungry hodag lurks in the woods around **Rhinelander,** a town where tall tales could be true. At least the only place in the world where you'll see a hodag is in the logging museum in the city's Pioneer Park. The mythical monster was dreamed up in 1896 by some of the loggers who worked in the forests. They supposedly captured a 7-foot-long hairy beast with huge horns and teeth, keeping it "alive" in a pit behind the house of one of the practical jokers. Nobody was too upset to discover that the men had assembled the beast with ox hides and claws made from bent steel rods. The hodag had captured the town's interest and became a local legend.

The **Rhinelander Logging Museum** is at the junction of Highways 8 and 47 (715–369–5004). In addition to the hodag, the museum shows off equipment used by frontier woodcutters. The museum is open daily 10:00 A.M. to 5:00 P.M. from Memorial Day through Labor Day, and admission is free.

Adjacent to the logging facility is the **Civilian Conservation Corps Museum,** which should bring back memories to anyone who served in the CCC during the Depression. The replica of a typical camp located in a one-room schoolhouse was opened in 1983 for the fiftieth anniversary of the government-sponsored conservation work brigade. More than three million persons worked in the corps between 1933 and 1942, preserving and maintaining forests and waterways. Former CCC volunteers staff the museum from Memorial Day through Labor Day, telling about their work in the woods. Photos, uniforms, and tools from the era are displayed in the barracks and other buildings. Donations are accepted.

On the last Saturday in September, the folks in Minocqua celebrate **Beef-O-Rama,** where anyone who wants to fix a giant pot roast (provided by the local Chamber of Commerce) can compete for prizes. Celebrity judges get to sample upwards of sixty roasts before choosing a winner. Prior to announcing the victors, the chefs parade down the main street to a local park where the meat is made into sandwiches.

I took daughter Kate and one of her friends plus son Steve there for a recent party. We couldn't look at another roast beef for months.

Minocqua and Milwaukee, incidentally, have launched into a Sister City tourism promotion to encourage a rural-urban getaway experience.

Polk County

On the outskirts of St. Croix Falls along Highway 8 is the **Ice Age Interpretive Center** at Interstate Park. Some splendid geological formations in the park's canyonlands are sure to get camera shutters clicking. A highly instructive film on the impact of the glaciers throughout the region should capture the attention of even the most wiggly tyke. The center is open year-round from 9:00 A.M. to 4:00 P.M. during the summer, otherwise hours vary. You'll need a state park sticker for admission, which can be secured at the center (715–483–3747).

But if the film still doesn't keep the kids' attention, drive 3 miles west on Highway 8 to *Fawn Doe Rosa Park,* where they can feed and pet deer and other animals. The park is open 9:30 A.M. to 8:00 P.M. mid-May through September. Call (715) 483–3747 if you need more information.

Price County

Timm's Hill, the highest point in Wisconsin, is 6 miles east of Omega, just before you get to the crossroads village of Spirit. Timm's Hill is 1,951 feet (594.8 meters) above sea level. An observation tower rears over the treetops for an even more expansive view of the countryside. On a blustery autumn day, middle son Steve and I climbed up there as the wind tugged our coattails. A hint: Don't look down. But once on the top, the sight was spectacular . . . even if it was a white-knuckler.

Wisconsin Concrete Park on Highway 13 South in *Phillips* is definitely a difficult—or should I say hard—place to miss. Some 200 statues made from concrete portray cowboys on horseback, deer, bears, Native Americans, and a plethora of other items from the imagination of the late Fred Smith. When Smith retired from logging, he took up sculpture and today is considered one of America's foremost folk artists. For a special effect Smith put bits of broken glass into his dozens of whimsical forms, all of which seem to smile back at the observer. The park is open year-round; admission is free. For information call (715) 339–4505 or (800) 269–4505.

St. Croix County

Hudson looks much like the Hudson River Valley of New York State. At least that's what the original settlers in the area thought, so they figured the name would fit their community as well. The *Octagon House* is the local history center, at 1004 Third Street (715–386–2654), on the north end of the town's business district off Highway 35. There's a magnificent old grand piano in the old home's living room. Looking at it, one would never guess that it was twice dumped into the Mississippi River on its delivery run here in the mid-1800s. The Octagon House is open May 1 to October 31, and then open for three weeks after Thanksgiving for a holiday display. The house is closed for the remainder of the year. The hours are Tuesday through Saturday from 10:00 A.M.

Lutfisk Lunching

Norwegian, Danish, and Swedish influences are still strong throughout Wisconsin's Northland, with more guys in hunting jackets nicknamed "Swede" than probably anywhere else in Wisconsin. And many of the churches in the North, especially around Burnett County's Grantsburg, still stage lutfisk suppers as fund-raisers. Vacationers will find these fjord feasts loads of fun.

Kokt lutfisk is dried cod that has been preserved in lye and soda and softened into a glutinous mass by letting it sit in saltwater for about a week. It is then boiled and served with a white sauce *(mjolksds)* along with boiled potatoes. Everything is liberally dosed with salt and white and black pepper. *Lefsa,* a rolled and sugared pancake, is the typical side dish.

For the times and dates of these suppers, check the local newspapers. Among them are the *Inter-County Leader,* which is published in Frederick in Polk County, and the *Burnett County Sentinel,* published in Grantsburg. The weeklies can be purchased at grocery stores, gas stations, bait shops, and similar retail outlets.

to 4:00 P.M. and Sunday from 2:00 to 4:30 P.M. Admission is $5.00 for adults, $2.00 for ages thirteen to nineteen, and $1.00 for twelve and under.

Near the city, a puffing, rumbling, rocking, and rolling engine swings quickly around the track. A full head of steam greets the passengers waiting for a ride on the **St. Croix Railroad.** Everyone piles on, a bit cramped maybe, but ready to roll. It's not a hard run, with only a 4-foot-high engine and several 6-foot-long passenger cars traveling more than 7,000 feet of track. But that's the fun of it. The "toy line" railroad is Bob Ahrens's plaything, a train set to end all train sets, with an engine that burns crushed charcoal. In fact, the entrance to this place has a sign that reads CAUTION—MAN AT PLAY. He laid the aluminum rails himself, spacing them through his eight acres of valleyland. The train runs the last Sunday of each month from noon to 4:00 P.M. Call (715) 386–1871 for more information.

The **Apple River** in Somerset is the best place in the state to try your hand, or bottom, at tubing. Numerous outfitters throughout the area rent inner tubes for swift rides along the flowage. The water isn't usually deep, but be sure to wear tennis shoes because of the rocky river bottom. Even kids can enjoy the ride, swirling as they do through the eddies and across quiet pools. The rental companies will pick you up at the end of the hour or half-day run. Watch out for sunburn, however. The glare from the stream can bake fair skin quicker than a microwave.

One good outfitter in the area, a member of the Hudson Area Chamber of Commerce (800–657–6775), is the **Apple River Campground** (800–637–8936 or 715–247–3378). Rates for tubing are $8.50. You need to add an extra dollar for Saturday and Sunday. Runs are offered during daylight hours Monday through Friday and on weekends May through August.

Sawyer County

There was a time when the North Woods attracted another tourist element, one that was not really welcomed. Chicago mobsters often came to the quiet lakes and woods to escape the literal and figurative heat of the Windy City. They brought their nervousness with them, however. *The Hideout* was one of the most extensive retreats used by mobster Al Capone, who favored fishing almost as much as rum running. Fieldstone pillars guard the entrances to a 400-acre estate near Couderay where he used to rest and recuperate. The architecture inside the grounds includes a gun tower, bunkhouse, cell, and other buildings utilized by gang members when they vacationed in Sawyer County. An eight-car garage on the property has been converted into a restaurant and bar. Don't be surprised to see a mannequin of the notorious gangster in the main lodge, seated at a table in the dining room.

The Hideout (715–945–2746) is open for tours daily from 11:00 A.M. to 5:00 P.M. the weekend before Memorial Day through mid-September. Late in the autumn until the third weekend of October, the site is open only Friday, Saturday, and Sunday. Tours cost $9.75 for adults and $4.75 for children seven to twelve. The place is still secluded, set in the woods 17 miles southeast of Hayward. To get there take County Trunk B east to NN, south on NN to N, east on N for 2 blocks to CC, then east on CC 0.5 mile to the entrance.

The world's largest muskie rears over the trees in *Hayward,* marking the site of the *National Fresh Water Fishing Hall of Fame.* The five-story glass-fiber structure houses a large portion of the museum, with its dated outboard engines, lures, and stuffed fish. The lower jaw of the giant muskie is a platform on which several weddings have been held. Even if you aren't die-hard fisher-folks, wandering among the exhibits makes a good layover for anyone on a rainy weekday afternoon when vacation time is running short. Admission is $6.50 for adults, $6.00 for seniors, $3.75 for kids under eighteen, and $2.75 for youngsters ten and under. The museum is open daily in June, July, and August from 10:00 A.M. to 5:00 P.M. In April, May,

funfacts

For a copy of the *Visitor's Guide to Wisconsin's Cultural Events & Attractions,* contact the Wisconsin Department of Tourism, 201 West Washington Avenue, Madison 53703 (800–432–8747). Enclose $1.00 for handling.

National Fresh Water Fishing Hall of Fame

September, and October, the hours are 10:00 A.M. to 4:00 P.M. Only the offices are open in winter. The museum is located on the south side of Hayward at the corner of County Trunk B and Highway 27 (715–634–4440).

Hayward is also site of the **Lumberjack World Championships** held each July, with contestants from Australia, New Zealand, and the United States. They compete in ax chopping, tree climbing, bucksawing, and other robust events. This is a chance for you to wear red flannel shirts, overalls, and wide suspenders. Everyone else in town does. For information contact the Hayward Area Association of Commerce, Highway 63, Box 726, Hayward 54843-0726, (715) 634–8662 or (715) 634–6923.

Trempealeau County

Trempealeau County's western boundary is the turgid, mud-black Mississippi River. Catfish roll to the surface, and muskrats splash in the backwater sloughs. The waterway, fed by the fast-flowing Black River, anchors the bottom of the county and gives life to its surroundings.

We love watching fat barges swinging downstream, loaded with grain, lumber, or petroleum products from the Twin Cities, heading to the far Southland and the Gulf of Mexico. The barges, shepherded by a rumbling tugboat, are aimed carefully for the entrance to **Lock and Dam No. 6** at Trempealeau, one of the major links on the upper river's navigational channels.

An overlook near a parking lot alongside the dam provides a great vantage point for watching the river traffic during the spring to autumn shipping season. You almost can stand on top of the barges as they are pushed through the locks. Then, all of a sudden, the barges drop down to the lower level and continue on their journey to New Orleans. In addition to the bigger vessels, more than 6,000 pleasure craft use the locks each year. Lines of little fishing boats, sleek canoes, and jaunty cabin cruisers hug the lock walls like a convoy of ducklings before they also are dropped or raised to the next level. The complex consists of a main lock and an auxiliary structure recently completed by the Army Corps of Engineers, plus a concrete dam and an earthen dike extending across the wet bottomlands. The foot of the spillway near the Minnesota side provides good fishing.

While in town stay at the comfortably funky old **Trempealeau Hotel** (608–534–6898). Owner Bill King takes very good care of his guests. Eight rooms are available above the restaurant for $35 to $40 a night. A shared bathroom is down the hall. Or you can opt for a suite with a whirlpool and bathroom in either the Doc West House or the Pines Cottage for $100 during the week and $120 on the weekend. Kingfisher rooms, four riverside motel rooms, are also an option. They go for $55 to $65. In the hotel's restaurant, try the signature walnut burgers, made from English walnuts. The Trempealeau also hosts a regular lineup of music.

North of Trempealeau is Galesville, at the junction of Highways 35/54 and 53. The town's **Backyard Patio and Cafe** is just across Beaver Creek from High Cliff Park and its bluffside hiking trail.

The restaurant has some delightful off-the-beaten-path eats, drinks, and music. New Ulm's Ulmer Lager beer and build-your-own turkey sandwiches with sprouts and tomatoes go down well when listening to High and Outside or other bluegrass/folk music groups.

The Lehmann's are the owners of the eatery and have comfortably cluttered the Backyard Patio and Cafe with farm-auction and garage-sale treasures. Be sure to stop in and enjoy the music, atmosphere, and friendly service, even if it is just for dessert. Homemade pies, cakes, and muffins are baked fresh every day.

Trempealeau National Wildlife Refuge (608–539–2311; midwest.fws.gov/Trempealeau/), near Trempealeau, is managed by the U.S. Fish and Wildlife Service. There is no way that anyone could see the entire 6,000 acres of the refuge in a weekend or even a week, but take the kids along the 5-mile self-guided auto tour around the park that skirts the edge of the Mississippi River. There is also a well-marked 0.5-mile nature trail and a marsh to explore. White-tailed deer, bald eagles, ducks, geese, and other creatures can readily be seen.

Perrot State Park is another marvelous outdoor preserve to explore along the Mississippi River, located between the town of Trempealeau and the national refuge. Most of the trails here take hikers to the bluffs overlooking the river. Be aware that they have steep, challenging climbs up steps or stairways so be sure to bring appropriate hiking boots or shoes. For a closer look at the river, we've always enjoyed the Riverview Trail, a 2.5-mile trek that is accessed from the campgrounds. If you are into cross-country skiing or mountain biking, the most challenging route is the 3.1-mile Prairie Trail. The park has 9 miles of cross-country possibilities and 7 miles open for bikers. Skate skiing, however, is only allowed on a marked 2-mile section in the campground area. Canoeing opportunities take guests deep into the watery preserve for the chance to spot all sorts of wildlife. Bring sunscreen and a hat because the day's rays can scorch tender skin. Perrot, dedicated in 1928, is one of the state's oldest parks and is named after French fur trader Nicholas Perrot who traversed this area in the 1600s.

Vilas County

Life in the North Woods isn't just about bears and camping out. It can be civilized, too. After all, Jason Meinholz operates **Soda Pop's** in Eagle River, serving up 120 different varieties of refreshing beverage (715–479–9424).

The town of **Eagle River** has long been one of the state's premier tourist attractions, playing up the "get away from it all" image that downstaters really appreciate. The highly touted Eagle River chain of twenty-eight lakes is considered one of the world's largest such systems. It's all part of Vilas County's watery spread of 1,300 large, countable bodies of water, plus seventy-three rivers and smaller flowages.

Of course, the locals claim that the fish always bite up here and that the living is constantly easy. Yet drawing in that record muskie can still take a bit of work, to say nothing of the walleye, perch, and bass. Many fisherfolk these days advocate the "catch-and-release" form of outdoor entertainment, whereby finny critters attracted to the hook are freed to come back another day. That ensures fun for the next generation. Plenty of guides are available for showing vacationers the best locales for tossing in a line. Contact the **Eagle River Guides Association** for details on reeling in the big ones (715–479–8804).

Winter in the Eagle River area is also loaded with plenty of outdoor opportunities, including ice fishing, of course. The county is called the Snowmobile Capital of the World because of its extensive trail system, which reaches more than 500 miles. Consequently, Eagle River is a natural for the home of the **International Snowmobile Hall of Fame.**

If you take County M north out of Boulder Junction to County B West, you'll find yourself in Presque Isle. **Presque Isle Heritage Society Museum** (715–686–2481), with a fine collection of artifacts and clothing from the area's logging days, is located in downtown Presque Isle. Continue your drive up Main Street and you'll discover the old Presque grade school, and down a grassy path

putonice

From Christmas through New Year's Day, the Eagle River Area Fire Department and volunteers construct an Ice Palace with more than 2,500 10-inch blocks of ice cut from Silver Lake. There is a new design each year. At night the palace is illuminated with colored lights. Call (800) 359–6315.

is the historic "Shanty Boy Hill" cemetery. It is named so because of the ramshackle shanties and houses the loggers lived in while working in the forests. The largest walleye-rearing ponds, where more than ten million walleye fingerlings have been produced for transplanting, can be visited daily. For more information about any of these attractions, contact the Presque Isle Chamber of Commerce at (715) 686–2910.

Don't get the wrong idea if I mention **Hintz's North Star Lodge** (715–542–3600) in Star Lake. We are not related to Bill Hintz, the young guy who purchased the old resort in 1984, but we've spent some pleasant vacation hours there. Daughter Kate and middle son Steve still talk about the frog-jumping contest they organized on the patio to the rear of the main building. Son Dan reeled in enough fish to keep us in brain food for the entire week. I read, loafed, swam, and sunburned for seven glorious days.

The place was built in 1894 as a retreat for railroad and lumber magnates and their guests. Bill does his own cooking, which includes fresh walleye and regular weekday specials. While we usually ate in our own cabin, we tried his Sunday brunch, a table-groaner that included homemade sweet rolls, eggs, sausage, bacon, pancakes, chicken, fried potatoes, dessert, and a ton of salads and other fixings. The eleven cabins at North Star Lodge range from $450 to $1,500 per week, sleeping from four to eight persons.

Not far from Star Lake is **Sayner,** home of the **Vilas County Historical Museum** (715–542–3388), open daily from 10:00 A.M. to 4:00 P.M. through the autumn color season. The free museum has an extensive collection of old and contemporary snowmobiles, seen in the winter through picture windows in the rear of the facility. The lighted display opens up to a snowmobile track that runs behind the building, so visitors can have a look even during a nighttime jaunt.

The world's first commercial snowmobile was built by the late Carl Eliason of Sayner, whose family now runs the hardware store and lumberyard across the street from the museum. In 1924 he used a small gasoline motor—attached to a long toboggan mounted on front and rear tracks—to help him get through the drifts. The idea caught on so well that now the snowmobile is the Northland's main form of winter recreational transportation. The prototypes of Eliason's vehicles are in the exhibit.

The annual **World Championship Snowmobile Derby** is always a big affair in Eagle River and celebrated its fortieth anniversary in 2003. On the third weekend each January, pro racers flock to the track that has been coated with 16 inches of solid ice. Speeds of more than 100 mph have been clocked on the 0.5-mile banked oval. For information and ticket prices about upcoming derbies, call (715) 479–4424.

The complex is owned by Audrey and Dick Decker, a lively couple who also run Deckers' Sno-Venture Tours. They have taken snowmobile riders to Finland, Iceland, Canada, Yosemite, and other exotic locales, as well as on lengthy trips around northern Wisconsin and into the Upper Peninsula of Michigan. A Decker tour is something special, bonding a disparate group of folks of all riding skills who come from around the country. The Deckers also put together special packages for corporate groups, providing long, challenging rides for CEOs and their staffs who want a different sort of getaway from the office.

Some of the best memories I had on a recent five-day Decker trip from Eagle River to Bayfield and back again were the roasted hot dogs in a warming cabin in Chequamegon Forest, grouse exploding out of the thickets near Iron River, and the sight of the vast frozen waters of Lake Superior just before the sun came up. For details on tours write to the Deckers at Box 1447, Eagle River 54521

Loon Business

The eerie cry of the loon is one of the most thought-provoking sounds in the North Woods. These powerful waterbirds have red eyes, a green-black head, a long beak, and black and white plumage. The common loon is the only one of the four types of loons found in Wisconsin. The others are denizens of Canada and Alaska. Trivia lovers: Want to know why the bird has red eyes? The color is caused by a pigment in the bird's retina that filters light when loons dive beneath the water's surface and allows for sight. And it is impossible to tell the sex of a loon without looking at its internal organs.

At the risk of driving you loony, here are some more loon facts:

They weigh between seven and ten pounds.

They require a 0.25 mile of smooth lake surface in order to become airborne.

A loon can fly upwards of 80 mph.

Loons are believed to mate for life. It is believed that loons return to the same lakes every year. First the male arrives and waits for the female. She usually lays two eggs.

There are four types of loon calls (wail, tremolo, yodel, and hoot).

Gangsters led by bank robber John Dillinger once paused at the *Little Bohemia Resort,* near *Manitowish Waters* and 20 miles north of Minocqua on Highway 51. In 1934 the thugs were escaping from a holdup in Racine and made it to Little Bohemia for a rest stop. Apparently it was the only place open between Mercer and Minocqua, so the gang stayed for a long weekend.

Acting on a tip, the police arrived to smoke out the notorious crew. By the time the gunfire was over, three locals who had been sitting at the bar were shot dead, and several sobbing girlfriends had been left behind by the gang. The thugs had hightailed it into the woods and escaped. The current owner, Emil Wanatka Jr., is the son of the man who operated Little Bohemia when Dillinger checked in—and out.

It's much quieter these days, but you can still see a small building on the restaurant grounds that contains items abandoned by the criminals, including underwear, some tins of laxatives, and other odds and ends.

The building itself is peppered with about one hundred bullet holes. Little Bohemia (715–543–8433) opens daily (except Wednesday) at 4:00 P.M.

Part of *Woodruff* lies in Oneida County, but the bulk of the community and its neighbor, Arbor Vitae, are on the southern edge of Vilas County. The crossroads towns share a common school district, with the main grade school in Woodruff. On the playground a block west of Highway 51 is a *giant concrete penny.* The town claims it is the world's largest coin, weighing in at 17,452 pounds and standing 10 feet tall. The statue was erected in 1957, recalling a fund-raiser for the local hospital that brought in a million-plus pennies. In 1952, kids in Otto Burich's geometry class wanted to see a million of something. So he suggested they count a million pennies and contribute the money as a kick-off donation for a clinic.

Snow Schlepping

The *Midwest Snowshoe Championship* series features twelve races, including six in Wisconsin in January and February. There are men's and women's divisions. The goal of the program is to increase visibility of snowshoeing in the Midwest. Call (800) 522–5657.

The Wisconsin legs of the series include the 5K and fun run Snowshoe Rendezvous and Race in White Lake; the Perkinstown Tramp, with 3- and 6-mile men's and women's races, as well as a kids' race, in Medford; the Sasquash Snowshoe Race, with 5K and 10K events, in Wisconsin Rapids; the New World Snowshoe Championship half marathon and 10K and 2-mile fun run in Luck; the Snowshoer/Asaph Wittlesey 10K in Washburn; and the Chequamegon Snowshoe Championship 10K at the American Birkebiner in Hayward.

The medical facility was long sought by Dr. Kate Newcomb, the "Angel on Snowshoes," who delivered babies by the bushel-basket throughout the county regardless of the weather. Newcomb appeared on the old *This Is Your Life* television program and told about the fund-raising efforts. Naturally that led to more donations and the eventual construction of a clinic. Several years later, an uncle of actress Elizabeth Taylor gave the community more funds with which to build a larger medical unit. He had vacationed in the Woodruff–Arbor Vitae area for years and wanted to help the towns.

Woodruff celebrated its centennial in 1988, with a re-creation of the first ***Penny Parade,*** the one launching the children's efforts three decades earlier. Dr. Newcomb's refurbished home on Second Street, just around the corner from the school and the giant penny, also was opened as a museum.

Log rolling, wood chopping, and tree climbing are a few of the events presented on the grounds of ***Scheer's Lumberjack Show*** (715–634–6923; www.scheerslumberjackshow.com) in downtown Woodruff on State Highway 97 East. The program of logger skills is open mid-June through late August. Tickets are $7.95 for adults, $5.95 for youngsters four to eleven, and $6.95 for seniors. Fred Scheer, a world champion log roller; his brother Bob, a record holder in pole climbing; and their sister Judy, the seven-time world's record holder in women's log rolling, form the core of the entertainers' troupe. There are two different sites to view the timber talents. Days and times of the shows vary, so be sure to call for verification.

funfacts

If you think Wisconsin is nothing but cows and cheese wheels, guess again. The state is replete with oddities and weird goings-on. To find the how, the what's, and the where's, read *Wisconsin Curiosities: Quirky Characters, Roadside Oddities & Other Offbeat Stuff* by Michael Feldman and Diana Cook (Globe Pequot, 2004). They'll tell about a talented worm that played basketball and the best place to find locally made limburger. The Web site, www.weird-wi.com/oddities, will connect the curious to other sites that describe the ongoing exploration for pyramids under Rock Lake or mysterious cobwebs that fell from the sky over Milwaukee, Green Bay, and several other eastern Wisconsin cities in 1881. Another site, www.associatedcontent.com, tells where to find Wisconsin's largest talking cow, as if there were a smaller bovine somewhere in the state. It also describes other peculiarities in the Cheese State. Well, you get the picture.

Washburn County

The ***world's largest warm-water fish hatchery,*** according to the Wisconsin Department of Natural Resources, which runs the place, is located in Spooner. The sprawling facility is south of downtown on Highway 63, across two bridges.

The DNR has a nice picnic area on the grounds, where you can put up your feet and watch the fingerlings splish and splash. Several varieties of game fish are raised here for stocking North Woods lakes. It's enough to make you want to bring a fishing pole.

Places to Stay in Northern Wisconsin

MINOCQUA

Comfort Inn,
8729 U.S. Highway 51 North,
(715) 358–2588
Inexpensive to moderate.

New Concord Inn of Minocqua,
320 Front Street,
(715) 356–1800 or
(800) 356–8888
Inexpensive to moderate.

Pine Hill Resort,
8544 Hower Road,
(715) 356–3418
Moderate

NEILLSVILLE

The Heartland Motel,
7 South Hewett,
(715) 743–4004
Inexpensive

RHINELANDER

Holiday Acres,
South Shore Drive on Lake Thompson, 4 miles east of Rhinelander. Take Highway 8 and follow signs,
(715) 369–1500
Moderate

Miller's Shorewood Vista,
4239 West Lake George Road, (715) 362–4818
Moderate

Three G's Resort,
4134 Business 8 East,
(715) 493–2293
Moderate

SHELL LAKE

Bashaw Lake Resort,
3215 Lakeview Church Road, (715) 466–2310 or
(877) 306–3501
Moderate

SPOONER

Best Western-American Heritage Inn,
101 Maple Street,
(715) 635–9770 or
(800) 780–7234
Inexpensive

Country House Motel and R.V. Park,
717 South River Street,
U.S. Highway 63,
(715) 635–8721
Inexpensive

Green Acres Motel,
N4809 U.S. Highway 63 South and Highway 253,
(715) 635–2177
Inexpensive

Inn Town Motel,
801 River Street,
(715) 635–3529
Inexpensive

Person's Dunn Lake Resort,
7815 Dunn Lake Road,
(715) 635–9557
Moderate

WOODRUFF

Indian Shores Camping & Cottages,
Highway 47 East,
Box 12C, Woodruff,
(715) 356–5552
Moderate

Indian Shores/ Shoreline Inn,
7750 Strongheart Road,
(715) 356–5552
Moderate

Madeline Lake Resort,
8902 Madeline Lake Road,
(715) 356–7610
Moderate

Places to Eat in Northern Wisconsin

AMERY

A&W Restaurant,
326 South Keller Avenue,
(715) 268–4500
When it's hot outside, a frosty mug of root beer usually hits the spot. Be sure to try the A&W chili dogs, a cheeseburger, platter of fries, or onion rings. And then get out and run a mile back home or to your camping site. Work it off, but it's so good when the taste buds first are tempted.
Inexpensive, so it's a good food destination for a car full of kids. Inexpensive.

Village Pizzeria of Amery,
210 Keller Avenue North,
(715) 268–7010
Nothing's better than a cheese, sausage, mushroom, green pepper, black olive pizza no matter the time of year. The Village Pizzeria has 'em all when it comes to the popular round Italian dish. Go for the large pizza and save the extra pieces for breakfast. Yummy. Open daily. Inexpensive.

BAYFIELD

Bayfield County Market,
18071 County Road 501,
(970) 884–0844
For Mexican food fans, the Bayfield County Market presents a lively, family-style restaurant. Lunch and dinner specials bring a South of the

Border feel to northern Wisconsin. Yet you can still get a top sirloin, a salad, and pasta. The relaxed ambience of the casual restaurant is conducive to fun, making it an enjoyable night out for the family. Open daily. Inexpensive.

Greunke's Restaurant,
17 Rittenhouse Avenue,
(715) 779–5480
Blueberry pancakes are prime breakfast favorites that attract diners of all ages to this popular down-home restaurant. Burgers, salads, and soups are luncheon pluses. Trout, whitefish livers, and pizzas add pizzazz for the dinner crowd. Greunke's serves breakfast, lunch, and dinner April through October. Stepping into this place is like slipping into the 1940s, with all the Coca-Cola memorabilia, a working Wurlitzer organ, and an old soda fountain. Open daily. Inexpensive to moderate.

CHIPPEWA FALLS

Golden Eagle Restaurant,
16760 County Highway X,
(715) 723–2948
As expected, the Eagle flies with a full menu of food for its customers who come from around the Chippewa Falls area. Noted for good portion sizes, strong coffee, and homemade desserts, the restaurant is a favorite for vacationers as well. Burgers, hot dogs, hearty soups, burgers, and other traditional American fare are served by long-time waitresses who are a cheerful bunch. Open daily. Inexpensive.

EAGLE RIVER

Aerio Club,
1530 Highway 45 North,
(715) 479–4695
Since the 1930s, the Aerio Club has been a hub of Eagle River social life. The comfortable little eatery offers a full dining complement of tasty appetizers, thick sandwiches, hearty pizzas, and its broasted chicken that is famous throughout the North Woods. The Friday night fish fry and Wednesday and Saturday night prime rib specials go over great with winter snowmobilers who drop by after exiting the Eagle River Trail Pit Stop #35. Summertime vacationers also appreciate the hefty portions and fine flavoring. The wide open dining room features tables and chairs. Open daily. Inexpensive to moderate.

Chanticleer Inn,
1458 East Dollar Lake Road,
(715) 479–4141
The Chanticleer offers a smoke-free, air-conditioned dining room overlooking scenic Lake Voyager. Boats putter past in the summer and, sometimes, you can see deer carefully treading across the ice in winter. The menu includes a noted Chantiburger, plus lobster and a Friday fish fry. The extensive salad bar seems to stretch for miles, yet you can also work from a light sandwich menu. Outdoor lakeside dining is available in the Beer Garden, where visitors can come by boat or car. Free docking, by the way. Brats, hot dogs, burgers, rib sandwiches, grilled chicken sand-

wiches, and salad. The Inn is also a regular snowmobilers' stop. Open daily. Moderate.

HAYWARD

Angler's Bar & Grill,
10547 Main Street,
(715) 634–4700
The Angler's has been a popular spot on Main Street for more than sixty-five years. The grill part of the facility features homemade soups, salad bowls, and char-grilled sandwiches. Outdoor patio dining and a beer garden are open in the summer. For a different twist, the Angler's also offers tacos and other Hispanic specialties, as well as pizza for an Italian touch. The Friday fish fry is always popular. When not eating, try your hand at one of the four bowling lanes or just puddle around the game room. Open daily. Kitchen closes at 10:00 P.M. nightly. Inexpensive.

Karibalis Restaurant,
10563 North Main Street,
(715) 634–2462
Talk about longevity. The Karibalis has been one of the area's finest restaurants for generations. Gus Karibalis, who originally hailed from North Dakota, opened the place in 1922. According to legend, Karibalis won the building in a poker game. He started as a "pool emporium" with the current bar, plus seven pool and three billiards tables, making it a gathering place for the area's farmers and lumberjacks. During Prohibition, he began serving food. In 1939, Karibalis offered 5-cent beers and 10-

cent hamburgers, which brought in customers by the drove. Its self-described "world famous" burgers are still popular, as are the steaks and seafood. The place now claims to have Hayward's largest salad bar. A lounge and outdoor deck also draw patrons. Open daily from 11:00 A.M. to 9:00 P.M. Inexpensive.

MANITOWISH WATERS

Pea Patch Motel and Saloon,
County Highway West,
(715) 543–2455
The Pea Patch is 0.5 mile off of U.S. Highway 51 on County Highway West, adjacent to the dam in downtown Manitowish Waters, which gives it the right to claim it serves up the "best dam burgers" in Wisconsin. For snowmobilers, the saloon is next to Wisconsin Snowmobile Trail #8. Open daily. Inexpensive.

Swanberg's Bavarian Inn,
County Trunk West,
Downtown,
(715) 543–2122
Swanberg's features large wine and beer lists, plus powerful martinis and other cocktails. Veal, chicken, pork, seafood, steaks, and pastas are prepared to order. The cozy fireside setting makes it perfect for winter nights. The Inn is accessible by boat through Koller Park or snowmobile (trail #6) in the summer. Nightly specials and a children's menu are available as well. On hot August nights, the air conditioning is much appreciated. Open

daily year-round, with dinners starting at 5:30 P.M. Reservations appreciated. Moderate.

MINOCQUA

The Belle Isle,
301 Front Street,
(715) 356–7444
Music at the Belle Isle is "food for the soul," serving up a platter of live music, ranging from known local bands and the midwest's finest classic rock, reggae, and blues headliners. Karaoke also draws a crowd. Lunch and dinner are served, featuring daily specials and a Friday fish fry. Inexpensive to moderate.

Bosacki's Boat House,
At the Bridge,
(715) 356–5292
Breakfast, lunch, and dinner bring the crowds to Bosacki's, a Minoqua landmark for four generations. The original building was built by the Jossart family in 1896, and the original dream of combining a comfortable place to dine with great food has never changed. Baked chicken and mashed spuds are traditional North Woods comfort food, served in abundance here. Dinner is served until midnight every day, with a Sunday brunch delicious enough to keep anglers off the lakes for another hour or so. The old-fashioned soda fountain is a great draw for kids and, okay, adults. Bosacki's also features one of the longest bars in town. Great lake views too. Moderate.

Mama's Supper Club,
10486 Highway 70 West,
(715) 356–5070
When mama says, "eat!" you want to here . . . because the Italian and American cuisines are delicious. Pastas of all kinds, with the best homemade tomato sauces, are on the menu, along with steaks, seafood, and fresh salads. After a meal at Mama's, guests are often spotted talking with their hands. Open daily, with a well-stocked Sunday brunch. Moderate.

Paul Bunyan's Northwoods Cook Shanty,
8653 Highway 51 North,
(715) 356–6270
Paul Bunyan's features lumberjack-sized meals in a backwoods setting. That doesn't mean you need to catch your own meal. Hamburgers, grilled chicken, and fried walleye sandwiches are on the menu. The facility is open for breakfast, lunch, and dinner, served family style. This Bunyan's is a relative of that in the Wisconsin Dells, with a similar feel. All you really need to know is that the food is hearty, plentiful, and value added. Open daily. Inexpensive to moderate.

PHILLIPS

Skyline Supper Club,
784 North Lake Avenue,
(715) 339–3355
You can get a good look at Wisconsin's lake country from the Skyline. This is a popular hideaway for anglers and snowmobilers, depend-ing on the season. Regardless of the time of year, however, the club's wide range of entrees, soups, salads, and sand-wiches is bound to please. Numerous business and social groups meet here for parties, so be prepared to find some evening crowds. Open daily. Moderate.

RHINELANDER

Rhinelander Cafe & Pub,
33 North Brown Street,
(715) 362–2918
It's always sandwich time at the cafe and pub, with burg-ers, dogs, turkey, and chicken available, along with hefty servings of soup and chili. The pub is a happening place with all the fish stories in the summer. In the winter, the snowmobile crowd tells about derring-do on their heavy duty machinery. Open daily. Inexpensive.

The Al-Gen Dinner Club,
3428 Faust Lake Road,
(715) 362–4032
The club has a woodsy feel, with the interior logs provid-ing a rustic ambience. Steaks, broasted chicken, fish, homemade soup, and, oh-so-sweet desserts are big draws. Hosts Rob and Amy Swearingen make sure that their Friday night fish fry and comprehensive wine list are attractive both to regular Oneida County patrons and newcomers. The baked onion soup is among the best in the North Woods. The cocktail lounge and the dining room are closed Mondays. Moderate.

RICE LAKE

Lehman's Supper Club,
2911 South Main Street,
(715) 234–2428 or (715) 234–9911
You can't miss the supper club, located as it is across from the Cedar Mall. Lunches and dinners feature some of the finest beef in the North Woods. When hungry, ask for a full rack of barbe-cued ribs. Or try the walleye for lighter fare. Noon and dinner specials are posted daily. It's great fun to relax in the lounge after hiking, bik-ing, hunting, fishing, or snowmobiling in the area. Closed Mondays. Moderate.

ST. CROIX FALLS

Logger's Bar & Grill,
2071 Glacier Drive,
(715) 483–2504
Friday fish fry, homemade pizza and soup, sandwiches, and lunch and dinner spe-cials have contributed to the success of the Logger's Bar. Steak, rib eye, T-bone, and sirloin are delicious. The bar offers drink specials in the spacious bar, which is deco-rated with logging tools, mounted deer heads, and photos of the old days in the lumber camps. Pool tables and a game area make for fun every day of the week. Inexpensive.

St. Croix Valley Golf Course,
2200 U.S. Highway 8,
(715) 483–3377
Chef Curt Berends and his staff always put out a good spread, to keep their golfing clientele "on the ball." A chili

buffet is always a fun favorite during the club's annual Chili Open in October. Located a little more than 4 miles east of Stillwater, Minnesota, the club is a draw for duffers and their guests. Because of its location and scenery, the restaurant is host to many types of events such as weddings, rehearsal dinners, and reunions, in addition to holiday parties and business meetings. Dining room open to the public only during spring-autumn golf season (dates vary); open for parties the rest of the year. Inexpensive to moderate.

SUPERIOR

Barker's Island Inn,
300 Marina Drive,
(715) 392–7515 or (800) 344–7515
Steak and seafood specialties such as smoothly flakey whitefish ensure a steady clientele from around the Superior-Duluth area. A good view of Lake Superior provides special ambience for diners appreciating a good time, good food, and good drinks. Comfortable table seatings provide a value added touch, making any night out a true occasion. Open daily for lunch and dinner. Moderate.

Fullers Family Restaurant,
5817 Tower Avenue,
(715) 392–7510
Burgers, chicken, seafood, soups, tasty salads, and mouthwatering cakes and pies are on the menu at Fullers, a Superior tradition for families seeking a night out with good value and hearty servings. Kids are certainly welcome, and no one minds babies. Breakfast begins at 6:45 A.M., followed by lunch and dinner. Closed Sundays. Inexpensive to moderate.

SELECTED CHAMBERS OF COMMERCE

Chequamegon National Forest, Park Falls Ranger District, U.S. Department of Agriculture,
1170 South Fourth Avenue (Highway 13), Park Falls 54552, (715) 762–2461

Eagle River Chamber of Commerce Information Center,
116 South Railroad Street,
Eagle River 54521-1917,
(715) 479–6400

Hayward Area Chamber of Commerce,
101 West First Street, P.O. Box 726, Hayward 54843-0726, (715) 634–4801

Minocqua–Arbor Vitae–Woodruff Chamber of Commerce,
Box 1006, Minocqua 54548,
(800) 446–6784 or (715) 356–5266

Mississippi Valley Partners,
c/o Village Clerk, 508 Second Street, Pepin 54759, (715) 442–2461

Rusk County Information Center,
205 West Ninth Street South,
Ladysmith 54848,
(800) 535–7875 or (715) 532–2642

Shawano Area Chamber of Commerce,
213 East Green Bay Street,
Shawano 54166-0038, (715) 524–2139 or (800) 235–8528

Waupaca County Chamber of Commerce,
c/o Parks and Recreation,
221 South Main Street,
Waupaca 54981,
(715) 258–7343

The Shack Smokehouse & Grill,
3301 Belknap Street,
(715) 392–9836
Hickory pit barbecue plus salads, sandwiches, seafood, and choice steaks have been hits here since the 1980s. Appetizers such as spinach-artichoke dip and french onion soup are guaranteed to get a meal off to a marvelous start. You can build your own burger, starting with a half-pound of meat and adding loads of condiments for a mouth-stretching delight. Some 1,450 wines are stocked in the cellar, so there should be no problem selecting a perfect complement to whatever dish is ordered. In the Smokehouse's adjacent dinner theater, the Wine & Dine Players offer a full season of romantic comedy, spoofs, and other light-hearted fare to go along with a meal. Open daily except for Christmas. Moderate.

Eastern Wisconsin

The eastern portion of Wisconsin near Lake Michigan has the greatest concentration of population in the state, but there are still secret treasures of travel waiting there for you. For an extensive overview of what the nation's inland coast has to offer, take the Lake Michigan Circle Tour. For 1,000 miles the route carries tourists through Wisconsin, Michigan, Indiana, and Illinois. Wisconsin's 300-mile connection begins at Highway 32 south of Kenosha and concludes at Highway 41 in Marinette. Many lakeshore towns have designated "spur" routes off the main Circle drive, to show off their home neighborhoods.

The route is marked by 3-by-3-foot green-and-white signs set about every 5 miles. In most areas the route meanders close to city beaches, harbors, and marinas, so be sure to bring a fishing pole and suntan lotion. Angling licenses can be secured at most bait and tackle shops, so don't let the initial lack of the right paperwork be an impediment.

For your reference, here's the Wisconsin leg of the Circle route: Highway 32 through Kenosha, Racine, Milwaukee, and Port Washington to its interchange with I–43 north of Port Washington; I–43 to the interchange with Highway 42 south-west of Sheboygan; Highway 42 through Sheboygan to the

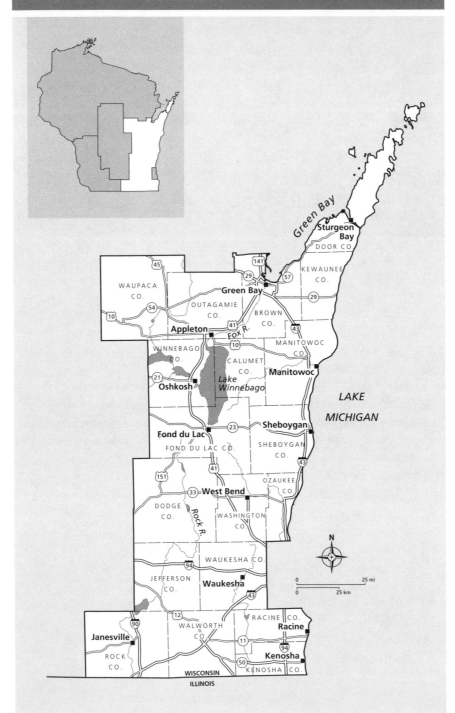

junction with I–43 northwest of Sheboygan; I–43 to its interchange with Highway 151 southwest of Manitowoc.

Take Highway 151 to downtown Manitowoc, then to Highway 10 and its junction with Highway 42 north of the downtown. Drive Highway 42 through Two Rivers, Kewaunee, and Algoma to Sturgeon Bay; Highway 57 up the east side of Door County to Sister Bay; Highway 42 down the east shore of Green Bay back to Sturgeon Bay.

Then move on Highway 57 to its junction with Highway 29 in Green Bay; Highway 29 through downtown Green Bay to its interchange with Highway 41 in Howard; Highway 41 west along the shore of Green Bay to Marinette and the Michigan border.

You'll go through communities in Kenosha, Racine, Milwaukee, Ozaukee, Sheboygan, Manitowoc, Kewanee, Door, Brown, Oconto, and Marinette Counties on your Circle adventure. En route you'll hit restaurants, museums, lodgings, and other attractions that blend in perfectly with the lakefront milieu.

Brown County

The **Oneida Nation Museum** in **De Pere,** a Green Bay suburb, offers keen insights into the lives of this Native American tribe, which came to Wisconsin

EASTERN WISCONSIN'S TOP HITS

American Club	Outagamie Museum and Houdini Historical Center
Aztalan State Park	
Bristol Renaissance Faire	Peterson's Hamburgers
Chain O'Lakes	Pioneer Village
Emma Carlin Hiking Trail	Point Beach State Forest
Experimental Aircraft Association Fly-in	Rock Aqua Jays
Green Bay Packer Hall of Fame	Seven Mile Fair & Market Square
Hoard Historical Museum and Dairy Exhibit	Southern Kettle Moraine Forest
Hobo's Korner Kitchen	Walleye Weekend
Houdini Plaza	Washington Island
Old World Wisconsin	Wisconsin Maritime Museum

in the 1820s. There's a hands-on room in which kids can play a drum and try on an eagle-feather headdress. The museum is located at the intersection of Highways E and EE. It's open 9:00 A.M. to 5:00 P.M. Tuesday through Friday, closed Saturday, Sunday, and Monday. Call (920) 869–2768 for more details. The tribe also operates a giant bingo parlor and casino adjacent to its Radisson Hotel across from the airport in Green Bay.

The De Pere Historical Society maintains **White Pillars,** the state's first bank building. The structure, located at 403 North Broadway, was built in 1836 to house the currency and records of the De Pere Hydraulic Company. The firm was then building a dam across the Fox River in De Pere. Over the generations the old bank building was alternately a barbershop, an Episcopalian meetinghouse, and a newspaper office before becoming a home. It was returned to its original look in 1973. The bank is open Tuesday through Friday from noon to 4:00 P.M. and Saturday from 1:00 to 5:00 P.M. Admission is free. For more information call (920) 336–3877.

While in **Green Bay,** don't miss the remodeled **Green Bay Packers Hall of Fame,** in Lambeau Field on Lombardi Avenue. The museum, open 9:00 A.M. to 6:00 P.M. daily, honors all the players who have worn the gold and green of the city's pro football team over the years. You can even try kicking your own field goal there. In July and August the team has practice sessions open to the public in the nearby stadium. (A giant statue of a ball-grabbing Packer atop a football that used to stand on the lawn in front of the old museum building was

AUTHORS' FAVORITES

Aztalan State Park,
Lake Mills

Experimental Aircraft Center Museum,
Oshkosh

Golden Rondelle,
Johnson's Wax, Racine

Great Lakes Dragaway,
Union Grove

Green Bay Packers Hall of Fame,
Green Bay

Hoard Historical Museum and Dairy Exhibit,
Fort Atkinson

Lake Michigan shoreline

Lambeau Field/Stadium tour,
Green Bay

National Railroad Museum,
Green Bay

Old World Wisconsin,
Eagle

Oneida Nation Museum

Orchards in Door County

moved in November 2003 to the front of the Neville Public Museum, 210 Museum Place.) Call (920) 499–4281. There is an admission fee.

The *National Railroad Museum,* just off Highway 41, is a nationally known train museum. While train buffs may already be aware of the history of its rolling stock, the rest of us might not be as knowledgeable. One locomotive on display, called "Big Boy," weighs in at 600 tons and is 133 feet long. Another engine pulled Gen. Dwight Eisenhower's command train in World War II.

For details on the railroad museum, call (920) 437–7623 or www.national rrmuseum.org. The facility is open year-round from 9:00 A.M. to 5:00 P.M. Monday through Saturday, from 11:00 A.M. to 5:00 P.M. Sunday. From May 1 through October 15, train rides are offered at 10:00 and 11:30 A.M. and at 2:30 and 4:00 P.M. Summer admission is $9.00 for adults, $8.00 for seniors (sixty-two and older), $6.50 for youngsters four through twelve, and free for kids three and younger. During the winter season, October 15 through April 30, admission is generally half price because the train ride is not available.

For flower and plant lovers, the *Green Bay Botanical Garden* is a definite must-see. The garden is located on a sixty-acre site adjacent to the Northeast Wisconsin Technical College campus on the west side of Green Bay. The rolling hills, spring fed pond, and excellent soil make it an ideal dwelling for a wide spectrum of plants, from formal rose gardens to the fairytale-like atmosphere of the children's garden. Impressive architecture includes graceful bridges, domed gazebos, and even an English cottage. Workshops, programs, and special events are offered throughout the year. The garden is open daily May through October, 9:00 A.M. to 8:00 P.M., and Monday through Friday, November through April, 9:00 A.M. to 4:00 P.M. For more information call (920) 490–9457; or visit www.gbbg.org.

For eating, *Chili John's* (920–494–4624) is famous for its namesake food, ranging from spicy enough to curl hair to milder versions for daisy-weights. The place has been in the same family for three generations. It's located at 519 South Military Avenue in the Beacon Shopping Center, at the intersection of Highway 54. Take-out is available. Some wags claim you can use the hottest version for fueling a motorboat, but don't believe 'em. Just eat and be satisfied.

Dodge County

Dodge County is rich in farmland, layered with rolling hills, and spotted with lakes. Westford, Mud Lake, Shaw Marsh, Theresa Marsh, and Horicon Marsh wildlife areas and the *Horicon National Wildlife Refuge,* as well as Fox, Emily, Beaver Dam, and Sinissippi Lakes, are the county's pride and joy. Outdoors fans flock here regardless of the season for bird-watching, hunting, fishing, or just plain loafing.

Our favorite canoeing jaunt is deep into the Horicon Refuge, angling for bullheads and watching for blue herons and sandhill cranes. The wildlife refuge has several large rookeries of each, accessible only by water. The **Blue Heron Landing,** near the Highway 33 bridge over the Rock River, has canoe rentals April through September and pontoon boat tours from May through the end of October.

Call (920) 485–4663 or visit www.horiconmarsh.com for details. Public boat-launching sites are located at River Bend Park below the Horicon Dam in town, Ice House Slough off Chestnut Street, Arndt Ditch Landing off Highway E northwest of Horicon, and Burnett Ditch Landing on the west side of the marsh.

If you have kids too little to take into the marsh, let them fish for bullheads from the grassy west-side riverbank across from the John Deere plant, near the Highway 33 bridge west of downtown. Pubs in the neighborhood offer pickled eggs and pig's feet, two gourmet treats for the macho set.

Canada geese use the county's cornfields and swamps for a regular autumn pit stop on their way south. They fly from the Hudson Bay in Canada to their winter layover where the Ohio River joins the Mississippi. Up to 100,000—sometimes more—birds are counted in the marsh each year. Subsequently, on some weekends, traffic is bumper- to-bumper along the county roads ringing the marshes as rubberneckers strain to see the giant fowl. Some of the feathered fliers weigh in at an impressive eighteen pounds or more, with a wingspan of 6 feet. If you can, take a middle-of-the-week jaunt around the Horicon instead of a Saturday or Sunday run. You'll be able to stop and stare to your heart's content at the sky-blackening flocks without worrying about backed-up traffic.

The town celebrates its link with the environment during **Horicon Marsh Days** in July, with activities ranging from street sales to a drum- and-bugle-corps competition that attracts groups from around southeastern Wisconsin. In September the Autumn Art on the Marsh show is held in Discher Park, on Cedar Street. The show provides an opportunity to stock up on Christmas presents.

Founded in 1907, the **J. W. Jung Seed Company** in Randolph is another Dodge County attraction, located 40 miles northeast of Madison. Each winter, while planning for planting, gardeners eagerly look forward to the company's nationally distributed mail-order vegetable and flower catalogs. The firm prints its own catalogs, up to 2.5 million copies a year, with 5,000 orders for seeds and plantings per day during the peak spring season. Few people realize that tours of Jung are available if you call ahead (800–247–5864). There's also the opportunity for green thumbers to stop in at the company's garden store, open 8:00 A.M. to 4:30 P.M. Monday through Friday and 8:00 A.M. to 4:00 P.M. Saturday. It sells shrubs, evergreens, seeds, fruit trees, and plants.

TOP ANNUAL EVENTS

Walleye Weekend,
Fond du Lac, early June,
(920) 923–6555

Laura Ingalls Wilder Children's Day,
Old World Wisconsin, Eagle,
late July, (262) 594–6300

America Fest,
Green Bay, Fourth of July,
(888) 867–3342

Sawdust Days,
Oshkosh, early July,
(920) 235–5584

Salmon-O-Rama,
Racine, mid-July, (262) 634–1931

Experimental Aircraft Association Fly-In, Oshkosh, July,
(800) JOIN–EAA

Festival of the Trees,
Racine, November,
(262) 634–6002

Snowshoe Workshop at Retzer Nature Center,
Waukesha, December 1–2,
(262) 896–8007

Specialists are on hand to answer questions about plantings, soil conditions, and all those similar tough details that are necessary to help create the perfect vegetable or flower garden. To ensure the continuation of its fine stock, the company has test plots for many varieties of plants, from gladioluses to seed corn.

The firm's founder, J. W. Jung, died in 1988 at age one hundred. Even after he had hit the century mark, however, Jung was often out speaking to his customers, spending a full day at work. The company currently is run by grandson Richard Zondag and other members of the family.

The *Dodge County Fairgrounds* (920–885–3586; www.dodgecountyfair grounds.com) in *Beaver Dam* has racing and demolition derbies at various times in the summer. The track is 3 miles east of Beaver Dam on Highway 33.

For a quieter but a buzzing good time, there's the *Honey of a Museum* on Highway 67, 2 miles north of *Ashippun.* More than two million pounds of honey are produced each year at the apiary located there. Spigots in the museum allow you to taste the different flavors of honey, from tart wildflower to bitter brown buckwheat and smooth golden clover. Honey is sold in a shop on the grounds, with numerous varieties from plain to that spiced with apricot bits. The museum (920–474–4411) is open year-round from 9:00 A.M. to 3:30 P.M. Monday to Friday. From mid-May through October, it is also open from noon to 4:00 P.M., Saturday and Sunday.

If all that noise isn't one's cuppa tea, then it's time to delve back into history where it is really quiet. The *Rock River Archeological Society* was established in 1998 to study the ancient Native American heritage of Dodge County and nearby areas. The group holds meetings, leads tours, and hosts

At Death's Door

The stretch of water between the tip of the Door Peninsula and Washington Island, 7 miles offshore, is called the **Porte des Morts Passage.** This literally means "Passage of Death" or "Door of Death," from which Door County gets its name. The rockbound coast, the shoals, and the reefs have chewed up dozens of ships over the generations. While the name is appropriate, it originally had nothing to do with shipwrecks. Early French traders called the treacherous passage by that handle in honor of a group of Native American friends who died there during a storm.

events that help participants better understand the land and waterways of the region. Especially interesting are visits to the numerous effigy mounds that can be found throughout the county.

The group meets at 7:00 P.M. on the third Wednesday of each month between September and May at the Department of Natural Resources service center on Highway 28 between Mayville and Horicon. Contact them through their Web site at www.dnr.state.wi.us/org/land/wildlife/reclands/horicon/edcntr/rrarchsoc/.

Door County

Door County (920–743–4456; http://doorcounty.org) has often been called the Cape Cod of Wisconsin. The rocky coast juts like a thumb into the frosty waters of Lake Michigan, separating the lake from Green Bay. It's a harsh landscape, one that artists love. Scandinavian farmers and fishers settled the vicinity, appreciating its environmental kinship to their homeland. We like the county regardless of the season. Spring has the fragrance of cherry and apple blossoms. Summer's hard heat is beaten only in the cool woods or by swimming.

We just wish that some of the small towns were not becoming so commercialized, with what appears to us an overabundance of mini-malls featuring crafts, candles, ribbons, and trendy hiking wear. All these shops have become too much of a good thing. So we prefer to hit the back roads, where it's more relaxing.

Autumn's colorama in Door County is considered among the best in the state. A drive around the peninsula in October provides the last opportunity to scour the county's antiques shops before they close for the snowbound winter. Winter? Well, there's cross-country skiing, followed by a huddle in front of the fireplace with a hot toddy.

The city of **Sturgeon Bay** (800–301–6246; www.sturgeonbay.com) is the entry point for the county, where Highways 42 and 57 link to cross the ship channel. To get there any other way, you'll have to swim, sail, or fly; all of which are excellent options, of course, if you have your own fins, yacht, or plane. Regardless of the transport mode, the county has facilities to accommodate anyone's arrival.

Door County is noted for its many excellent inns and guest houses. Among the best in Sturgeon Bay are the White Lace Inn, 16 North Fifth Avenue (877–948–5223); the Bay Shore Inn, 4205 Bay Shore Drive (800–556–4551); the Inn at Cedar Crossing, 336 Louisiana (920–743–4200); and the Scofield House, 908 Michigan (920–743–7727). In Ephraim try the French Country Inn, 3052 Spruce Lane (920–854–4001).

Inn on Maple, 414 Maple Drive, Sister Bay (920–854–5107), is an excellent lodging on the peninsula. One of the most popular in Door County is Jan and Andy Coulson's White Gull Inn, P.O. Box 160, Fish Creek (920–868–3517; www.whitegullinn.com). Hospitality and moderate pricing are the name of the game for all these accommodations.

Of all the Door County traditions, the fish boil is the most famous, harkening back to the area's Scandinavian heritage. Almost every roadside restaurant and inn offers some version of this popular summer "event." The chef boils a huge pot of salt water over an outside blaze. Depending on his or her inclinations as to what ingredients go in when, next usually comes seasoning, potatoes, and onions that cook for about fifteen to twenty minutes. Bunyan-size chunks of whitefish are then boiled in the mix for another seven to ten minutes or so. No eyes of newt or wing of bat are needed—this is your basic stick-to-the-ribs

Inn on Maple

food. The water bubbles over from the pot, causing a dramatic explosion of steam and great photo opportunities. The boil carries off all the fats with the scalding foam.

You can then sit down for a breeze-touched picnic. Add homemade bread and jam, coleslaw, corn-on-the-cob, and a slab of freshly baked Door County cherry or apple pie. A la mode helps make this concluding part of the meal truly decadent. But what the hey? Mmmm, grand! For a listing of several regional restaurants offering this combo of showmanship and good eats, check out www.doorcountyvacations.com/html/generalInfo/fishBoils.htm.

Washington Island is reached by ferry only from Gills Rock on the Door County mainland. The island has been discovered by tourists, which has led to an overabundance of gift shops near the harbor mouth. But once you get away from the ferry landing, the island is delightfully pretty. Spend a day driving around the island's back roads or rent a bike at the dockside. I was running late during one exploration and had to catch the night's last ferryboat. With about a minute to spare, I got from the north end of the island to the south end. I don't recommend a careening drive like that on a regular basis because the roads are too twisting and narrow. But at least I made the boat landing in time.

Rock Island is the next island out from Washington, also reached by ferryboat only. No cars are allowed in this state park, so be prepared to hike. Without the noise of autos to compete with the surf and the wind rustling the beech leaves, you can spot the deer and other wildlife that live on the

Backpacking Only

Newport State Park is a semiwilderness on the far tip of Door County. A century ago the logging village of Newport stood where the park is now. The village eventually died and reverted to fields and forests. While hiking there we've found the ruins of several cabins and foundations of houses far back among the pines. The park has 11 miles of shoreline along Lake Michigan, including a 3,000-foot-long beach.

The best part about the park is that it allows only backpacking at its campsites, which range along the lakeside for quiet, if not five-star resort comfort. But we never went for that, preferring to rough it. The dawn up from the side was worth the strain of humping in all our gear. The wildflowers in spring and the explosion of leaf color in autumn means repeat trips. The park is located 5 miles northeast of Ellison Bay on Highway 42. Then turn east on County Highway NP. The park is open daily from dawn to dusk year-round. For further information contact the Park Superintendent, Newport State Park, 475 South County Highway NP, Ellison Bay 54210, (920) 854–2500; www.dcty.com/newport.

craggy spit of rock and sand. Pack a lunch and sit on the north beach looking out over the lake. The view is tremendous. Archaeologists have been poking around the island for several years, discovering ancient Native American villages and burial places, as well as checking out abandoned pioneer settlements. The sites are well marked, but don't go around digging on your own. They're all legally protected.

Fond du Lac County

Ripon proudly struts the fact that the Republican Party was formed here when a group of disgruntled politicians met on March 20, 1854. The building in which they got together is now called the *Little White Schoolhouse.* The building on Blackburn Street is open daily throughout the summer and early autumn.

The city of *Fond du Lac* is on the southern rim of Lake Winnebago, with a large white lighthouse at the Lakeside Park to act as a focal point for outdoor events. The city's *Walleye Weekend* each June attracts anglers from all over the Midwest to compete for cash prizes and the adulation of fellow fishing fanatics. For details call the Fond du Lac Convention and Visitors Bureau, (920) 923–3010 or (800) 937–9123, or the Fond du Lac Festival at (920) 923–6555.

findthebadger

In case your geography is a bit askew and you need to locate the Badger State on a map, Wisconsin is bounded on the north by Michigan's Upper Peninsula and Lake Superior, on the west by Iowa and Minnesota, on the south by Illinois, and on the east by Lake Michigan.

Jefferson County

The *Emma Carlin Hiking Trail* is one of the state's best for hiking and biking, beginning in a parking lot on County Trunk Z, south of Highway 59 and only 2 miles east of Palmyra. The trail offers three loops of varying distance, with a pond, meadows, and plenty of wildlife. Eagles are often spotted high in the air over the aspen and basswood groves that are scattered between the oak stands. Sometimes turkey vultures can be seen swooping and soaring overhead as well.

After a brisk hike on the trail, indulge in all the creature comforts at the *Fargo Mansion Inn* (920–648–3654) in *Lake Mills.* Enoch Fargo, a descendant of the stagecoach family, built the home at the turn of the nineteenth century. It became the town's social center, complete with towers, woodwork, a lavish foyer, and a huge kitchen with a walk-in freezer. The neighbors were amazed when Fargo put in a cement sidewalk out front, supposedly the first in Wisconsin.

After a succession of owners, including one family that hosted eighty foster children (over the years, not all at once), the building was listed on the National Register of Historic Places in 1982 and made into a guest house in 1986. Five bedrooms are on the second floor, reached by a staircase worthy of Cinderella. The rooms are named for former occupants of the mansion. Another four to five suites have been added to the building's third floor by owner Barry Luce and his partner, Tom Boycks.

The inn has tandem bikes for use in the summer, for pedaling along the nearby Glacial Drumlin Trail. Prices at the inn are moderate and include a continental breakfast.

Near Lake Mills is **Aztalan State Park** (920–648–8774) and the southern unit of Kettle Moraine Forest. On summer weekends dirt-bike racers zoom near the park on a twisted, turning motocross track that can be seen from I–94. Their roaring engines, however, can't be heard at the site of a prehistoric village to the south. The tribe that settled here is thought to be an outpost of ancient mound builders who lived in southern Illinois.

Artifacts found throughout the region show that the inhabitants were great traders. Shells, precious metals, and implements not indigenous to central Wisconsin have been found in farm fields and along riverbanks. The artifacts and pioneer tools are displayed at the **Lake Mills–Aztalan Historical Society Museum** (920–648–4632), 3 miles east of Lake Mills on County Trunk B. Two pioneer churches and other nineteenth-century pioneer buildings are on the museum site, which is open noon to 4:00 P.M. Thursday through Sunday from mid-May through late September. There is a modest charge.

The state has erected a palisade where the village once stood, similar to one that archaeologists say protected the tribe from marauding enemy bands. Excellent markers and signage around the grounds tell the story of the Aztalan tribe. A picnic site is nearby at the foot of a hill leading down to a creek. On one of our excursions there, the kids spent half a day fishing after reading how the Native Americans used the same waterway for their fish traps and netting. It is possible that this community was somehow related to the Cahokia Mounds people of southwestern Illinois. Archaeologists have discovered many similar artifacts and building styles at both sites.

Fort Atkinson is home of the **Hoard Historical Museum and Dairy Exhibit,** 407 Merchants Avenue (920–563–7769). The museum is open Memorial Day through Labor Day, Tuesday through Saturday, 9:30 A.M. to 4:30 P.M. and Sunday, 11:00 A.M. to 3:00 P.M. Winter hours are 9:30 A.M. to 3:30 P.M., Tuesday through Saturday. The exhibits trace the development of the American dairy industry, with plaques honoring famous scientists and dairy operators. Fort Atkinson has long been famous as a dairy and agricultural publishing center, where such important magazines as *Hoard's Dairyman* are produced.

The Hoard Museum also traces the action of the U.S. Army and militia in the Black Hawk War of 1832. Several skirmishes took place in Jefferson County between pursuing troops and their quarry, the Fox and allies who were led by the famed warrior Black Hawk.

Young Abraham Lincoln was one of the militiamen who chased the Native Americans to the Mississippi River, where they were massacred while trying to escape by swimming across. A large map in the museum shows where soldiers and Native Americans camped as they jockeyed back and forth.

The town also has a replica of Fort Koshkonong, originally built to protect settlers during the Black Hawk War.

Nearby are several prehistoric Native American markers, one of which resembles a huge panther. That intaglio (a design cut into the surface of the earth) was probably constructed around A.D. 1000. The Fort Atkinson form is believed to be one of only two such earthworks remaining in the world (another intaglio in the shape of a panther is in Ontario). The design is rare, because most of the patterns made by the Native Americans were in mounds, rather than in depressions in the ground. The intaglio is located on the west bank of the Rock River, on Highway 106 at the west edge of town. Actually, you will have to use your imagination in "seeing" the beast, because at least 25 feet of the tail was destroyed by construction of a driveway in 1941. The depression is grass covered, near some hedges and sidewalks at 1236 Riverside Drive.

On Highway 26 on the south side of town is the **Fireside Dinner Theatre** and restaurant (920–563–9505 or 800–477–9505), which stages live theater-in-the-round productions, many of which are well-known musicals. The theater is popular with tour groups. The country's top folk and acoustic musicians perform regularly at the **Café Carpe,** a club operated by well-known singer Bill Camplin and co-owner Kitty Welch at 18 South Water Street West (920–563–9391). Not quite a throwback to the coffeehouse days of the 1960s, but it's close enough. The Café Carpe has a soothing ambience, good vibes, and hearty, reasonably priced food. A place to call a musical home.

In Watertown, on the county's north side, is the restored building that was the nation's first kindergarten, celebrating its 150th anniversary in 2006. A German teacher, Margarethe Meyer Schurz, brought this form of teaching youngsters to the United States in 1856. The structure was originally in down-town Watertown but was moved to the site of the **Octagon House Museum** in 1956, which had its 150th birthday in 2004. Both museums are open daily.

Summer hours are 11:00 A.M. to 4:00 P.M.; winter hours are 11:00 A.M. to 3:00 P.M. (919 Charles Street, 920–261–2796). Admission is $7.00 for adults, $4.00 for students six to seventeen, $6.00 for seniors and AAA members, and $15.00 for a family. Kids five and younger get in free.

Peterson's Hamburger Stand and Ice Cream Parlor, (920) 674–3637, on U.S. Highway 18, 1 block east of downtown in Jefferson, is burger nirvana. Peterson's is open from 10:30 A.M. to 9:30 P.M., from mid-March until mid-October. This tiny shack (and its predecessors) has been a staple for Jefferson burger fans since the 1920s. A couple of hot, steamy kids flip burgers on a small grill in the cramped shack. But they do a great job. Fast, as well. I always ask for fried onions. The mix can't be beat, even though you don't want to talk closely with anyone for awhile. Wooweee! Be prepared to wait, especially on summer evenings, because the place is so popular. There's no indoor seating, so perch outside on a long bench stretching alongside an adjacent building, which houses an ice-cream parlor. On the way home to Milwaukee, I once drove six hours from Minneapolis to Jefferson, just for a couple of Peterson's cheeseburgers.

While in **Watertown,** stop for ice cream at **Mullen's Dairy and Eatery** on West Main Street (920–261–4278). The dairy still produces its own creamery products. Scattered around the room are old advertising materials, glass milk bottles, and similar items from the company's past. It's open Monday to Friday from 9:00 A.M. to 9:00 P.M. and weekends until 10:00 P.M.

Kenosha County

Kenosha County is tucked into the far southeastern corner of the state, where Lake Michigan laps along its miles of beach frontage. The rolling waters provided opportunities for trade and fishing, so pioneer settlers plunked down their log cabins along the shoreline. Eventually, a string of mansions grew up along the lakeside, especially in **Kenosha,** the county seat. They include the **Kemper Center,** once a girls' school, renovated as a conference center and banquet hall at 6501 Third Avenue (262–657–6005), home of an annual Oktoberfest in October, usually featuring the Dorf Kapelle Village Band; and the Kenosha County History Center and its famous lighthouse, 220 Fifty-first Place (262–654–5770). From 1957 to the autumn of 2003, the Alford Mansion was home to the Society for the Preservation and Encouragement of Barber Shop Quartet Singing in America (SPEBSQSA)—or, saying that with less of a mouthful—the Barbershop Harmony Society. The Tudor-revival building, built in 1928, is a private residence again. After the sale, the society moved its headquarters to 7930 Sheridan Road.

If gazing at older buildings isn't your forte, perhaps fishing is. The county boasts the largest catch rate of coho salmon and lake trout along the Wisconsin side of Lake Michigan. Cohorama, a celebration of that fabled fighting fish, is usually held in mid-June and features a fishing contest. What else?

The primo hamburger joint in town is **Ron's Place,** 3301 Fifty-second Street (262–657–5907). It's inexpensive, with a delicious half-pound burger called the "5x5" that is guaranteed to show up any national fast-food chain's poor excuse for a sandwich. The burger costs around $4.25 and is worth every penny. Ron's has other eats as well, of course, but when it comes to burgers, I won't eat anywhere else in Kenosha.

The **Bristol Renaissance Faire** in Bristol Township is a fun step way, way back into history. Jugglers, whipcrackers, troubadours, poets, and minstrels put on shows on weekends from mid-July through Labor Day. The eighty-acre site is near the Illinois-Wisconsin border just off I–94. From Chicago take I–94 west to Highway 41 north and exit at Russell Road.

From Milwaukee take I–94 east, exit at County Road V, and follow the Frontage Road. There's usually a College of Wizards, bawdy comedy, games of skill (get the kids to slay a dragon), and a sword fight or two. For tickets contact the Faire, (847) 395–7773 or www.renfair.com.

Kenoshans appreciate their well-maintained beaches, although they are not staffed by lifeguards. Folks of all ages love swimming, tanning, and loaf-

Great to Hike

Bong Recreation Area is named after Wisconsin native Richard I. Bong, the number-one fighter pilot for the United States during World War II. In the mid-1950s the government purchased 5,540 acres in Racine and Kenosha Counties for an air force base. The project was abandoned at the end of that decade. In the 1960s, 1,000 acres of the vacant land were purchased to convert to forestland and a county park. In 1974, 4,515 additional acres were set aside as the state's first recreational area that included nontraditional uses of parkland. For instance, sky gliding, dog training, hot-air ballooning, and model-rocket launching are allowed. But we go for the hiking opportunities around the park's small lake.

The Blue Trail (South Loop) is one of the most interesting treks, taking us along a nature trail with excellent signage. The marshy areas in the middle of the recreation site are excellent for bird-watching, so bring some binoculars. This is an easy trek for little kids. From I–94 get off at the Highway 142 exit and drive west about 8 miles. The park is 1 mile west of Highway 75. Kenosha is the largest nearby city, 17 miles to the east on Lake Michigan. For more information contact the site manager, Bong State Recreation Area, 26313 Burlington Road, Kansasville 53139, (262) 878–5600; www.dnr.state.wi.us/org/land/parks/specific/bong/.

ing at Alford Park, 2901 Alford Drive; Eichelman Beach, 6125-3rd Avenue; Pennoyer Park, 3601-75th Avenue; Simmons Island Park, 5001 Simmons Island; and Southport Park, 7825-1st Avenue. You'll also have to bob about on your own; no flotation devices can be used in swimming areas.

Locals also love their parks and nature areas. Anderson Park, 8730-22nd Avenue, has a playground, as well as baseball and soccer fields. In the summer, the public swimming pool here is busy with two water slides. In the winter, an ice skating rink is set up. A ninety-five-acre fishing pond also attracts young anglers, helped by grandparents. Charles Nash Park, 5909-56th Street, is geared toward the active Kenoshan, with its fifty-two acres hosting four baseball diamonds, a soccer field, horseshoe pits, playground, and skateboard park. Yet it does have a spacious picnic area for after-game gatherings. The twenty-four-acre Kennedy Park, 4051 Fifth Avenue, also has a picnic area, with a hiking/biking trail to use for working off the brats and burgers. Lincoln Park, 7010-22nd Avenue, features the lovely Warren J. Taylor Sunken Garden, with its fifty-plus varieties of annual plantings in thirty-one formal beds. During nice weather, you can almost stumble over the wedding parties using the grounds as photo backdrops.

For more details, call the parks department (262–663–4080) or check www.kenosha.org/departments/parks.

The community has two marinas, each with beautiful nearby beaches for swimming. The **Simmons Island Marina** (262–653–4052) and the **Southport Marina** (262–657–5565) host boaters from around Lake Michigan, who appreciate the accommodations there for their vessels. On balmy summer Saturdays, the lakefront is home to **Harbor Marketplace,** an extended farmers' market that offers fresh produce and entertainment (262–653–4030).

Speaking of food, don't miss dropping by **Tenuta's Delicatessen and Liquors,** a real down-home Italian grocery store on the west side of town at 3203 Fifty-third Street (262–657–9001). Go for the two-for-one wine buys found at the rear of the store, augmented by homemade meatballs, pasta, and other wonders from the vast coolers. Mmmmm, great.

Kewaunee County

Algoma is a photographer's dream on early summer mornings, especially as the state's largest charter fishing fleet sets out from the harbor. The city claims record lake-salmon catches every year just offshore. Who's to argue when boat after boat returns with hefty catches after a full day on the choppy Lake Michigan waters? It's not uncommon to haul in twenty-pound chinooks off Algoma Shores.

Von Stiehl Winery, at 115 Navarino Street in Algoma (920–487–5208 or 800–955–5208; www.vonstiehl.com), is open for tours daily from 9:00 A.M. to 5:00 P.M. May through October. The winery store is open throughout the year, with complimentary tastings. Tours run every half hour, beginning at 10:00 A.M. Tickets are $3.00 for adults, seniors are $2.50, and kids under sixteen are free. Perusing the collection of toy trolls on display is almost as much fun as visiting the sampling room. The winery specializes in sweet and semisweet wines and has won several national and international awards.

Kewaunee County can promise dolls, wine, and huge fish. It also can show off the world's largest grandfather clock, located on Kewaunee's north side. The old timepiece, which stands 35 feet tall, is the trademark of Svoboda Industries (920–388–2691 or 800–678–9996), a one-hundred-year-old firm that specializes in all sorts of wood products. The clock is on the facade of the factory, chiming every fifteen minutes. The Svoboda plant is located on Highway 42 North and makes smaller versions of the grandfather clock in addition to furniture, carvings, and other wooden household accessories.

Manitowoc County

The county fronts the rolling waters of Lake Michigan, with a string of towns along the shore that look like diamonds, with lights sparkling at night. The coastline, although lost in darkness, glimmers when you're putt-putting along in a powerboat. The best view is from 0.5 mile or so offshore on a lazy summer evening.

The city of *Manitowoc* must be one of the few towns that has its own submarine. The USS *Cobia,* acquired by the *Wisconsin Maritime Museum* from the U.S. Navy in 1970, has been outfitted just as it was during combat in World War II. Recorded battle sounds, accurate to the shouts of "dive, dive, dive," lend reality to the tight quarters. The 311-foot-long vessel had a distinguished career, sinking thirteen Japanese vessels in 1944 and 1945. After being

landho!

The first sailing vessel to reach the upper Great Lakes was the *Griffon,* a galleon captained originally by famed explorer René-Robert Cavelier, Sieur de La Salle. In 1679 he visited several of the Door County islands and collected furs. However, the ship went down in a raging storm on its return trip to Niagara. Subsequently, the *Griffon* also was the first of many recorded vessels to be sunk on Lake Michigan.

decommissioned, the sub was assigned as a training ship for Milwaukee's submarine reserves unit. Manitowoc secured the *Cobia* as a memorial to the factory workers who built twenty-eight subs in city plants during the war.

The museum itself celebrates life on Lake Michigan, with exhibits of shipwrecks, model vessels, diving gear, photographs, and artifacts. It opened in 1969 but moved to new quarters in 1986, a building complete with a "street" that includes a ship chandlery, post office, and other storefronts.

One of the most interesting displays is a full-scale section of a sailing ship as it would have appeared during construction in 1854. The beams, spikes, and caulking are all in their proper places, detailing the intricate work that went into the rugged lake vessels.

The museum (920–684–0218; 866–724–2356; www.wisconsinmaritime.org) is located at 75 Maritime Drive in downtown Manitowoc. The museum is open seven days a week from 9:00 A.M. to 6:00 P.M. and is closed for major holidays. Tickets for both the museum and the USS *Cobia* submarine tour are $12.00 for adults, $10.00 children, and free for youngsters under six.

The *Inn on Maritime Bay* (920–682–7000 or 800–654–5353) is the place to eat in Manitowoc, featuring fish and steak. General menu prices are moderate. The inn is on the shore in downtown Manitowoc and offers short "getaways" such as the Waterfront Retreat and Castaway Package. The latter includes a box lunch for fishing or sailing, two of the most popular sports in town.

Speaking of eating, it's obvious that no one need ever go hungry in Manitowoc, especially when strolling into *Beerntsen's Candies* at 108 North Eighth Street (920–684–9616). This quaint candy shop with its ice-cream parlor has been a tradition in the city since, well, let's say since when chocolate was invented. In 1932, Joseph Beerntsen founded the company, which is now in its third generation of the family. The Beerntsens opened a second outlet in Cedarburg in 1984. Homemade temptations line the shelves in all their caloric splendor. Beerntsen's hot fudge is so lusciously thick and rich, it makes a lava flow look like skim milk. Hours are 9:00 A.M. to 8:00 P.M., Monday through Friday; and from 10:00 A.M. to 4:00 P.M., Saturday and Sunday year-round.

Mishicot is a Native American word for "place of shelter." The city is tucked into farmland at the junction of Highways 147 and 163. Lake Michigan is about 10 miles to the east. *River Edge Galleries* (920–755–4777) has one of the most extensive collections of the work of Wisconsin fine artists of any state showplace, regularly displaying Karen Gunderman, Patrick Farrell, and other state personalities. The two-story gallery on the East Twin River is located at 432 East Main Street.

A great state-owned property along Lake Michigan in Manitowoc County is perfect for anyone who enjoys rambling outside and communing with the birds and bees. Although maintained by the county, the 123-acre *Fischer Creek State Recreation Area,* 4319 Expo Drive, offers wooded bluffs, expansive grasslands, and creature-filled wetlands, along with almost a mile of Lake Michigan shoreline on which to tramp. No camping is allowed, but for other details on what to see and do, call the Manitowoc parks folks at (920) 683–4185.

Point Beach State Forest (920–794–7480) is just south of the power plant. It covers more than 2,800 acres of prime timber bordered by 6 miles of sand dunes along Lake Michigan. The woods contain beech, hemlock, maple, yellow birch, and numerous other varieties of trees. There are 127 wooded campsites, seventy with electricity, and all are a short walk to the beach. For campsite reservations, call (888) 947–2757. They are open year-round.

Wildlife is abundant, ranging from deer and fox to mink and muskrat. Naturalist programs are held regularly there throughout the summer. The lighthouse is a major attraction at Rowley Point, in operation since 1953.

The ice-cream sundae was supposedly invented in Two Rivers, about 6 miles north of Manitowoc on Highway 42. On a steamy Sunday in 1881, Ed Berner, owner of a local soda fountain, was asked to top off a dish of ice cream with chocolate sauce. The sauce was usually used only for sodas, but the new concoction took off in popularity once the town's youngsters tried it. A glass vendor saw potential in the product and ordered special sets of canoe-shaped dishes for Berner, calling them sundae dishes. A plaque marking the event stands downtown. Berner's fountain at 1404 Fifteenth Street is gone now, replaced by a parking lot for Kurtz's Vintage Wine Cellar.

Outagamie County

The fate and future of Outagamie County, linked to Calumet and Winnebago Counties to the south, are closely tied to Lake Winnebago and the Fox River. Since pioneer times the county has been a commercial center. The waterways brought explorers, settlers, and traders into the heart of Wisconsin from Green Bay and Lake Michigan.

The **Outagamie Museum and Houdini Historical Center,** run by the county historical society, is different from many of its sister museums around the state. This facility concentrates on the industrial and corporate heritage of the Fox River Valley. The displays cover electricity, papermaking, financial services, agriculture, and communication, as well as local history. *Tools of Change,* depicting technology's impact on culture between 1840 and 1950, is fascinating. The standing exhibit is a must-see for kids, who can tour a machine shop, a doctor's office, and other "rooms" to see how various tools are used. First edition books written by Pulitzer Prize-winning author Edna Feber are also on display. The museum is located at 330 East College Avenue in Appleton (920–735–9370 or 920–733–8445). Admission is $5.00 for adults, $4.00 for seniors and students,

Wildlife at the Edge

If nature is your game, then the **Riveredge Nature Center** is the place to stroll. It's one of our most popular near-to-home getaways for bird-watching, deer sighting, and woodchuck counting. The center is a 350-acre stretch of woodland and prairie along the Milwaukee River. The property offers 12 miles of hiking and cross-country ski trails. In addition, naturalist programs, photo shows, and environmental classes keep outdoors lovers occupied. We trekked the property, with a special kinship for the trails along the river because of the scenery and wildlife-viewing opportunities. Bring bug goop for muggy summer hikes; swarms of pesky skeeters can be an irritant.

The main property behind the old barn that serves as center headquarters is ablaze with prairie flowers in spring and summer and is lacking the mosquito problem that you might encounter along the riverbank trails. I've never seen so many daisies as are on display at the center. The yellow carpet seems to spread from horizon to horizon. The center is only 1 mile east of Newburg on County Highway Y. Trail fees are $4.00 for adults and $2.00 for kids agaes four to thirteen iwth a family rate of $12.00. Guests are asked to register at the visitor center. The center is open 8:00 A.M. to 5:00 P.M. Monday through Friday and noon to 4:00 P.M. on Saturday and Sunday. Contact Riveredge Nature Center, 4458 West Hawthorne, Box 26, Newburg 53060-0026, (800) 287–8098 or (262) 675–6888; www.riveredgenc.org.

$2.50 for children five to seventeen, and $12.00 for a family. A ticket includes admission to the Houdini Historical Center. Hours are Tuesday to Saturday 10:00 A.M. to 4:00 P.M., and Sunday noon to 4:00 P.M. The museum is closed Mondays except in June, July, and August.

A few years ago, the state's tourism motto was "Escape to Wisconsin." That led to all sorts of bad jokes, of course. But the **Houdini Historical Center** is no laughing matter. The facility, dedicated to Appleton's favorite son, has a wide selection of his memorabilia and artifacts. Demonstrations and hands-on exhibits let you test your own agility and ability. Let me tell you that "escapism" isn't as easy as it looks. The museum is open daily 10:00 A.M. to 5:00 P.M. Call (920) 735–9370.

To tour **Appleton,** exit Highway 41 on College Avenue and park at the city ramp at the Paper Valley Hotel. Walk down the steps at Jones Park for a look at the locks and dam on the Fox River and cross the river on the Oneida Skyline Bridge. Return to the Appleton Center office building and walk through it to **Houdini Plaza,** which commemorates Appleton's famous native son, magician Harry Houdini. There is a sculpture in the plaza of the noted performer, who was born in the city in 1874 as Erich Weiss. The young man took the name of the famous French magician Houdin when he launched his career as an escape artist. Each fall, an annual magic festival called Houdini

Days draws internationally-renowned magicians. The event features perform-ances and workshops.

Appleton is also home to Lawrence University and the Fox City Performing Arts Center, a 2,100-seat proscenium-style theater. The center has an extensive schedule of local and national performers. For a lineup, call (920) 730–3760 or check www.foxcitiespac.com.

Ozaukee County

Take a step back one hundred years, whizzing over the crest of County Road I. The Wisconsin frontier of the 1840s pops out of the farmland at the Ozaukee County *Pioneer Village,* on the north edge of Hawthorne Hills Park in Saukville.

Twenty settlers' buildings from around the county, including houses, barns, the Cedarburg railroad station, a chapel, and trading post, were moved to the site and reassembled into a village, bordered by an 1860s split-rail fence from the Alvin Wiskerchen farm. The rails are mostly cedar, but there are some oak and ash as well. The village is open from noon to 5:00 P.M. Saturday and Sunday from Memorial Day through mid-October. The last tour is 4:00 P.M. Curators demonstrate pioneer skills such as log trimming, weaving, bread bak-ing, and iron working. All the buildings are furnished in styles from the 1840s to the early 1900s, depending on the structure.

There's nothing fishy about *Port Washington,* 25 miles north of Milwaukee on the shores of Lake Michigan, except that it offers excellent angling for coho and lake trout. The city has a relatively new marina, built in 1982, that has a fish-cleaning station at the waterfront, plus boat-launching facilities. You also can fish from the breakwater and along the piers. Keep an eye on the kids, however, because the chill lake water runs deep and fast even close to shore. Fourth of July fireworks are popped off at the marina, making a blazing spectacle over the harbor entrance.

Port Washington celebrates what it claims is the *World's Largest One-Day Outdoor Fish Fry* on the third Saturday of each July. Having attended several of these events, I'm not one to offer a challenge. You want fish, you get fish. Seemingly tons of it. Plus the usual french-fried potatoes as a side delight. Fish-fry aficionados love the smoked fish eating contest, an activity I prefer to pass on.

The local firefighters usually have a hose war, trying with their streams of water to push a beer barrel across a wire strung between two poles. The oppos-ing side attempts to push it back, making for a wet time for all participants. A hint: don't stand close. The teams sometimes will playfully squirt the crowd, especially if it's a hot day.

Port Washington has several excellent restaurants specializing in fish. Among the best is *Smith Brothers,* 100 North Franklin (262–284–5592). Its prime location overlooks the Port Washington harbor, with the best view of the sailboats in the marina from the restaurant's top deck. In addition to sit-down dinners (in the pricey range), a fish market there has almost any kind of finny fella—fresh—you can imagine. After a full meal at the restaurant, stroll down to the wharf to watch the anglers.

"The Port" has become a destination for cyclers, many with food in mind after a long trek. *Dockside Deli,* 222 East Main Street (262–284–9440) serves breakfast and lunch, with cookies-to-die-for, including a delight known as the Snickerdoodle. *Harry's Restaurant,* 128 North Franklin Street, is another popular spot attracting bikers. Hungry diners often line up outside for a taste of Harry's down-home cooking. Call (262) 284–2861.

The city's downtown chamber of commerce building on Grand Avenue is called the *Pebble House.* On the National Register of Historic Places, the old home was built in Greek Revival style with rubble stone walls 20 inches thick. The foundation of the building was constructed of pebbles and rocks collected along the shoreline by original owners Elizabeth and Henry Dodge in 1848. The house was moved to its current location in 1985, pebbles and all. To reach the chamber of commerce, call (262) 284–0900.

The last remaining authentic covered bridge of what had been forty in the state is in Ozaukee County's *Covered Bridge County Park.* The bridge over Cedar Creek was built in 1876 and "retired" from service in 1962. You'll find the structure by going west of downtown Grafton on Highway 60 to the junction with Highway 143. Turn north there on Covered Bridge Road.

In 1999 Donald Tendick Sr., donated 142 wooded acres interspersed with rolling farmland to Ozaukee County, with the idea that a park be developed. Although the philanthropist died in 2000, his memory lives on with *Tendick Nature Park,* located on County Highway O, approximately 2 miles north of Saukville. Its amenities include an archery range, disc golf course, access to the Milwaukee River for canoeing, nature trails, hiking/ski trails, and a winter sled-ding hill.

Hobo's Korner Kitchen, 100 East Main Street in Belgium (262–285–3417), is one of those truck stops where the food is plentiful, the conversation bois-terous, and the music preference is country-western. There is plenty of room to park, move, stretch, and grin. The stop is directly to the west of Highway 43, the main four-lane road to Sheboygan, at exit 107. On Fridays there is an all-you-can-eat codfish fry, including fries, two slabs of bread, coleslaw, a cup of soup, and enough tartar sauce to fill a ten-gallon pail. If you want to go fancy, try the Poor Man's Lobster with vegetables and potatoes.

Racine County

Racine has long been host to one of the county's largest colonies of Danish immigrants. And someday a poet will compose an ode honoring the delightful, delicious Danish kringle, the most delectable pastry of them all. Racine is the Kringle Capital of the Universe, with at least eleven bakeries where even a quick stop adds pounds to thighs and hips. The Racine Chamber of Commerce estimates that the bakeries, most of which are run by families of Danish descent, produce upwards of a million kringles annually. Many are shipped around the world for Christmas giving.

Kringles are oval-shaped layers of buttered dough, weighing about a pound and a half. They feature a variety of fillings such as pecan, walnut, raspberry, chocolate, rhubarb, cheese, cherry, apple, custard, and even peanut butter.

Today's kringles are smaller than the 3-by-8-foot pastries made in nineteenth-century Denmark. Austrians taught Danish bakers the technique of layering thin sheets of butter and dough, letting the concoction sit for a day or so before flattening it with large rolling pins. Most of the initial work is still done by hand, but better rolling machines and high-tech ovens ensure easier production and consistency. Some large plants can make 1,500 kringles an hour, a boon during holiday time.

Stop in for a take-home munch at Bendsten's Bakery, 3200 Washington Avenue (262–633–0365; www.bendstensbakery.com); Larsen Bakery, 3311 Washington Avenue (262–633–4298); Lehmann's Bakery, 2210 Sixteenth Street (262–632–2359; www.lehmanns.com); or O&H Danish Bakery, 1841 Douglas Avenue (866–637–8895 or 800–227–6665; www.ohdanishbakery.com) or 4006 Durand Avenue (866–554–1311).

Yet after a generation or two in Racine, kringle making is no longer exclusively Danish. Joe Polentini Sr., of Polentini's Bakery (6100 Washington Avenue, 262–886–3392), is proud of his Italian heritage. "You don't have to be Italian to make good Italian bread," Polentini jokes.

Green between the Toes

Milaeger's Inc.'s greenhouses in southeastern Wisconsin are among the largest in the state, located at 4838 Douglas Avenue in Racine or at 8717 Highway 11, Sturtevant. Both properties are open daily from 9:00 A.M. to 8:00 P.M. Monday through Friday, 8:30 A.M. to 5:00 P.M. Saturday, and 9:30 A.M. to 5:00 P.M. Sunday. Guests are free to browse amid the potted this-'n'-thats that are growing everywhere. Perennials are the big things here, with a total of seventy-one greenhouses to check out. I've always dreamed that my plants would be this lush. Call (262) 639–2040.

When in Racine, ride through the city's historic downtown and business district aboard one of the *lakefront trolleys.* They operate daily 10:00 A.M. to 5:00 P.M. Memorial Day through Labor Day. There are also special pub-and-grub tours to local restaurants and bars on Friday and Saturday night during the summer. Call (262) 637–9000 or (800) 317–4333.

Speaking of the lakefront, we always enjoy taking Lighthouse Drive between Three- and Four-Mile Roads in Racine. The *Wind Point Lighthouse* there is a familiar sight (site) for Racine residents and has been painted and photographed so often it probably has its own museum wing somewhere. Built in 1880 for a cost of $100,000, the 112-foot tower helped guide ships into the Racine harbor during its merchant fleet heyday. Before the lighthouse was built, a solitary tree on the point served as sentinel. The building now serves as the municipal offices for the village of Wind Point, surrounded as it is by the larger city of Racine. Note that the interior is not open to the public, but the grounds are available for strolling. Stunning views of Lake Michigan seen from the area are worth at least one Kodak Moment. I suggest you go for more.

The *Golden Rondelle* at the S. C. Johnson & Son Inc. plant in Racine offers tours on Friday by reservation. Contact the Guest Relations Center at the company, 1525 Howe Street, Racine 53403 (262–260–2154). The Golden Rondelle Theater was initially used by Johnson Wax at the 1964 World's Fair in New York as part of its display building.

Tours of the firm's main administration building, designed by Frank Lloyd Wright, also start at the Golden Rondelle Theater.

The Johnson company, better known as Johnson Wax, was started in 1886 as a manufacturer of parquet floors and moved into the wax business when customers asked for ways to protect their underfoot investment. Currently, the firm markets more than 200 products and carries out continuous research. A display of these items fills an exhibit room.

Racine's theater scene is known throughout the region for its wide selection of drama and music. Among the community creative venues are the *Prairie Performing Arts Center,* 4050 Lighthouse Drive, (262) 260–3845; and the *Racine Theater Guild,* 2519 Northwestern Avenue, (262) 633–4218. The *Over Our Head Players* operates the *Sixth Street Theater,* emphasizing contemporary comedy. The latter's playhouse is located at 318 Sixth Street, (262) 632–6802.

The *Racine Art Museum,* affectionately known as "RAM," is the repository of a significant collection of contemporary craft works, showcased in major exhibitions of new work, as well as with a permanent collection. RAM emphasizes ceramics, fibers, glass, metals, and wood. Such artists as ceramic sculptor Toshiko Takaezu are highlighted, showcasing fourteen human-sized sculptures in his *Star Series*. Wisconsin artists Dona Look, Alex Mandli, Michael Pugh, and Tom Rauschke are also featured. For details and schedules of exhibits, lectures, and workshops, contact RAM, 441 Main Street, (262) 638–8300, or check its Web site at www.ramart.org.

The **Seven Mile Fair & Market Square** in **Caledonia** is a bizarre bazaar. As in the old Arlo Guthrie song "Alice's Restaurant," you "can get anything you want" (at Seven Mile Square). Antique hammers, old postcards, collector buttons, car parts, discounted beauty products, tools by the ton, and the occasional fresh vegetables in season fill the booths. I remember the good old days when the entire ten acres was outdoors and bargain hunters flocked there in rain or shine. Today a large metal building houses several hundred exhibitors, with an overflow outside. The new place doesn't quite have the feel that the old locale did, when it was a cross between the Arab Quarter in Jerusalem and Coventry Gardens. Now there is more of a Shopping Network atmosphere to the place. But don't let that turn you off, because Seven Mile Fair is still wonderful for meandering. You can get lost for hours wandering up and down the aisles. I once purchased a complete set of handmade antique iron fireplace utensils (tongs, shovel, brush, wood carrier) for some outrageously low price.

Start in the 60,000-square-foot Market Square, which offers antiques and collectibles (one person's junk is another's treasure).

Specialty vendors lay out a menu of Mexican and Chinese foods, plus cheesecakes, ribs, and (on Friday) a magnificent fish fry. In the old days, you were lucky to get a hot dog. So I guess progress has made a difference.

The sprawling facility is open Saturday and Sunday year-round from 9:00 A.M. to 5:00 P.M. Admission is $1.50 for adults and $1.00 for seniors, youngsters eleven and under are free. Free admission to Market Square on Friday. The fair is located at 2730 West Seven Mile Road, just off I–94. Look for the marked exits if you are on the freeway. The place is always an "almost-home" landmark whenever we drive back north from Chicago to Milwaukee. The expanse of parking lots and the signage always signal that home and hearth are getting close. Call (262) 835–2177.

Burlington is proud of its reputation as home of the world-famous **Burlington Liars Club** (262–763–4640), which annually hosts a competition to see who can tell the tallest tales and the biggest lies. The awards are usually given out in a local restaurant, after judges cull through thousands of submissions. Submit your best "lie" with a $1.00 entry fee to the Burlington Liars Club, P.O. Box 156, Burlington 53105.

The community also calls itself "the Chocolate City" because of its chocolate plant. Annually in mid-May, the locals host **Chocolate Fest** to celebrate the city's history of chocolate manufacturing. The Nestle Corporation has a large

Wright Way Wingspread

Frank Lloyd Wright considered Wingspread, 33 East Four Mile Road, the last of his "prairie houses." The building, on Racine's north side, is now a major international conference center and think tank sponsored by the Johnson Foundation, where scholars, politicians, and others gather to debate great topics and to freshen their minds. I've taken in several programs over the years at the facility, with discussions covering the Arab-Israeli conflict to the state of higher education. Wingspread was once the private residence of H. F. Johnson, of Johnson Wax fame, and is the largest house of this design that famed architect Wright ever assembled. Tours are free, offered 9:00 A.M. to 4:00 P.M. by appointment. Call (262) 639-3211.

plant in town and is a large supporter of the event. Everywhere you turn is chocolate to eat or buy: dark, light, white, flavored—everything to satisfy the most discerning sweet tooth. Festgoers love watching a carver produce intricate designs from large hunks of the luscious stuff. A lucky raffle winner can even be awarded his or her weight in chocolate. Each night, bands on several stages ensure that everyone is up and moving. Hypnotists, comics, and magicians also hold forth. Be sure to watch the chainsaw artist produce whimsical bears and other critters from large logs. A carnival, bike ride, run/walk, and fireworks round out the fun. For details, go to www.chocolatefest.com.

I always stock up on chocolate whenever taking a drive along any one of the seven official Rustic Roads that grace the county. You never know when you might need a snack. Among the best tours in the state is the drive north from Burlington along Honey Lake Road, Maple Lane, and Pleasant View Road. This route eventually takes you to County Highway D and on to State Highway 83. The **Wehmhoff Woodland Preserve** on the route is a great place for muskrat watching. Another scenic backcountry expedition is along Oak Knoll Road from County Highway DD to County Highway D, adjacent to the Honey Creek Wildlife District. Wheatland Road from State Highway 142 south to Hoosier Creek Road and on to County Highway JB is also pleasant on a warm summer afternoon. Stop for fishing along the Fox River.

Nitro-powered dragsters, with plenty of accompanying fire and smoke, screech down the track at the **Great Lakes Dragaway** in Union Grove (262–878–3783). Broadway Bob (yep, that's his name) held sway as owner-manager-fan-magnifico from his timing tower overlooking the rubber-scarred pavement where jet cars rock and roar. He's now retired, but the facility is still going strong. The track is in the eastern outskirts of the city, easy to find with all the signage or simply by following your ears. Parachutes often have to be used to slow down the vehicles at the end of their 0.25-mile runs.

Whenever we need a motor fix (not tune-up, folks), the Great Lakes Dragaway is the place to go. The Hintz clan has regularly made it to the track —one of the best in the Midwest—for a day of watching the action. One time, Steve (middle son) and elder Hintz were allowed access to the timing tower. The whole thing rocks when the race cars framing it on the track below rev their engines. Flames shoot skyward, smoke is everywhere—and then they're off! Our eardrums still reverberate at the memory.

Several years ago, Kate (daughter) and elder Hintz collaborated on writing a series of drag-racing books for a children's publisher. Naturally, Great Lakes was on the list of must-see places to revisit. We actually tooled down the track (not at 200 mph, however), talked with drivers and pit crews, chatted with management, and generally had a grand time amid the turbo-jet vehicles and funny cars. Kate, being a modern young woman, naturally knew the difference between a piston head and camshaft. So she carried on a great conversation. But I admit, I was lost by the time we got to the intricacies of pressure gauges.

You can even rent the track's "Back 40," a long open field, for weddings, family reunions, and other shindigs. Call (847) 436–0333.

Rock County

Rock County is the sixth largest county in Wisconsin, located along the Illinois border. Enter the state on I–90 from the Lincoln State, where there is a Wisconsin Tourist Information Center at Rest Area 22. You'll get loads of details on activities and attractions in the county and elsewhere in Wisconsin. The information building is open 8:00 A.M. to 4:00 P.M. Sunday through Thursday and until 6:00 P.M. on Friday from mid-May throughout October. From November to mid-May the facility is open only from 8:00 A.M. to 4:00 P.M. Tuesday through Saturday.

The county has more than 1,500 sites listed with the National Register of Historic Places. Two towns in the northwestern part of the county are considered historic districts. The entire community of Cooksville (at the junction of Highways 138 and 59), with its splendid redbrick buildings, is on the list. Most of nearby Evansville (intersection of Highways 213 and 14) is also a historical site. Ask at the tourist information center for locations and details on similarly designated sites in the vicinity.

Beloit is the first major town you'll encounter, home of the **Hanchett-Bartlett Homestead.** The museum, 2149 St. Lawrence, is on the city's west side. It's an old Victorian–era farmhouse built in the 1850s, featuring period furniture. The grounds include an old one-room schoolhouse. The museum

(608–365–7835) is open Friday through Sunday 1:00 to 4:00 P.M. from June through August.

At *Beloit College* the *Logan Museum of Anthropology* is packed with prehistoric tools, axes, and clubs; arrowheads; and other artifacts from early Native Americans. Beloit College, chartered in 1846, and its surrounding neighborhood are also listed as a National Register of Historic Places district. The Logan Museum (608–363–2110) is open 11:00 A.M. to 4:00 P.M. daily, except Mondays. Admission is free. Since the facility is on a college campus, it is closed on the usual school holidays. You can also take a self-guided tour of twenty-three effigy mounds built from A.D. 700 to A.D. 1200 by Native Americans.

The *Angel Museum,* 656 Pleasant Street, houses what is considered the world's largest collection of angels with more than 12,000 figures. Among them are 900 black angels donated by broadcast star Oprah Winfrey. The museum is open from May through October, 10:00 A.M. to 5:00 P.M., Monday through Saturday, and from 1:00 to 4:00 P.M., Sunday. From November through April, it is open 10:00 A.M. to 4:00 P.M., Tuesday though Saturday and closed Sunday and Monday. Call (608) 362–9099 for holiday hours.

For a quick picturesque drive from Beloit, drive northeast out of town on County Road X to the little crossroads communities of Shopiere and Tiffany in the Turtle Creek Valley. The latter town has a photogenic five-arch bridge over Turtle Creek. The "Tiffany Bridge" is the only such remaining five-arch railway bridge in the world. Then angle north to Janesville on either I–90 or Highway 51, exiting on Highway 14 to the *Tallman Restorations,* a villa built in 1857.

The old house includes many household conveniences that were the marvels of their day. For instance, running water was supplied by an attic storage tank rather than by the typical outside pump. The place even had its own working observatory. Abraham Lincoln slept here in 1859, long after his forays in the Jefferson County Indian wars.

The Lincoln-Tallman House (608–752–4519 or 608–756–4509) is open daily from 9:00 A.M. to 4:00 P.M., from June through September, and weekends from 9:00 A.M. to 4:00 P.M., year-round. Holiday tours are held daily from November 20 through December 31, although they are closed on Christmas. Tours of the property are led hourly beginning at 9:00 A.M. with the last one at 3:00 P.M. Admission is $8.00 for adults, $7.50 for seniors, and $4.00 for children six to eighteen.

North of downtown along Parker Drive is Traxler Park, where the *Rock Aqua Jays* national champion waterskiing team demonstrates its skills at 7:00 P.M. Sunday and Wednesday nights in June and July and 6:30 P.M. in August on the Rock River. For information contact Forward Janesville, (608) 757–3171 or (800) 48PARKS. The Web site is www.rockaquajays.com.

Sheboygan County

The *Rolling Meadows Sorghum Mill* in Elkhart Lake is the largest working plant in the state. Tours of the facility are held during business hours from Memorial Day through October 31. Once inside, you'll see how the manufacture of sweet sorghum has evolved from the use of horse presses to modern equipment. A mill is adjacent to a broom factory that opened in the early 1990s, with an exhibit showing the manufacturing evolution of brooms. Talk with owners Richard and Cheryl Wittgreve for all the latest in the wonderfully sticky business of sorghum making. And they sweep up afterwards, of course! The mill is located at N9030 Little Eklhart Lake Road. Call (920) 876–2182.

The *Kettle Moraine State Forest—Northern Unit,* with forest headquarters in Campbellsport (262–626–2116), is a warren of hiking and biking trails through the rocky, rolling countryside formed by glaciers 10,000 years ago. Learn how the topography came together by visiting the Henry S. Reuss Ice Age Visitor Center (920–533–8322). The center is open weekdays from 8:30 A.M. to 4:00 P.M., and weekends and holidays from 9:30 A.M. to 5:00 P.M. The center, with its twenty-minute film on the Ice Age, extensive exhibits, and great views, is closed Christmas Eve and Christmas Day. The Ice Age center is located 0.5 mile west of Dundee on Highway 67. The knowledgeable staff there provides information focusing on the forest, as well as naturalist tours.

You may spot the likes of actor/racer Paul Newman roaming the pit area at the *Road America* track in Elkhart Lake, an hour's drive north of Milwaukee. He often comes to drive, sign autographs, and greet friends such as the Andrettis, Unsers, Sullivans, and other top drivers who

funfacts

Wisconsin has about 110,000 miles of highways and paved roads. In 1917 the state was the first to adopt the number system for highways, a practice soon followed elsewhere.

always turn out for the September running of the Road America race. But don't miss the lineup of other events held on the twisting course throughout the summer, such as the Super Cycle Weekend and the Chicago Historic Races, the latter sponsored by the *Chicago Sun-Times* newspaper (800–365–RACE).

The track is one of the greatest locales for people-watching in eastern Wisconsin, as well as for watching classic race vehicles.

You get there from Milwaukee by taking I–43 north to Highway 23, go west to Highway 67. Take 67 north to County Trunk J. Road America gates are 2 miles up the road on the left side. The grandstand near gate 4 provides some of the best viewing, near the Corvette Corral.

A stroll along the Rotary Riverview Boardwalk on Sheboygan's Lake Michigan waterfront can be a relief from the roaring engines at Elkhart Lake. The jaunt, on South Franklin Street, goes past a historic fishing village that was once a vibrant part of the city harbor. A pleasant time for such a walk is on Sheboygan Bratwurst Day, always the first Saturday in August. Enter the eating contest: Participants see how many double-brat sandwiches they can wolf down in fifteen minutes.

The **Kohler Design Center** (800–4–KOHLER [456–4537]; www.us.kohler .com/designkb/designcenter/designcenter.jsp) in the village of Kohler, opened in 1985, showcases the innovative bathroom appliances built by the company that gave its name to the town. The firm is one of the world's leading manufacturers of plumbing accessories. One wall in the center is creatively stacked with red, white, black, and gray toilet bowls and bidets, framed by bathtubs, whirlpools, and similar appliances in a display called the Great Wall of China. The exhibit takes the mundane and transforms it into nifty art. Marine engines and other implements made by the company also are shown off. The center is open 8:00 A.M. to 5:00 P.M. Monday through Friday and 10:00 A.M. to 4:00 P.M. Saturday, Sunday, and holidays. Admission is free.

Kohler itself is a planned community just to the west of Sheboygan, built at the turn of the twentieth century to house plant staff. Winding streets, ivy-covered walls, and streetlights provide a charming element. The old dorm where the workers lived has been converted into a posh resort called the **American Club.** Prices match the elegant ambience.

The annual pre-Thanksgiving chocolate festival, called "In Celebration of Chocolate," at the American Club is a study in delightful decadence. The secret to a successful foray at the groaning board is developing a slow, easy pace around the torte table, picking up speed at the chocolate-covered fruit, and then gaining momentum at the cakes. I've learned this through experience and training (building up stamina with chocolate-covered cherries over several months of a preseasonal holiday push). The chefs make their own chocolate, which is whipped, whirled, and swirled into everything imaginable when it comes to desserts.

One of the American Club ballrooms is set aside for the early-December festival. Ablaze with candles and dazzling with

funfacts

Wisconsin's shoreline extends 381 miles along Lake Michigan. For those wanting to learn the metric system, that translates to 613 kilometers. The shore along Lake Superior is 292 miles (470 kilometers). The two vary greatly in appearance: There are high bluffs and sandy beaches along Lake Michigan, while Lake Superior offers more low-lying hills and pebbled beaches.

crystal, the site is transformed. I like to vary my chocolate selections with sherbert and fresh pears or apples. This freshens the mouth and prepares me for the next go-around. Be aware that this is more of a social, to-see-and-be-seen soiree rather than a stampede to the trough. It is inexcusable, although tempting, to fill one's pocket or purse with leftovers.

For resort packages that include the festival, Call the American Club for all the details, (800) 344–2838 or (920) 457–8000.

From culinary art to art-art, it is always relaxing to visit the *John Michael Kohler Arts Center,* 608 New York Avenue, which was established in 1967 to encourage and support innovative explorations in the arts. The Center is proud of being a lab for the creation of new works, an originator of exhibitions, and a performing arts producer. It offers a wide range of art-related activities in space that never seems to slow down. Check its offerings by calling (920) 458–6144 or peruse its Web site at www.jmkac.org.

For the sports-minded, the nearby **Whistling Straits** golf course north of Kohler was host of the 2004 PGA Championship and will be the site of the 2007 U.S. Senior Open, 2010 PGA Championship, 2015 PGA Championship, and 2020 Ryder Cup. Designed by Pete Dye, the facility opened in 1998, offering two rugged courses along the Lake Michigan shoreline. Duffers have to work hard here for that special hole-in-one. (800–618–5535; www.destination kohler.com/ws/ws.html).

Walworth County

Delavan is Circus City in a state that gave birth to more than 135 shows over the past 150 years. Between 1847 and 1894, the city was winter quarters for twenty-eight of those circuses, including P. T. Barnum's first. You'll know the town's favorite image once you pull into downtown: A statue of a giant, rearing elephant stands on the town square.

Delavan's Spring Grove Cemetery and Old Settlers Cemetery has about one hundred famous entertainers and less-well-known workers and administrative personnel buried there. Gordon Yadon, a retired postmaster, offers free tours of circus sites around town during the town's Circus Days Festival each July.

For a fine scenic overlook of the nearby Ice Age Trail, visit the **Whitewater Lake Recreation Area** ranger station, west of Walworth County Highway P on Kettle Moraine Drive. Walk up the moraine on a dirt road past the gravel pit, and take the roadway about 0.5 mile to the first open viewing area on the ridge's crest. One hundred feet below are Rice and Whitewater Lakes and rolling moraines that reach to the horizon. The view is magnificent.

An artesian well on Clover Valley Road, about 3 miles south of Whitewater, is popular with hikers and others who appreciate fresh, cold water. The place has been known for the past eighty or more years.

The lakes area of Walworth County, especially around Lake Geneva, is a popular resort area for Chicagoans and other Midwesterners. Fontana, Williams Bay, and **Lake Geneva** are small, touristy towns bordering the main lake. Larger facilities such as Lake Lawn Lodge (with several major Native American mounds on its property), Interlaken, The Abbey, and Americana Resort are well known for their spas, massages, tennis courts, horseback riding, restaurants, and meeting/convention rooms with rates to match. Try the more manageable, laid-back **Eleven Gables Inn** on Lake Geneva (262–248–8393 or www .LKgeneva.com). Only 2 blocks from downtown Lake Geneva (463 Wrigley Drive), the bed-and-breakfast inn has an unobstructed view of the water and its own pier for swimming and fishing.

The **Geneva Inn** on the eastern shore of Lake Geneva is another great layover for the road-weary. The property has thirty-seven guest rooms, each is snug and cozy, along with a marvelous restaurant with lakeside dining and lip-smacking meals. The Geneva Inn offers all sorts of packages throughout the year, making it easy for budgeting. Call (800) 441–5881 or check its Web site at www.genevainn.com.

For a different sort of stay, there's the **End of the Line.** I don't know if you would call the place a motel or hotel because accommodations are in real cabooses (caboosi?). Each railcar has its own bathroom, beds, and the usual guest amenities. The registration lobby is called the Roundhouse, and the Side Track gift shop has an assortment of railroad-themed gift items. The place is located at 301 East Townline Road (262–248–7245).

For Scandinavian food there's **Scuttlebutts,** at 831 Wrigley Drive (262–248–1111) on the lakefront. This family restaurant lays out the largest stacks of Swedish pancakes in town. **Popeye's Galley and Grog** and **Popeye's Restaurant** on Lake Geneva's waterfront opened in 1972. Call (262) 248–4381 to review its range of menu items. In the nearby quiet of tiny Williams Bay, **Chef's Corner Bistro** (262–245–6334) on Geneva Street has excellent homemade soups and German cooking. Chef's Corner is open only for dinner. **Kirsch's** in the French Country Inn, W4190 West End Road, won the *Wine Spectator* Award of Excellence from 2000 to 2005. Call (262) 245–5756.

For a different way to see Lake Geneva, the **Lake Geneva Cruise Line** (800–558–5911) has a hiking tour in conjunction with a spring and autumn luncheon cruise. A shoreline footpath extends all 23 miles around the lake, only 3 feet from the water.

For the full lake package, park at the Riviera Boat Docks in Lake Geneva. Numerous ticket options are available. You'll be cruising past the Victorian–era

OTHER ATTRACTIONS WORTH SEEING

Bear Den Zoo,
Waterford

Bjorklunden Chapel,
Baileys Harbor

Blackwolf Run Golf Course,
Kohler

Door County Maritime Museum,
Gills Rock

Door County Maritime Museum,
Sturgeon Bay

Jackson Harbor Maritime Museum,
Washington Island

Manitowoc Museum of Sculpture

Racine Zoological Gardens

River Bend Nature Center,
Racine

homes of the Wrigley chewing-gum heirs, the Swift meat-packing clan, and the Montgomery Ward Thorne family.

Even with all that walking, it's an easier job than the one held by the "mailgirls" on the *Walworth II*. Working as regular summertime postal carriers, the two women leap from moving boat to dock and back again while delivering mail to homes on the lake. They have to jump to shore, run the length of a pier, drop off the mail, and leap back on the moving vessel before it gets too far away. The delivery process is a tradition that has been going on for more than seventy-five years.

Nobody has fallen into the water in recent years, but all the eager tourists on the early morning run take bets on the possibility of a damp plunge. Many different tours are available, ranging from $16.00 to $19.00 for adults without a meal, and $34.95 to $54.00 with a meal.

The two-and-one-half-hour cruise operates seven days a week between mid-June and mid-September, beginning at 9:00 A.M. from Lake Geneva Cruise Line docks. When not jumping from boat to pier, the mailgirls act as guides, describing the mansions along the shore. Call (262) 248–6206 for reservations (www.cruiselakegeneva.com).

Washington County

Washington County is just north of Waukesha and Milwaukee Counties, taking in the northern unit of the Kettle Moraine Forest. Follow the Kettle Moraine Drive by car or bike over landscapes carved out by glaciers 15,000 years ago. *Holy Hill* is the most prominent physical attraction in the county, perched high overlooking the surrounding countryside. The church looks as if it slipped off a page from a Bavarian calendar. Carmelite priests maintain a retreat center there, where you can get a great view of the forestland.

The surrounding farms and villages were first populated by Irish immigrants, including my great-grandfather and his brothers. When they emigrated from Ireland around the time of the Civil War, English agents in Canada asked them to stay there when they paused to pick up supplies. "Not on your life," swore great-grandpops Russell. "I've lived under English rule long enough," he added as a parting shot and boarded a Lake Michigan steamer bound for Milwaukee.

From Beer City he hoofed it into the Holy Hill area, where other relatives from the Auld Sod had already settled. His experience is typical of that of many of the people still living there.

The town of *Erin* is a rural township with country roads named after Irish cities and provinces. Each year the old traditions are renewed with a hilarious *St. Patrick's Day Parade.* The floats, horses, and marchers travel about a 3.5-mile course through the countryside, beginning at the Town Hall (corner of Highways 167 and 83) and concluding at the corner of County Trunk K and Donegal Road. To give you an idea of the "seriousness" of the event, one recent parade featured My Wild Irish Nose, a float built like a giant green schnoz; a green llama; a hillbilly band made up of grandmothers; and similar silliness. The only orange you'll ever see on parade day is the color of Washington County trucks loaded with snow fences. For information call (262) 673–6226.

The Irish cemetery at K and Emerald Drive is crowded with Whelans, Fallons, Purtells, McGraths, O'Neills, Coffeys, Mahoneys, McConvilles, Sullivans, and Hagertys. The wind sighs off the hilltops as you drive from the unfenced graveyard along Emerald, another of the state's Rustic Roads.

Waukesha County

Old World Wisconsin, operated by the Historical Society of Wisconsin, is on the map when it comes to tourist attractions. Yet its ongoing displays, programs, and activities often are overlooked. That's a shame, because Old World is a great place to touch the living history of Wisconsin. More than forty buildings from around the state, originally built by immigrant settlers, have been relocated to the rolling Kettle Moraine highlands. Old World calls itself "America's Largest Outdoor Museum of Rural Life."

A motorized tram takes visitors around the 576-acre site. You can get on or off at leisure to explore the farmsites and buildings dotting the landscape. I like the museum because each community is separated from the other, to pre-serve the national identity. Interpreters in the appropriate costumes demonstrate crafts and chores you'd find in a typical mid-nineteenth-century household. There are plenty of cows, pigs, sheep, chickens, ducks, and other critters in the pastures and pens to keep up the interest of city kids.

Seasonal events help keep the Old World feeling on the appropriate track: spring plowing, summer planting, and autumn threshing with the era's appropriate horse-drawn equipment; Fourth of July oratory, parades, and band concerts. We've always

Old World Wisconsin

found it fun in the winter to cross-country ski around the buildings and over the fields. Many of the structures are open for visiting, even when the snow is drifting around the doorway. Each offers homemade ethnic cookies or breads, plus hot cider or hot chocolate to ward off the cold.

The museum (262–594–6300) is on Highway 67 outside the village of Eagle, about a half-hour drive south of I–94. It is open weekdays from May 1 to October 31 from 10:00 A.M. to 4:00 P.M. and weekends from 10:00 A.M. to 5:00 P.M. Admission for adults is $14.00, children five to twelve are $8.50, seniors are $12.80, and a family pass for $39.00 includes all-day tram transportation and an electronic tour guide.

The *Clausing Barn Restaurant* is an octagonal barn built in 1897. It is a cafeteria-style restaurant (262–594–6320).

Adjacent to the museum are the 16,600 acres of the *Southern Kettle Moraine Forest,* with a drive that tests your skill as a motorist. The ridges and valleys throughout the region were created by Ice Age glaciers. Today's roads barely tame the landscape as they loop and swirl over the ridges.

Not far from the edge of the state forest is the Genesee Depot, home of famed theatrical couple Alfred Lunt and Lynn Fontanne. Driving into the main courtyard of the sprawling complex called *Ten Chimneys* brings alive their flamboyant stage era. Lunt, who died in 1977, and Fontanne, who died in 1983, furnished their house with antiques and interesting art objects.

Visitors can now either tour the three-story main house, which consists of eighteen rooms ($28) or explore the entire estate ($35). Hours are 10:00 A.M. to 4:00 P.M., Wednesday through Sunday, April through October (262–968–4161).

Drive north from Eagle on Highway 67, cross I–94 on the overpass, and head into **Oconomowoc.** At the turn of the twentieth century, the town was a popular resort for Chicago-area business tycoons and their families, who flocked to the numerous lakes dotting the vicinity. Their elegant mansions border Lac La Belle and line the streets leading away from the water. Contemporary Oconomowoc has outgrown its quaint stage and is now a bustling community surrounded by subdivisions. The main street, however, has several excellent galleries, antiques shops, and crafts stores that carry unusual items.

The **Oconomowoc Gallery, Ltd.,** 157 East Wisconsin Avenue (262–567–8123 or 800–494–2878), carries wildlife art, contemporary and traditional fine art, sculpture, vintage French posters, creative custom framing, and gifts.

At 8:00 P.M. each Wednesday in June, July, and August, the Oconomowoc city band revs up a concert for the folks who come to the lake edge to listen. Bring your own lawn chair or blanket for a night outing. Sometimes bug spray is necessary.

Wisconsin on Ice

The Kettle Moraine glacial areas of southeastern Wisconsin are fabulous for the hiking and skiing opportunities. The state has some 46,000 acres of forestland with various forms of landscape created during the Ice Age. Wisconsin's ice sheets retreated only a mere 10,000 years ago. Among the most obvious landmarks are the **moraines.** These are hills or snakelike ridges marked by debris left when the glaciers retreated. In other words, they are a glacial garbage dump. One of the moraines in the region is 100 miles long and 300 feet high. The moraines that mark the most advanced position of the glaciers are called terminal moraines.

Drumlins are long ridges or oval-shaped hills formed by glacial drift.

Kames are steep, conical hills created when meltwater flowed into funnel-like holes in the ice. The water carried debris that piled up like sand in an hourglass. Some of Wisconsin's kames tower more than 100 feet above the surrounding flatlands.

Kettles are depressions in the ground, formed when blocks of ice that were buried by earth and rock eventually melted. The ground collapsed when the ice melted. Such hollows are now lakes, marshes, or small valleys.

Eskers are ridges of sand and gravel that were dumped by rivers flowing underneath a glacier.

I've always thought that the **Golden Mast Inn** (262–567–7047 or 800–232–8688) has one of the best views in the state, having written about the place for *Wisconsin Trails* magazine. Owned by German restaurateurs Hans and Maria Weissgerber and sons Hans Jr., and Jack, the Golden Mast looks out over Okauchee Lake with its convoys of ducks and dozens of sailboats. The food matches the scenery, with loins and schnitzel as house specialties. The place is located on Lacy's Lane at Okauchee Lake, just off Highway 16 on Oconomowoc's east side. The restaurant is one of four the family owns in Waukesha County.

The **Olympia Resort and Conference Center** (800–558–9573 or 262–567–0311) to the south of Oconomowoc is well known in southeastern Wisconsin as a great place for a comfortable rejuvenation. But the place is a secret to many outsiders. Massages, steam rooms, pools, facials, exercise classes, and meals help keep visitors trim and alert. I enjoy the eucalyptus room whenever I have a head cold; the pungent steam quickly clears my head and soothes my lungs. Rates are reasonable.

The **Hawk's Inn,** 426 West Wells Street, (262–646–4794) in nearby Delafield was built in the 1840s as a stagecoach stop. It has been refurbished as a museum, open from May through October. Tours are from 1:00 to 4:00 P.M. Saturday.

County seat **Waukesha** has made strides to keep its downtown alive and interesting, not wanting to be caught in the all-too-often downward spiral of smaller towns. There are numerous interesting shops, including one with magician's supplies. A gazebo/bandstand, called the Silurian Springhouse, was built as a hub for the one-way streets, which zoom off in several directions. This makes it difficult for a downtown drive-through, especially if you are unfamiliar with the area. I'd suggest you park and walk.

Waukesha means "fox" in Potawatomi, the language of one of many tribes that lived here over the generations. There are several mounds, built by earlier Native Americans, on the front lawn of the refurbished Central Library. The mounds are the only remaining ones of dozens that had been around the county prior to settlement. Most of the others have been plowed up or built over in the years since whites came into the region.

The fifty-plus mineral springs in and around Waukesha made it the center of the state's nineteenth-century spa trade. The regenerative effects of the water were supposedly discovered by Col. Richard Dunbar, a local landowner. The good gentleman was not feeling well while out for a stroll one afternoon and took several drinks from a spring he discovered on his jaunt. Dunbar then napped under a nearby tree and allegedly woke up cured of everything that ailed him. From then on, bathhouses and health facilities sprang up, touting the wonders of Waukesha's water.

Background on these old properties can be found at the ***Waukesha County Historical Museum,*** 101 West Main Street (262–521–2859). The facility is open from 10:00 A.M. to 4:30 P.M., Tuesday through Saturday. Admission is $2.00 for adults. The region's pioneer history is explored, along with the growth and development of Waukesha and its outlying areas. To see firsthand how the good old days really were, drop by ***Nashotah House,*** 2777 Mission Road (414–646–6500), in nearby Nashotah. The complex is now an Episcopal seminary, but self-guided tours of its historic buildings are available when you make a reservation through the school's development office.

More sites are available for touring by contacting the ***Western Ethnic Settlement Trail,*** 101 West Main Street (414–521–2859), which highlights numerous historic properties throughout Waukesha County.

On the east side of town is the ***Inn at Pine Terrace.*** High on a hill overlooking Oconomowoc's lakes, the property was appropriately secluded and comfortable, with a great breakfast. The inn is located at 351 East Lisbon Road (262–567–7463).

Waupaca County

Waupaca is a fantastic year-round getaway for anyone who loves the outdoors. The best-known attraction is the ***Chain O'Lakes,*** which consist of twenty-two interlocking, spring-fed lakes that range in size from 2.5 to 115 acres. The waterways—packed with fish, of course—are from 8 to 100 feet deep. The first settlers arrived in the area in 1849 to establish a flour mill to serve neighboring homesteaders. In honor of the earlier Native Americans who lived in the region, the new residents selected the name Waupaca, supposedly after a local tribal leader, Wa-Puka (meaning "watching"). Historians, however, claim the name was derived from *waubeck seba,* meaning "clear water."

Regardless of whence the name, the town of Waupaca knows how to have fun. In mid-June is the Strawberry Festival, followed on July 4 with Hometown Days. A Fall-O-Rama is held the last weekend in September. For details on events and activities, contact the Waupaca Area Chamber of Commerce, 221 South Main Street, Box 262, Waupaca 54981 (715) 258–7343 or 888–417–4040 (www.waupacaareachamber.com).

Waupaca is home to ***Hartman Creek State Park,*** which includes the Whispering Pines picnic area. Located 5 miles west of town on Highway 54, the 1,320-acre park offers tent and RV camping (101 sites) and a group campground.

Glacial oak hills, lakes, and ponds offer a plethora of color-photo opportunities while you are hiking or biking. Call the park offices (715–258–2372) for the latest information on wildlife discussions led by naturalists. Some 5 miles of the state's 1,000-mile Ice Age Trail system are also within the park boundaries. When cross-country skiing in the park, remember that the glaciers retreated from here a mere 10,000 years ago.

For a more "motorized" vacation stop in Waupaca County, *Iola* holds an annual *Old Car Show and Swap Meet* early each July. More than 2,500 show cars are displayed, with hundreds of pre-1983 vehicles up for sale. Call (715) 445–4000. Admission is charged. Iola is located at the intersection of State Highways 49 and 161. You can't miss the showgrounds—just follow the hundreds of bright posters and arrows leading to the site or pull the family sedan into a procession of flashy sporters that usually putt-putt around town during the show weekend. They'll get you to the right locale.

Winnebago County

The *Bergstrom-Mahler Museum* in *Neenah* has more than 1,500 glass paperweights on display as part of the Evangeline Bergstrom collection. The display features handmade weights from French, English, and American manufacturers dating back one hundred years. The museum offers research facilities for other collectors by appointment. The library is filled with material, and there is a workroom in which to look over samples and talk with curators. The museum is located at 165 North Park Avenue, Neenah 54956, (920) 751–4658. Admission is free.

The *Doty Cabin* on Webster and Lincoln in Neenah is a replica of the home of Wisconsin's second territorial governor, James Duane Doty. The building houses numerous pioneer artifacts, including many of the governor's own possessions. The cabin is open noon to 4:00 P.M. from mid-June to mid-August and Memorial Day and Labor Day weekends. Call the Neenah Parks and Recreation Department, (920) 751–4614, for more information. Admission is free.

Oshkosh, home of OshKosh B'Gosh, is also home of the world's largest fly-in event: the *Experimental Aircraft Association (EAA) Fly-in,* held at the end of July at Wittman Field. The fly-in attracts upwards of 700,000 guests. Warbirds, mini-aircraft, gliders, and regular private planes jam the fields surrounding the airport. The EAA aviation center museum is located at 3000 Poberezny Drive (920–426–4800), with hundreds of aircraft and accessories on display.

From Oshkosh drive northwest on Highway 110 to tiny Zittau, where some of the best cheese curds in Wisconsin can be found at the *Union Star Cheese Factory* (7742 County Road II, 920–836–2804). Non-Wisconsinites always wonder about the lumpy-looking curds, which make a delightfully squeaky sound when chewed. The curds are especially good with smoked catfish, crisp rye crackers, and freshly squeezed lemonade or a just-tapped beer. The factory is open Monday through Saturday, 7:00 A.M. to 5:00 P.M., and Sunday, 10:30 A.M. to 5:00 P.M.

Places to Stay in Eastern Wisconsin

APPLETON

Candlewood Inn,
4525 West College Avenue,
(920) 739–8000,
(866) 270–5110
Moderate

**Comfort Suites/
Comfort Dome,**
3809 West Wisconsin
Avenue,
(920) 730–3800,
(800) 228–5150,
fax (920) 730–9558
Moderate

Copper Leaf Hotel,
300 West College Avenue,
(920) 749–0303
Moderate

**Country Inn & Suites
by Carlson,**
355 Fox River Drive,
(920) 830–3240
Moderate

Hampton Inn,
350 Fox River Drive,
(920) 954–9211,
(800) HAMPTON (426–7866),
fax (920) 954–6514
Moderate

Residence Inn,
310 Metro Drive,
(920) 954–0570,
fax (920) 731–6343
Moderate

BAILEY'S HARBOR

**Bailey's Harbor Yacht Club
Resort,**
8151 Ridges Road,
(920) 839–2336,
(800) 927–2492,
Moderate to expensive.

CAMPBELLSPORT

Inn the Kettles,
W977 Highway F,
(920) 533–8602
Moderate

CLINTONVILLE

Clintonville Motel,
297 South Main Street,
(715) 823–6565
Moderate

DE PERE

James Street Inn,
201 James Street,
(920) 337–6135,
(800) 897–8483
Moderate

DELAVAN

Delavan Inn,
215 East Walworth Avenue,
(262) 728–9143,
fax (414) 728–1444
Moderate

EGG HARBOR

The Alpine Inn & Cottages,
7715 Alpine Road,
(920) 868–3000
(phone and fax)
Moderate

EPHRAIM

Edgewater Resort Motel,
10040 Water Street,
(920) 854–2734
Moderate

FISH CREEK

Beowulf Lodge,
3775 Highway 42,
(920) 868–2046,
(800) 433–7592
Moderate to expensive.

GREEN BAY

AmericInn of Green Bay,
2032 Velp Avenue,
(920) 434–9790
Inexpensive to moderate.

Bay Motel,
1301 South Military Avenue,
(920) 494–3441
Inexpensive to moderate.

Quality Inn & Suites,
321 South Washington
Street,
(920) 437–8771
Moderate

Wingate Inn,
2065 Airport Drive,
(920) 617–2000
Moderate

JANESVILLE

Best Western Janesville,
3900 Milton Avenue,
(608) 756–4511,
(800) 334–4271
Moderate

Hampton Inn,
2400 Fulton Street,
(608) 754–4900
Moderate

KENOSHA

Value Inn,
7221 122nd Avenue (I–94,
exit 344),
(262) 857–2622,
fax (414) 857–2375
Moderate

MANITOWOC

Birch Creek Inn,
4626 Calumet Avenue,
(920) 684–3374,
(800) 424–6126
Moderate

Inn on Maritime Bay,
101 Maritime Drive (Highway
42),
(920) 682 7000,
(800) 654–5353
Moderate to expensive.

RACINE

Racine Marriott,
7111 Washington Avenue,
(262) 886–6100,
fax (414) 886–1048
Moderate

SISTER BAY

County House Resort,
715 North Highland Road,
(920) 854–4551,
(800) 424–0041
fax (920) 854–9809
Moderate

STURGEON BAY

Bridgeport Resort,
Business Highway 42/57,
(920) 746–9919,
(800) 671–9190
Moderate

WAUPACA

Green Fountain Inn,
604 South Main Street,
(715) 258–5171,
(800) 603–4600
Moderate

Rustic Woods
Campground,
E2585 South Wood Drive,
(715) 258–2442
Inexpensive

Places to Eat in Eastern Wisconsin

ALGOMA

Breakwater,
527 Fourth Street,
(920) 487–3291
For a quick bite, the
Breakwater serves breakfast,
lunch, and dinner daily.
Check out its Wednesday
night family-style chicken
dinner. Its hamburgers also
get rave reviews from aficionados of the ubiquitous
beef patty. Add tomato, let-
tuce, ketchup, mustard, rel-
ish, pickles, and onions and
patrons have a feast fit for
kings or queens. Anglers
often make a stop here
before heading out to their
charter boats for a salmon
run on Lake Michigan. On
weekends, the restaurant is
open until 2:30 A.M. for the
late night crowd . . . or work-
night bunch. Inexpensive.

KEWAUNEE

The Cork Restaurant
& Pub,
306 Ellis Street,
(920) 388–2525
For a wide range of food and
prices (dinners range from
$5.00 to $25.00), the Cork is
a hopping place with occasional live music and nightly
specials including Wednesday's sixteen-ounce lobster
tail special. From mid-June
through October, the Cork is
open seven nights a week.
It's closed Monday early
November through June 15.
But that doesn't seem to
faze the locals who flock in
on other days to indulge
themselves with the Cork's
hearty portions of chicken,
steak, and other seafoods.
Good chef salads are also a
popular item. Inexpensive to
moderate.

DE PERE

A's Restaurant &
Music Café,
112 North Broadway,
(920) 336–2277
A's lives up to its name, with
musical styles ranging from
jazz and blues, and from
cabaret to rock on most
Fridays and Saturdays. A
band or performer is usually
on tap on Wednesdays as
well, with foot tappin', hand-
clappin', and dance rhythms.
The food is eclectic. Seafood
and steaks top the popularity
grid, with a light fare option
of soup, salad, and an appetizer for those watching their
waistlines. A's is open for
dinner 5:00 to 9:30 P.M.
Tuesday through Saturday

and for lunch on Tuesday through Friday. Inexpensive to moderate.

Black & Tan Grille,
101 Fort Howard Avenue,
(920) 336–4430
The Black and Tan, a heady mix of Guinness stout and beer, was the inspiration for the restaurant's name, housed as it is in a tan-colored Victorian home. Take advantage of the homey atmosphere and relax at the comfortable bar while waiting for a table. By the end of the evening, everyone will know your name, just like in the old *Cheers* television show. Specials include king salmon, yellowfin tuna, game and seafood dishes, fresh sea-sonal vegetables, and the always-popular Black Angus steak. Open daily. Moderate.

Pasquale's International Café,
305 Main Street,
(920) 336–3330
Pasquale's is known for its authentic Chicago-style Italian fare including Italian beef, ravioli, pasta alfredo, antipasto, and an interesting menu selection tagged "Daddy's Favorite Ribs" for folks who like 'dem bones, 'dem bones. This is a finger-lickin' special, with no need to stand on ceremony. Dig in. For the Celtic crowd, the restaurant also serves a mouthwatering corned beef on rye guaranteed to make the diner dream of Donegal. Wall murals are painted by local artist Cheryl Bowman, with scenes reminiscent of the World War II era. The

restaurant serves lunch and dinner seven days a week. Inexpensive to moderate.

EGG HARBOR
Olde Stage Station Restaurant,
7778 Egg Harbor Road (Highway 42),
(920) 868–3247
Said to be once an authen-tic, old-time stagecoach-freight haulers' stop, the Olde Stage Station Restaurant is famous for its pizzas. The chef presents a special blend of seven Wisconsin cheeses, baked in stone hearth ovens, provid-ing a tantalizing taste base for other toppings. The Olde Stage is open daily from 11:30 A.M. to 9:30 P.M. The restaurant also boasts having the largest selection of tap and bottled beers in Door County, with dozens of brewski labels from which to choose. The Sunday break-fast buffet starts at 8:00 A.M., a table-groaning treat with its mounds of scrambled eggs, pancakes, and other early morning munchies. The Olde Stage is closed Tuesday and Wednesday during the winter months. Moderate.

ELKHART LAKE
Harvey's of Elkhart Lake,
191 South Lincoln Street,
(920) 876–2216
For those on the hungry man regimen, Harvey's offers all-you-can eat specials on Wednesday (try the bluegill), Thursday (gobble a pizza), Friday (back to the bluegill), Saturday (slabs o' barbecued

ribs), and a Sunday breakfast buffet designed to set up a diner for the rest of the day. Harvey's roast duck is known throughout the region as one of the best signature items served. Better consider a treadmill workout after eating here. Open daily 11:00 A.M. to 9:00 P.M. and 8:00 A.M. to 9:00 P.M. on Sunday. Moderate.

Sal's Elkhart Inn,
91 South Lincoln Street,
(920) 876–3133
Sal's offers fine dining in an "Old World" atmosphere, being known for its monster steaks, generous portions of seafood, and hearty sand-wiches. Sal's is open daily from 5:00 to 9:30 P.M., although it is closed Mondays from Memorial Day to Labor Day. Reservations suggested. Moderate to expensive.

EPHRAIM
Old Post Office Restaurant,
10040 Highway 42,
(920) 854–4034
The "Post Office" is located in a historic building, built in the late 1800s when resi-dents could only access the village of Ephraim via water. At the time, the local post office was located at the rear of Peterson's General Store. Now, the structure, located at the Edgewater Resort, has been transformed into the Old Post Office Restaurant, boasting of one of the best neighborhood views of nearby Eagle Harbor. A cupboard in the main room is stocked with

homemade jellies, dishtowels, and other gift items for sale. The menu "posts" fun titles for the food: Letter Opener Juices, Priority Fruits, Express Mail Eggs, and Mailman Muffins to name a few. Traditional fish boils are held Monday through Saturday, as well as on holiday weekend Sundays. Reservations are requested for the boils, which include Lake Michigan whitefish, red potatoes, and white onions boiled up in a huge outside vat. Top off one of these meals with homemade bread and freshly baked cherry pie. Be aware that no lunches are served. Outdoor seating is available during good weather. Inexpensive to moderate.

FISH CREEK

White Gull Inn,
4225 Main Street,
(920) 868-3517 or (888) 364-9542
This historic inn and restaurant in the waterside village of Fish Creek was established in 1896. As such, the folks here know how to prepare and serve food. Starting with breakfast, a must is the inn's eggs Benedict, but diners can also get granola, sides of hash browns, and piles of buttermilk pancakes. Traditional Door County fish boils are served Wednesday, Friday, Saturday, and Sunday evenings from May through October and on Friday evenings the rest of

the year. The explosion of fire and water at the conclusion of the boil, when the liquid holding the fish and potatoes is poured off, makes for a real show. Reservations are a must, although some standbys are occasionally accommodated as space allows. Lunches include the usual array of tasty sandwiches and soups. For dinners, Chef John Vreeke prepares excellent Wisconsin beef and duckling, accompanied by locally-grown Door County fruit and other produce. Some recipes have been handed down over the generations. Open daily. Moderate to expensive.

GILLS ROCK

Shoreline Restaurant,
12747 Highway 42,
(920) 854-2950
The Shoreline Restaurant is well known throughout Door County for its homestyle cooking with a gourmet touch. Every dining room table offers a relaxing water view so patrons can watch the charter fishing boats and pleasure craft coming and going from the adjacent marina. Lunch and dinner are served from 11:00 A.M. to 9:00 P.M., regularly offering whitefish, plus nightly specials such as delectable crabmeat pasta, seashells with tomato cream sauce, and even coconut shrimp tempura. The panfried perch is another noted dish. For a twist, the restaurant offers its lighter lunch menu throughout the dinner hours. It's

worth walking on water to get to the homemade desserts, including a key lime pie. Open daily May through October. Moderate to expensive.

GREEN BAY

Mavis Family Restaurant,
1241 Bellevue Street,
(920) 468-7901
Of course, take the family to Mavis Family Restaurant for some amazing French toast. Plus Mavis' omelet specials must be made from happy eggs, for their wonderfully puffed up look and wonderful flavoring. Toss in ham, green peppers, and other additions for a special touch. Mavis Family Restaurant is open every day 6:00 A.M. to 2:00 P.M. Inexpensive.

Sideline Sports Bar & Restaurant,
1049 Lombardi Access,
(920) 496-5857
You want sports, you get sports at the Sideline Sports Bar on the road named after the Green Bay Packers' legendary coach, Vince Lombardi. With its convenient location near the team's Lambeau Field, with thirty-three televisions tuned to games, it's appropriate that this pub has the word "bar" before "restaurant" in its name. Packer lovers pack the joint, not just on game days, but also anytime they crave a burger that can be ordered in three sizes. Choose from a mere third-of-a-pound up through a one-

pound behemoth. Light eaters may instead wish to tackle a Sideline salad, one of several styles of wraps, or even a chicken sandwich. Don't mind the roaring in the background whenever there's a quarterback sneak or a first down. Grab your plate each time the Packers score—it's bedlam! Open daily. Inexpensive.

JACKSONPORT

Square Rigger Galley at Square Rigger Lodge,
6332 Highway 57,
(920) 823–2408 or
(877) 347–4264
The Square Rigger tacks into the "Quiet Side" of Door County, on the Lake Michigan side of the peninsula just north of Whitefish Dunes State Park. While some fish boils require guests to perch on picnic tables in the sometimes chilly outside, patrons here can luxuriate in the cozy dining room overlooking the white-capped lake and enjoy hors d'oeuvres before dinner is brought to their table. The Rigger's fish boil includes corn-on-the-cob, coleslaw, and fresh pumpernickel bread, in addition to the standard whitefish, spuds, and onions. No way can you get away without a slab of the Rigger's Door County cherry pie a la mode. Non-fish-lovers can substitute grilled chicken if they wish, and a kids menu is also available. Open daily. Moderate.

JANESVILLE

Prime Quarter Steak House,
1900 Humes Road (East U.S. Highway 14),
(608) 752–1881
While it's fun to fix one's own steak, it can become a bit too busy in the Prime Quarter as patrons scamper from salad bar to table to grill and back to table. Gridlock can sometimes occur. But take the easy way out and have the chef prepare the meats. The chain, headquartered in Madison, has seven restaurants in Wisconsin. Yet as with any good, local establishment, the management prizes USDA prime beef, husky baked potatoes, and an unlimited salad bar presenting nearly two dozen items. For a challenge, try finishing the forty-ounce steak in less than one hour and fifteen minutes, including a trip to the salad bar, a baked potato, and Texas toast. If you survive, you will become a proud, but loggy, member of the restaurant's Beefeater's Club and receive a medallion marking the accomplishment. On a subsequent visit, the medal can be redeemed for a regular prime quarter dinner. Pass the Bromo, please. Open daily. Moderate to expensive.

Tibbie's Fine Dining and Wise Guys Pub,
3431 Milton Avenue,
(608) 756–2313
Located in the Ramada Inn, Tibbie's restaurant is a comfortable layover eatery whenever traveling becomes a grind. While it offers the usual steaks, seafoods, soups, and salads, the locale is convenient, the interior is attractive, and the food many notches above what can be standard motel eatery grub. Even locals patronize the facility, which means that its reputation is assured. The adjacent Wise Guys Pub is a good place to perch and watch a football or baseball game on one or the other— or all three—television sets. On Sundays, the bartender juggles switching between six or seven different NFL games being played at the same time. Too confusing? Then sip a chill frosty and head upstairs to bed. Tibbie's is open daily for breakfast, lunch, and dinner. Inexpensive to moderate.

Wedges,
2006 North Washington Avenue,
(608) 757–1444
Lunch and dinner is served seven days a week with regular specials, including a Saturday night prime rib dinner hearty enough to assure carry-home leftovers. Don't forget the fresh dinner bread. For music lovers this is a fun stopover—Thursday has the time for singers to shine with a memorable karaoke night. Live music is often scheduled on the weekends. Moderate.

KOHLER

The American Club,
Highland Drive,
(920) 457–8000 or (800)
344–2838
The American Club, a AAA
Five-Diamond resort, boasts
several award-winning
restaurants on site or on its
nearby golf courses. From its
showcase Immigrant
Restaurant and Winery to the
more casual Horse and Plow,
each offers special service,
different atmosphere, and
mouthwatering foods. Stews,
wild game, steak, chicken,
lobster, and other fare
demonstrates the variety
available. On the lighter side,
the Greenhouse, actually an
antique solarium, offers afternoon and evening snacks. All
are open daily. Moderate to
expensive.

MANITOWOC/TWO RIVERS

Copper Kettle,
1600 Washington Street,
(920) 794–1110
Open daily at 5:00 A.M., the
Copper Kettle is ready for
the earliest angler seeking to
hit the waters of Lake
Michigan or the hungriest
noontime business diner out
to make a deal. Serves up
the best hash browns in the
county, according to knowledgeable potato connois-
seurs. Sandwiches, soup,
chicken, steaks, and pastas
always make for filling,
home-cooked meals. The
restaurant is open for dinner
only Thursday through
Sunday, closing at 7:00 P.M.
Inexpensive to moderate.

PLEASANT PRAIRIE

Lighthouse Inn Hotel & Restaurant,
1515 Memorial Drive,
(920) 793–4524
There are few experiences
more pleasant than watching
the moon rise over Lake
Michigan, lapping merely 20
feet away, from a comfortable
table in the inn's Water's
Edge Restaurant. Deep-fried
lake perch is a house favorite,
served as it is with crispy
cole slaw, home baked
bread, and choice of baked
or mashed potatoes, french
fries, or rice pilaf. Some diners take a plunge and enjoy
the fettuccini alfredo or Ice-
landic haddock, which can
be baked or deep fried. Cold
water lobster tail is also a
prize-winner, as is the broccoli-
stuffed chicken breast. The
Gull's Nest Lounge makes a
perfect place to perch while
waiting for supper or for just
a nice night out on the town.
Open daily for breakfast,
lunch, and dinner. Moderate
to expensive.

Machut's Supper Club,
3911 Lincoln Avenue,
(920) 793–9432
Norman and Lorraine Machut
opened Machut's Supper
Club in 1961, and it remains
in the family. The place was
originally called Babe and
Norm's Bar, later it was
called Machut's, and then it
morphed into Machut's
Supper Club. (To get it right,
pronouce the "ch" in
Machut's with a hard "k.")
Hamburgers and Mexican
style chili were served at the
bar, with roast chicken even-

tually being added. Today,
Machut's is a full-service
restaurant accommodating
individual guests as well as
group events such as the St.
Peter the Fisherman Ladies
Sheepshead Marathon ban-
quet and various political
fundraisers. Open daily.
Moderate.

Ray Radigan's,
11712 Sheridan Road,
(877) 606–9779
Founded in 1933, Radigan's
is a converted farmhouse
easily discovered under the
red neon sign that glows
"Wonderful Food." You only
need to do three things here.
Think steak. Talk steak. Eat
steak. "Old Man" Ray
Radigan died several years
ago, and his son, "Young
Mike," now runs the restaurant and purchases entire
sides of prime beef, which he
ages and makes his own
cuts. A Ray Radigan's
twenty-eight-ounce T-bone is
a meat-lover's delight. The
location (50 miles north of
Chicago and 40 miles south
of Milwaukee) has kept the
restaurant busy serving regulars from both communities.
Closed Mondays. Moderate
to expensive.

Toby's Diner,
1424 Washington Street,
(920) 682–8757
Toby's offers quick meals,
early breakfasts, and fast
lunches for the speedy set.
In addition to table seating,
patrons appreciate the carryouts of broasted chicken,
barbecued ribs, pork chops,
and homemade soup. Closed
Mondays. Inexpensive.

Tony's Pizza,
2204 Washington Street,
(920) 682–TONY
You can dine in or carry out with a full array of Italian dishes, but the pizza is the name of the game here. Come casual and stay late. A full-service bar accommodates customers waiting for the aromatic pizzas to come out of the oven, destined for home consumption. Open daily. Inexpensive.

OSHKOSH

The Granary Restaurant,
50 West Sixth Street,
(920) 233–3929
Tucked into downtown Oshkosh, The Granary is located in the historic old Schmidt building, a 120-year-old local landmark. Renovations have retained the oak beams that accent the dining room. The restaurant is within walking distance from the Convention Center and the Pioneer Inn. Roasted scallop salad and chicken almond salads are different taste treats. Alaskan king crab and Canadian walleye are among the seafood offerings. T-bones, sirloins, and strip steaks are numbered on the meaty side. Owners Jackie and Steve Amato serve lunch Monday through Saturday, with dinner served Monday through Saturday until 10:00 P.M. The restaurant is open from 5:00 to 9:00 P.M. Sunday. The lounge is open Monday through Saturday from 11:00 A.M. to close and Sunday from 4:00 P.M. to close. Moderate to expensive.

Robbins Restaurant,
1810 Omro Road,
(920) 235–2840
Robbins Restaurant provides a taste of home cooking, offering smoke-free dining. Chicken, chops, steaks, and seafoods in many styles of preparation line the menu. Robbins in the host of numerous organization lunches and dinners, such as those held by the Oshkosh Rotary Southwest and the nearby EAA aircraft museum, so it's one of the main places in town to see and be seen. Open for lunch and dinner daily. Moderate.

PLYMOUTH

52 Stafford, An Irish Inn,
52 Stafford Street,
(920) 893–0552
The 1892 building was originally a hotel and is now listed on the National Registry of Historic Places. True to the heritage of owner Rip O'Dwanny who has other guest houses in Green Bay and Mayville, Wisconsin, and in Ireland, Irish root soup is a regular menu item. Fresh spinach salad, roasted chicken breast sandwiches, and Black Angus burgers are lunch favorites. For dinner the rack of lamb, roast duckling, steamed salmon and steer tenderloins make the grade. Pub platters such as fish and chips and corned beef sandwiches can also be ordered. Dinner and room packages are available, with live music Wednesdays in the pub. The restaurant is closed Sundays. Moderate to expensive.

RACINE

Chartroom Restaurant and Bar,
209 Dodge Street,
(262) 632–9901
Live music at various times throughout the week is a regular feature at the Chartroom, featuring local and regional bands. Specializing in fish with its motto "Charting a Course for Seafood," the Chartroom caters to hearty eaters. Yellowfin tuna, stuffed shrimp, lake perch, pike perch, clam strips, and walleye almondine are regular menu listings. But chicken dishes and steak sandwiches are also available. True to its nautical theme, the restaurant's open dining room is divided by a row of pilings, to separate the smoking from nonsmoking areas. Luscious desserts include Godiva chocolate brownie sundaes, the strawberry or chocolate cheesecakes, and the Granny Smith caramel apple pies. The Chartroom is open daily, with reservations recommended for weekends. Inexpensive to moderate.

DeRango's Pizza Palace,
3840 Douglas Avenue,
(262) 639–4112
By visiting DeRango's Pizza Palace, diners quickly become happy participants in the family's long-standing tradition of serving good, hearty Italian foods. Domenico DeRango and his wife, Mirella, came to the United States in 1959 from Calabria with their two children, Benny and Carmela. After a brief time working at

a foundry, Dominic found his calling at his brother's restaurant. Eventually, the family started its own operation. Chicken parmigiana, lasagna, manicotti (either cheese or meat), rigatoni, and other pasta dishes are served. New York strip, sirloin, and prime rib are among the major meats also served daily. Take home a family bucket of twenty-four chicken pieces or a 16 x 32-inch party pizza. Moderate.

SHEBOYGAN

Brisco County Wood Grill,
539 Riverfront Drive,
(920) 803–6915
Black Angus beef slow cooked over a charcoal and apple wood fire headlines an impressive menu that Includes kabobs, fajitas, stir-fry, rotisserie chicken, sandwiches, hamburgers, an array of salads, and loads more. The Grill is noted for its dangerously delicious margaritas and mind-blowing mai-tais. Beer lovers appreciate the well-stocked cellar of imported, domestic, and Wisconsin microbrew beers. Open daily. Moderate.

City Streets Riverside Restaurant,
712 Riverfront Drive,
(920) 457–9050
The restaurant is a short walk to the city's dock and marina area where fishing and pleasure boats bob from spring through autumn. Open for lunch and dinner daily, the facility features

wonderfully piled high sandwiches, plus refreshing soup and crisp salads. Inexpensive to moderate.

STURGEON BAY

Perry's Cherry Diner,
230 Michigan Street,
(920) 743–9910
Perry's recreates the look and feel of a traditional 1950s-style casual eatery and is Door County's only smoke-free diner. It serves up a full contemporary menu for breakfast, lunch, and dinner. Hand-built malts and comfort foods such as meat loaf, gyros, burgers, vegetarian items, wraps, smoothies, and appetizers are listed. Conclude a meal with "Perry's Cherry Pie." Groovy era music is always playing. Inexpensive to moderate.

Scaturo's Baking Company & Cafe,
19 Green Bay Road,
(920) 746–8727
This is another Door County casual eatery fresh-from-the-oven pastries and breads. A three-egg omelet is one of the many breakfast specials. All soups and chilis are made from scratch. Pan-fried perch is served on Fridays until 8:00 P.M. The cafe also has a traditional fish boil, with whitefish accompanied by cole slaw, carrots, onions, potatoes, and cherry pie, mid-May through June on Friday and Saturday night and July through mid-October on Friday, Saturday, Sunday, and Monday. Open daily. Moderate.

WATERTOWN

Mullen's Dairy and Eatery,
212 West Main Street,
(920) 261–4278
Mullen's restaurant is a family kickback place with wide tables and comfortable chairs, offering sandwiches and soups. Malts, shakes, sundaes, and sodas encourage visitors from surrounding counties who have been returning for years and are well aware of the ice cream's quality and smooth taste. Nothing like a hearty dose of butter fat to tickle the fancy. The restaurant is open from 9:00 A.M. to 9:00 P.M. Sunday though Thursday, and from 9:00 A.M. to 10:00 P.M. Friday and Saturday. Smoke free. Inexpensive.

WAUPACA

Simpson's Indian Room Restaurant,
222 South Main Street,
(715) 258–8289
For a state noted for unusual food items, the pickled mushrooms served at Simpson's Restaurant are Wisconsin ace, being served in some bar drinks, stuck on a toothpick for munching, or sold in jars. Also remember to spread the grilled garlic on the warm, buttered bread when served for dinner. A Friday fish fry draws a lot of the neighbors, as do steak and other seafood. Sandwiches and subs are available midday. Open daily for lunch and dinner with karaoke on Thursdays from 9:00 to 11:00 P.M. Moderate.

The Woods Restaurant,
815 Fulton Street,
(715) 258–7400
The Woods is located behind the Waupaca Woods Mall, making for plenty of parking. Follow your nose to the steaks, ham, chicken, shrimp and pork chops. A Wood's breakfast is geared to the working guy/gal with two farm fresh eggs served any style, along with two pieces of French toast and choice of bacon, ham, sausage links or patties. The grilled kielbasa sausage and two fresh eggs served with hash browns or American fries can also fuel the workday fire. Speaking of blazes, a fireplace makes the place cozy for wintery evenings. Open for breakfast, lunch, and dinner from 7:00 A.M. to 9:00 P.M. Monday through Friday, and from 7:00 A.M. to 3:00 P.M. Saturday and Sunday.

SELECTED CHAMBERS OF COMMERCE

Algoma Chamber of Commerce,
1226 Lake Street, Algoma 54201,
(920) 487–2041, (800) 498–4888,
www.algoma.org

Door County Chamber of Commerce,
Box 406, Sturgeon Bay 54235-0406,
(920) 743–4456, (800) 52–RELAX,
www.doorcounty.com

Fond du Lac Convention and Visitors Bureau,
171 South Pioneer Road,
Fond du Lac 64935,
(920) 923–3010, (800) 937–9123,
www.fdl.com

Forward Janesville,
51 South Jackson, Janesville
53547-8008, (608) 757–3160,
www.forwardjanesville.com

Green Bay Visitor and Convention Bureau,
1901 South Oneida Street,
Green Bay 10596,
(920) 494–9507,
(888) 867–3342 (toll-free),
www.greenbay.com

Racine County Convention and Visitors Bureau,
14015 Washington Avenue,
Sturtevant 53177
(262) 884–6400,
www.visitracine.org

Sheboygan Area Convention and Visitors Bureau,
712 River Front Drive,
Sheboygan 53081,
(920) 457–9495, (800) 457–9497,
www.sheboygan.org

Milwaukee and Environs

The Potawatomi Indians called **Milwaukee** the "Gathering Place by the Waters," indicating a neutral ground. Tribes from around the Midwest could relax on the shaded banks of the Milwaukee and Menomonee Rivers and compare notes on buffalo hunting, just as today's conventioneers do about sales figures. Wild rice was thick in the swamps, and a large bluff separated the river valley from Lake Michigan. The hard, sandy beach was perfect for racing horses.

Of course, that was all before the first European settlers moved into the region. The explorer-priest Father Jacques Marquette pulled his canoe up on the riverbank in 1674 (a site now called Pere Marquette Park, located behind the Milwaukee County Historical Society, 910 North Old World Third Street, 414–273–8288). He was followed later by French trappers, who in turn were followed by Yankee land speculators. Next came the settlers. Soon the swamps were gone, the bluff was covered with houses, and the beach was a lakefront park.

Yet Milwaukee still retains that gathering-place image, proud of the potpourri of heritages that make up the roster of residents. Any visitor to the city finds that out immediately. Ethnic festivals, parades, church events, lectures, exhibitions, folk fairs, and a host of other events celebrate Milwaukee's

dozens of nationalities. And it's a city of neighborhoods. Sherman Park, Merrill Park, Bay View, Walker's Point, Harambee, and the others have their different housing and lifestyle flavors. About 1.5 million persons live in the metropolitan area consisting of Milwaukee and its immediate suburbs. Of that, 596,245 were city residents in 2005, making it the largest in the state.

You should start a jaunt at **Visit Milwaukee**, 648 North Plankinton Avenue (800–231–0903 or 414–273–3950; www.milwaukee.org), for the latest in brochures and information on attractions and events. The bureau is across the street from the convention complex called MECCA, near the Wisconsin Center, kitty-corner from the Hyatt Hotel. Another visitor information center is located at General Mitchell Field, 5300 South Howell Avenue (414–273–3950). The Milwaukee County Transit System (414–344–6711) has summer tours around the city, with pickups at the major downtown hotels. The trip ($10.00 for adults, $8.00 for seniors and kids under twelve) beats driving and provides a good orientation for first-time visitors.

The **Historic Third Ward**, a revitalized district just south of downtown, even has a Web page. Check in with them at www.historicthirdward.org. The page tells what is happening in the warren of art galleries, eateries, ad agencies, and shops that have mostly taken over from the truckers and warehousemen of yore.

In fact, warehouses in the old produce market there are being turned into upscale shops and bars.

MILWAUKEE AND ENVIRONS' TOP HITS

African Center	Kehr's Kandy Kitchen
Art Smart's Dart Mart and Juggling Emporium	Lakefront Festival of the Arts
	Polaris Restaurant
Boerner Botanical Gardens	Summerfest
Dean Jensen's Gallery	Tony Sendik's
Derry Hegarty's Pub & Grill	Usinger's
Forelle Fish Netting Corporation	Wisconsin State Fair
Goldmann's Department Store	Woodland Pattern
Harry W. Schwartz Book Shop	
Havenwoods Environmental Awareness Center	

However, the **Milwaukee Public Market,** 400 North Water Street, which opened with much fanfare in 2005, keeps alive that tradition of peddling fresh fruits and vegetables. The facility is open from 10:00 A.M. to 7:00 P.M. Tuesday through Friday; from 8:00 A.M. to 5:00 P.M. Saturday; and 8:00 A.M. to 4:00 P.M. Sunday. It is closed on Monday. In addition to the quality corn and apples, the market offers breads, cheese, meats, fish, and a host of specialty food items. Tables are available for anyone wishing to forage the stalls and then eat. Regular cooking classes are offered on the second mezzanine, so you can get an answer to "Is Chilean sea bass really bass?" In addition to street parking, the Historic Third Ward operates nearby parking garages at 212 North Milwaukee Street and 255 East Chicago Street. Contact the market at (414) 336–1111 or www.milwaukeepublicmarket.org.

From here, you should be able to strike out to see the city, currently going through a downtown building boom that includes a major-league auditorium, a theater district, office towers, and hotels. Visitors who haven't been to Milwaukee in several years often find themselves turned around because the old landmarks have given way to the new.

You don't have to hit the shopping malls for interesting rummaging. There are favorite places where a shopper can count on excellent service, ease in access, unique items, and knowledgeable clerks. To find your way

Tread the Boards

Milwaukee's theater scene includes more than twenty drama, dance, and musical companies in town, including First Stage, (414) 267–2929, which gears its performances to children; the Milwaukee Repertory Theater, (414) 224–1761; Skylight Opera, (414) 291–7811; Milwaukee Chamber Theater, (414) 276–8842; Florentine Opera, (414) 291–5700; Milwaukee Ballet, (414) 643–7677; Wild Space Dance Company, (414) 271–0307; Theatre X, (414) 278–0555; Bialystock & Bloom, (414) 223–0479; Milwaukee Shakespeare Company (414) 229–4308; and the Next Act Theater, (414) 278–7780. Irish, Native American, and African-American theater companies keep the ethnic performance world vibrant and alive.

AUTHORS' FAVORITES

Ethnic festivals	Milwaukee lakefront
Historic Third Ward	Milwaukee Public Museum
Marcus Center for the Performing Arts	Wisconsin State Fair

around this world, there's the **Milwaukee Map Service,** 959 North Mayfair Road (414–774–1300 or 800–525–3822). The place is a magnet for geography buffs. Just the thing for *Off the Beaten Path* readers is the series of Wisconsin regional maps that show every road in the state. The sections cost between $6.00 and $10.00. The map store is open 8:00 A.M. to 6:00 P.M. Monday through Friday and 9:00 A.M. to 4:00 P.M. Saturday.

Now head for Milwaukee's South Side and the **Forelle Fish Netting Corporation,** which sells netting for soccer goals, fishing, and even curtains. Its customers include the Milwaukee County Zoo, commercial fishers, and interior decorators. The quiet little store is located at 1030 South First Street (414–672–5935).

everythinginsports

For sports fans, Milwaukee has the Brewers baseball club, (414) 902–4400, and the Admirals for hockey (414) 227–0550. Soccer fans enjoy the Wave (2597 North Downer Avenue, 414–332–3338) for pro indoor matches and the Milwaukee Rampage (414–448–5425) for pro outdoor games. Hoops fanatics love the Bucks (414–227–0500) and the college basketball teams. Indoor events are generally held in the Bradley Center, 1001 North Fourth Street, in downtown Milwaukee. The hall is big enough to hold a 747 jetliner. Even the nosebleed section provides great views. Television monitors mounted over the central floor help with close-up action.

For an eclectic mix of shopping, coffeehouses, bars, and restaurants, Milwaukeeans usually head to **Brady Street,** a historic boulevard that has gone through numerous changes over the generations. Reborn again in the late 1990s, some of the trendiest joints in the city can be found here. Sharply dressed dudes flock to **Aala Reed Men's Clothing,** 1320 East Brady Street, (414) 226–2252, while their foxy counterparts make their way to **Miss Groove,** 1225 East Brady Street, (414) 298–9185. For the retro look, there's **Orchid Annie's Vintage Vogue,** 1327 East Brady Street, (414) 347–0606.

Glorioso Brothers Grocery, 1020 East Brady Street, (414) 272–0540, and **Sciortino's Bakery,** 1101 East Brady Street, (414) 272–4623, keep memories alive of what was once primarily a neighborhood of Italian émigrés.

Poetry Slams

"Poetry slams," in which readers compete for applause at local clubs, are great fun. For more than twenty-five years, the Coffee House, in the lower level of Redeemer Lutheran Church, 631 North Nineteenth Street (414–299–9598), has had open stages in addition to regularly scheduled performers. Kids and grown-ups can test their theatrical panache in front of live audiences. Y Not II, 706 East Lyon Street (414–347–9972), also presents a regular round of slams.

Get plenty of laughs at the **Comedy Cafe,** 615 East Brady Street, (414) 271–5653, then head for the **Hi Hat Lounge,** 1701 North Arlington Street (at the corner of Brady and Arlington; 414–225–9330), where the mixologists know almost everyone by name by the second beverage. The **Nomad World Pub,** 1401 East Brady, (414) 224–8111, has a great summer street scene and a cozy inside ambience for winter. **Regano's Roman Coin,** 1004 East Brady Street, (414) 278–9334, has been in the same family for more than thirty years. The quintessential Milwaukee tavern was built in 1890 and opens weekdays at 7:00 A.M. and 10:00 A.M. on Sunday.

frozenyummies

Milwaukee's frozen-custard shops are known for variety, delicious smoothness, and simply yum-yum ambience. Since the Hintz resistance is low when it comes to custard, our cars make their own way up to any one of a dozen stands in town. (Several look as if they date from the 1950s, which they do.)

Here are our top picks:

Gilles, 7515 West Blue Mound Road, (414) 453–4875

Kopps, 7631 West Layton Avenue, (414) 282–4312; and 5373 North Port Washington Road, (414) 961–2006; (414) 282–4080 is the "flavor line"

Leon's, 3131 South Twenty-seventh Street, (414) 383–1784

Not far off Brady is another landmark bar, **Wolski's Tavern,** at 1936 North Pulaski Street, (414) 276–8130. Bumper stickers proclaiming "I closed Wolski's" show up around the world. Enter if you dare.

Whenever we think we have too many balls in the air, when the job seems overwhelming, when things start falling out of the sky, a quick fix comes at **Art Smart's Dart Mart and Juggling Emporium,** 1695 North Humboldt Street (414–273–DART). There's a psychological boost gained just by walking through the front door and knowing that many customers here drop a lot of things while perfecting their techniques. Glass cases are packed with Native American clubs, torches, beanbags, balls, and other similar tools. Hanging on the walls are darts, dart boards, wind-up airplanes, and a host of other geegaws. And kites! There are dragons, birds, and jets . . . red kites, yellow kites, blue kites, and rainbow kites. You can't beat it.

If you are into sausage in the wurst way, **Usinger's** in downtown Milwaukee (1030 Old World Third Street, 414–276–9100) has pounds and pounds of the stuff made the good, old-fashioned German way. Many of the clerks speak with a hint of a home-country accent. Hungry crowds pack the company's showroom on Saturday morning for their weekly purchases, so go midweek if you can to avoid the rush.

The **African Center** import and food store (1912 West Hampton Avenue, 414–263–6153) serves the growing Black Caribbean community in Milwaukee, as well as city residents originally from Kenya, Nigeria, Malawi, and other African nations. Vincent Awosika and his brother, Charles, have regularly sponsored fashion shows, featuring bright, contemporary designs from those regions.

Woodland Pattern (720 East Locust Street, 414–263–5001) presents an extensive selection of small-press and poetry books, feminist literature, international kids' books, and avant-garde music. A large hall doubles as an art/ photo gallery, as well as a stage for a regularly scheduled calendar of poetry readers and musicians.

Easter means chocolate eggs, jelly beans, and fairy food at **Kehr's Kandy Kitchen** (3533 West Lisbon Avenue, 414–344–4305). The weeks before the holiday, the tiny white building overflows with folks hunting for the per-

African Heritage

Take in an African and African-American museum experience while in Milwaukee. The **Milwaukee Public Museum** has an extensive Africa wing, with full-size dioramas of lion hunters and other displays. Early museum managers often made visits back to Africa to study cultures and bring back artifacts. We've always come away knowing more about life in rain forests and deserts than we ever thought possible. The museum is located at 800 West Wells Street, (414) 278–2702. The facility is open 9:00 A.M. to 5:00 P.M. daily. Admission is $9.00 for adults, $8.50 for seniors (sixty-plus), $6.00 for kids ages four to seventeen, and free for kids two and younger.

America's Black Holocaust Museum, 2233 North Fourth Street, is somber, but don't let that steer you away. The museum traces the pattern of racial hatred in the United States. The displays are powerfully serious. Call for hours, (414) 264–2500.

The **Wisconsin Black Historical Society Museum,** at 2620 West Center Street, highlights Black contributions to the state. It provides an intimate glance at the African-American cultural experience. Call for hours, (414) 372–7677.

Cross-Country Ski Fun

In many places, even in big cities like Madison and Milwaukee, skiers almost can ski out their front doors. Literally. When we lived only a few blocks from Milwaukee's Lake Michigan, it was simple to walk over to the parks rimming the shoreline. After strapping on our skis, we could cut along the top of the bluffs overlooking the lake or swoop down the slopes to the flatlands. It was then easy to cruise along the edge of the ice-packed lake. The ice, by the way, groans and sighs on a winter evening. This produces an eerie symphony, especially with the percussion of surf booming up from under the floes.

Personally, I dig nighttime skiing, with a hint of falling snow reflected in the street lights. This makes for a truly amazing adventure. It is a bracing way to get ready to turn in for the evening . . . after a cup of hot chocolate (and marshmallows!), of course. Then snuggle under the quilts!

Milwaukee's East Side hotels—such as the Park East, County Clare, Knickerbocker, Pfister, and Astor—are close to these lakeside parks. So bring skis on your next winter visit to town.

fect nest-filler for their kids, grandchildren, or themselves. Chocolate-covered cherries, white almond chocolate . . . ah, that list is tempting. It's great to see the staff carrying on the Kehr family's candymaking traditions.

There are several streets on which you'll find quite a number of specialty stores, eateries, and entertainment outlets that are must-visits.

Mitchell Street on the South Side has been tagged "bridal row" because of the numerous wedding shops there. You can get anything you've ever dreamed of in *Goldmann's Department Store,* 930 West Mitchell Street (414–645–9100). The firm has been a neighborhood staple there for generations. Wringer washing machines, corsets, and oversized jeans (large enough to hold three regular-weight men) are included in the stock.

The lunch counter is the best in town for people watching and listening for "Milwaukeese," the jargon of the city that warrants a chuckle. "Let's go down by Schuster's where the streetcar bends the corner around" is one of the most famous examples.

Take in a *Harry W. Schwartz Book Shop* in Milwaukee if you need extra copies of *Wisconsin Off the Beaten Path*. There are stores in suburban Brookfield, Shorewood, and Mequon and another at 2559 North Downer Avenue and 2662 South Kinnickinnic Avenue in Bay View.

If hunger strikes you, Downer Avenue is the place to be. *Gil's Café,* at 2608 North Downer Avenue (414–964–4455), is a two-story cafe that accommodates smokers on the second floor. The breeze off the lake can be enjoyed in the summer months on the patio with outdoor seating. Enjoy salads, sandwiches, and even pizza at Gil's.

Dream Dance is considered one of the city's best restaurants, even though it is located in the Potawatomi Bingo Casino, 1721 West Canal Street (414–847–7883). The menu features exotic items such as deer, raised on the tribal lands in northern Wisconsin.

Make sure you top dinner off right and stop at *LIXX,* 2597 North Downer Avenue (414) 332–3338. The best frozen custard and frozen yogurt in the area can be found in this corner sweet shop. Have a smooth butterscotch shake, or maybe an ooey-gooey turtle sundae is more to your liking. Of course, there are always regular, boring cones.

Tony Sendik's (2643 North Downer Avenue, 414–962–1600) is one of the largest fresh fruit and vegetable stores in the city. Ready-made bouquets are conveniently located by the front door, for shoppers and lovers in a hurry. Tony Sendik also runs a fresh fish shop in his store, where you can get hot carryouts of fish and chips.

In the 4600 and 4700 blocks of Burleigh Street on the near West Side, several kosher stores sell lox, bagels, and all the trimmings for a hearty breakfast.

The neighborhood around the intersection of West Lisbon and West North Avenues, where they connect diagonally, has an intercontinental flair, with an Indian grocery, two Greek and several Oriental restaurants, a Greek gift shop, a Black Muslim mosque, and a Chicago-style hot dog stand.

Milwaukeeans, like the army, travel on their stomachs. There must be more high-quality eating places in this city than almost anywhere else. The best skyline view is from the *Polaris Restaurant* atop the Hyatt Regency Hotel (333 West Kilbourn, 414–276–1234). You can whiz to the top of the hotel aboard one of those glass-enclosed elevators with the twinkling lights. This is an occasion eatery, for birthdays, anniversaries, and special tête-à-têtes. The room rotates a full turn every forty-five minutes, to give you a look at the City Hall, the downtown construction, the lake,

flemishlook

Milwaukee's city hall is considered one of the world's best examples of Flemish-Renaissance design. The building celebrated its centennial in 1995.

and the roadways leading into the city. There's nothing like it while dining on a lobster tail and sipping a rare vintage. Prices range from moderate to expensive. Also try *Blu,* at the top of the Pfister Hotel, 424 East Wisconsin Avenue (414–273–8222) for another look at Milwaukee's skyline.

What would Milwaukee be without its pubs? Some neighborhoods have a bar on each corner, plus an extra one in the middle, all of which have their regular clientele. Water Street downtown near City Hall now has a "strip" of bars and restaurants that attract the upwardly mobile set. But here are some special ones where neckties are certainly unnecessary and a down-home feel without pretension is prevalent:

An Irish touch can be found at **Mo's Irish Pub,** 142 West Wisconsin Avenue (414– 272–0721), featuring live entertainment, a good pouring of pints, and pub grub such as burgers. Try the Irish food, including stew and boxty, a potato griddle cake.

Derry Hegarty's Pub, 5328 West Bluemound Road, (414–453–6088), is located across the street from both a church and a cemetery—to ensure that any good Irishman has a direct, fast pipeline from the pub to heaven. Hegarty, originally of Cork, has been a fixture on Milwaukee's pub scene for more than two decades. Many is the wake, wedding, and fancy ball we've attended there

Have a Sip

Visitors often work up a thirst when visiting Milwaukee. One of the first questions always asked is "where are the breweries?" The title of Beer City, bestowed on Milwaukee years ago, is still strong. However, only Miller remains as the last of the big breweries in town. Filling in are several smaller boutique breweries and brewpubs. Tours are held at most locations.

Miller Brewing Company's Visitor Center is located at 4251 West State Street, (414) 931–2337 or (800) 944–5483 (LITE). Call for updated tour information. The plant is located on the city's North Side.

Sprecher Brewing Co. can be found at 701 West Glendale Avenue, Glendale, (414) 964–2739. Tours are at 1:00, 2:00, and 3:00 P.M. Saturday, and Fridays throughout the year at 4:00 P.M.; reservations required. In addition to its beer, Sprecher brews a mean root beer. It is so creamy and smooth that connoisseurs consider it a gourmet soda.

Lakefront Brewery is a small neighborhood brewery whose reputation for producing quality brew is growing. This is truly off the beaten path. You'll find Lakefront in the city's RiverWest neighborhood, just west of the Milwaukee River. The plant and tasting room is at 1872 North Commerce, (414) 372–8800. The Friday fish fry, complete with live polka music, is a must.

The Milwaukee Ale House is a 1997 addition to the Historic Third Water. An old warehouse was converted into the pub, which includes a restaurant. The elder Hintz likes Louie's Demise, a strong ale named after a long-ago relative of one of the owners. The fellow allegedly died in a barroom brawl. At least that's the family legend. Look for the big kettles in the alehouse windows at 233 North Water Street (414–226–2337). Water Street Brewery, 1101 North Water Street (414–272–1195), is comfortable, with great brew made on-site.

The Miller Inn at the Miller Brewing Company

in his backroom. Local politicos use his watering hole as a site for major fund-raisers. He serves exceptionally good pub grub, as well. For years, the place has been the appropriate gathering spot for Irish groups. The Ancient Order of Hibernians and the Emerald Society hold regular meetings in one of his down-stairs rooms, usually the snug one with the fireplace that is a favorite for win-ter sessions. Hegarty once had a great blustering Saint Bernard named Muldoon who loved beer. The dog has long since gone to its reward, yet Derry Hegarty's stays on and on and on. You just can't keep a good Corkman down.

Caroline's Jazz Club, 401 South 2nd Street, (414) 221–9444, presents some of the best sounds in town, located in the old warehouse district south of downtown across the Milwaukee River. Owner Caroline Rubitsky brings in top national talent, as well as provides a venue for local musicians. Beginning around 8:00 P.M. on Tuesday, Wednesday, and Thursday, smaller combos per-form, while Friday and Saturday nights are more wild with larger ensembles on stage. You can't beat Rubitsky's Martini specials either. For more jazz, *The Estate,* 2423 North Murray Avenue, (414) 964–9923, is a classic hideaway on

Milwaukee's Eastside that presents smooth music almost every night of the week. Call to see who is performing.

Food for the cultural soul can be had at the small galleries dotting the Milwaukee landscape. *Dean Jensen Gallery* (759 North Water Street, 414–278 –7100) was opened by the former art critic for the *Milwaukee Sentinel* newspaper. Wildlife art specialists are featured in the *Landmarks Gallery* at 231 North Seventy-sixth Street (414–453–1620). The *Tory Folliard Gallery* is at 233 North Milwaukee Street, (414) 273–7311; www.toryfolliard.com.

Augmenting the gallery scene are the dozens of art fairs around the community, ranging from the nationally renowned *Lakefront Festival of the Arts* in June, held on the grounds of the lakefront Milwaukee Art Center, to neighborhood and college fairs. The weather is usually cold and rainy for at least one day out of the three for the lakefront fest. Keep an umbrella handy, just in case. But since the fest is now held under tents, the iffy weather is less of a challenge.

Milwaukee also is known as Cream City, a legacy of the nineteenth century when many homes were constructed from a creamy-colored brick. The houses are easily spotted around town, with large concentrations in the older neighborhoods on the near South Side and along the lakefront. For a time, more workers labored in the brickyards than in the breweries, producing millions of bricks a year. For a peek at how the other half lives, take a jaunt along Lake Shore Drive (Highway 32 of Red Arrow Division fame) past Milwaukee's Gold Coast mansions. Some are of the distinctive Cream City brick.

extraevents

There are dozens of **Milwaukee-based events** held during the year that are geared to families. Don't forget Juneteenth Day, (414) 372–3770, celebrating the final liberation of slaves after the Civil War; Rainbow Summer, (414) 273–7206, on the grounds of the Performing Arts Center, a summerlong series of outdoor concerts; Milwaukee a la Carte, (414) 256–5412; the Grape Lakes Food and Wine Festival, (414) 224–3850; Briggs & Stratton Al's Run Marathon, (414) 266–6320; several Greek and Serbian festivals at outlying churches; and Jazz in the Park, (414) 271–1416, held every summer Thursday in the downtown Cathedral Square.

Even with the dense population, pockets of calm are easily found in a city that cherishes its parks and open spaces. *Havenwoods Environmental Awareness Center* (6141 North Hopkins Street, 414–527–0232) has a 240-acre tract of fields and woodlots with 3 miles of marked trails. The center is a twenty-minute drive from the central city. Many schools utilize the site for nature-study programs. Another getaway is the lakefront bike trail that wanders north from near the Henry W. Maier Lakefront Festival

Munchies at the Fair

The **Wisconsin State Fair,** at 8600 West Greenfield Avenue, West Allis, is held at the end of July and early August. The fair is more than one hundred years old, showcasing geese, horses, cheese, tractors, and geegaws. Dan says, "I have my plan. Always head straight for the Family Center, where the Wisconsin Potato and Vegetable Growers Association serves up huge baked spuds. Best ever!" Elder Hintz suggests, "Ask for the cherry toppings at the ice-cream booth run by the 4-H." We both agree that this is "eat on the cheap" and the way to go. After munching our way around the displays presented by the honey producers, pork farmers, and beef council, we roll out the door and head to the midway for carnival fun and to meet old friends. That's after a look at the rabbits, chickens, geese, pigs, horses, and Holsteins, of course. Call (414) 266–7000. In his callow youth, elder Hintz used to work for Royal American Shows, one of the country's major railroad carnivals, and played the Wisconsin fair venue. So a repeat visit to the show grounds brings back memories.

Park into the suburbs. The roadway is located on an abandoned railroad right-of-way, so the pedaling is smooth and easy. The three climate-controlled domes of the **Mitchell Park Horticultural Conservatory** (524 South Layton Avenue, 414 –649–9800) are well-known Milwaukee landmarks. Their floral displays, rain forest, and desert area are always worth a stop. **Boerner Botanical Garden** in Whitnall Park (9400 Boerner Drive, 414–525–5600) is another site where the bloom is always on the rose.

Growing Power (5500 West Silver Spring, 414–527–1546) is a great place to learn how to use worms in gardening. Owner Will Allen knows all the tricks.

The Department of City Development also has devised several **historic building tours** around Milwaukee, taking in the Bay View, Juneautown, Kilbourntown, North Point, Walker's Point, and West End neighborhoods. Flyers on each area include maps and point-by-point descriptions of famous old structures found along the way. Combine one of these jaunts with the MKE Neighborhood program, and you will really learn the face of the city. Be ready to stop in at any of the mom-and-pop groceries and restaurants found along the way. Copies of the flyers also can be secured from the DCD.

Milwaukee is noted as the City of Festivals. Kicking off the year are the **Scottish Highland Games** in Old Heidleberg Park behind the Bavarian Inn, 700 West Lexington Boulevard, Glendale. The events are held in early June, with sheep-herding demonstrations by border collies, bagpiping, and caber tossing. The latter is akin to throwing telephone poles end over end.

We always enjoy attending **Asian Moon,** another June extravaganza. As a chef, Dan likes to check out the menus, ranging from standard fried rice to such delicacies as sweet banana egg rolls, kung pao chicken, and spicy pork with green beans. Elder Hintz just likes to eat. The festival was launched in 1994, featuring music and foods from Chinese, Japanese, Hmong, Indian, Filipino, and other Eastern cultures. The fest is sponsored by the Wisconsin Organization for Asian Americans. The fest's offices are at 3920 South Taylor Avenue (414) 483–8530, or www.asianmoon.org.

June seems to be the heavy party month in Milwaukee because **Polish Fest** also occurs at this time. So limber up your polka legs and prepare for munching pierogies and smacznego. The festival's offices are at 6941 South Sixty-eighth Street in suburban Franklin (414–529–2140; www.polishfest.org).

The Big Daddy of Milwaukee's festivals is **Summerfest,** a musical blowout that runs for eleven days—from the end of June through the Fourth of July weekend. Summerfest, one of North America's largest music events, brings a wide range of music to the eighty-five-acre lakefront festival show grounds. Almost a million people attend each year to watch the world-famous talent and knosh their way around the vendor booths. The fest office is at 200 North Harbor Drive (414–273–3378).

discoverthemuseum

Tucked deep inside the heart of the Milwaukee Museum Center—far from the main entrance's beaten path—**Discovery World** is a popular "hands-on" learning place for kids of all ages. Displays emphasize science, economics, and technology. It's all in good fun. Discovery World, the James Lovell Museum of Science, Economics, and Technology, can be entered at James Street. The main Museum Center is at 815 North James Lovell Street (414–765–9966). The center itself is open daily from 9:00 A.M. to 5:00 P.M., but it's closed on the Fourth of July, Thanksgiving, and Christmas. Admission is $7.00 for adults, $6.00 for seniors (sixty-two-plus), $4.75 for kids ages three to fifteen, and free for kids two and younger.

For the French connection, **Bastille Days** can-can do a Francophile fun-fun job. For details contact the East Towne Association, 770 North Jefferson, (414) 271–1416. The city's French celebration is on Cathedral Square downtown. There's loads of oh-la-la and dang good music, from Cajun to Breton to the music of chanteuse Edith Piaf.

We love fireworks, so **Festa Italiana** is on the top of our summertime calendar for pyrotechnics. Every night of the four-day fest offers skybound starbursts that rival a Vesuvius eruption. Suggestion: take a blanket and a cooler of lemonade and hunker down on the grounds of the Milwaukee Art Museum, across the still waters of the Summerfest lagoon. When the displays go pop, bang, and whistle, you'll get the best views of anywhere in town. The reflections on the water are not to be missed. For entertainer information contact Italian Community Center, 631 West Chicago Avenue, (414) 223–2800.

OTHER ATTRACTIONS WORTH SEEING

Allen-Bradley clock tower	Joan of Arc Chapel, Marquette University campus
Annunciation Greek Orthodox Church	
Bradley Center	Milwaukee Antique Center
Brady Street pubs, shops, and restaurants	St. Josephat Basilica
	Slim McGinn's Pub
Grand Avenue shopping mall	University of Wisconsin union

German Fest is oompah-rich in yodeling, lederhosen, tuba playing, and spanferkel sandwiches. With a name like ours, OBP authors Hintz and Hintz make this a must-see almost every year. There is plenty to see: marching bands, the Milwaukee symphony, and heritage displays. Dog lovers howl over the antics of the Badger Dachshund Club and its ground-hugging Dachshund Derby. You can reach the fest offices at 8229 West Capitol Drive (414-464-9444). The fest is held in July.

To understand the wonders of the Black cultural experience, take in the *African World Festival,* one of the more exotic of Milwaukee's lakefront events. The opening ceremonies highlight rich African traditions where native priests bless the water and earth. The prayers are accompanied by dancers, drummers, and singers. This authenticity continues throughout the festival, covering everything from foods to music to displays. High points for the elder Hintz: peanut soup, blues, and bebop. Coauthor Dan digs the poets, rappers, and authors. Contact the fest at 2821 North Fourth Street, (414) 372-4567. The fest is held in early August.

For the quarter Irish in the Hintz clan lineage, *Milwaukee Irish Fest* offers an obvious Gaelic fix. The fest is the world's largest Irish music and cultural event, held annually on the third weekend in August. Irish Fest was around well before *Riverdance* and *Lord of the Dance,* the two hit Irish musical extravaganzas of the late 1990s. The show laid the groundwork in developing a fan system for such productions. The festival's headquarters are at 1532 Wauwatosa Avenue (414-476-3378).

Neither of us has entered the jalapeño-pepper-eating competition at *Mexican Fiesta,* but it is fun to watch. That is only one of the many activities as the Latino community struts its stuff on the lakefront. They have loads of great music and good food each August. For details you can reach Fiesta at 1220 West Windlake Avenue, (414) 383-7066.

First Typewriter

The typewriter was invented in Milwaukee by Christopher Latham Sholes, with the help of Carlos Glidden and Samuel W. Soule. The device, the first practical machine of its kind, was developed in 1867. You can see a plaque dedicated to Sholes and his typewriter at the corner of West State Street and North Fourth Street, behind the Milwaukee Arena and across the street from the *Milwaukee Journal–Sentinel* offices, 333 West State Street.

Colorfully costumed Native American dancers of all ages from around the country and Canada compete for top awards at *Indian Summer.* This fest holds its nationally recognized powwow in early September and is a major stop on the pro tour for the fancy, grass, and women's pro dance tour. Dan's grandfather used to teach Native American dancing way, way back in the 1930s. So we always go to see the latest versions of traditional steps. While there, the elder Hintz indulges in his fancy for buffalo burgers and Indian tacos. And there's more. Skilled native demonstrators share their handiwork. Observe them, then stroll through the four traditional tribal villages and look over the various types of huts and tepees. Dan is an Indian Summer music fan, soaking up its range of folk, country, and pop performers—all of whom are Native Americans. The fest headquarters is located at 7441 West Greenfield Avenue (414–774–7119). One of the newer festivals is *Arab World Fest,* offering the food and entertainment of the Middle East.

Later in the year, all this ethnicity is summed up at *Holiday Folk Fair,* one of the major events presented by the International Institute of Milwaukee County (1110 North Old World Third Street, 414–225–6225). Held at the Wisconsin State Fair Park in mid-November, the Folk Fair is a rainbow mix of all the city's international traditions: from Latvian to Serb, Hungarian to Latino. The fair is the oldest in the country, having started in the 1940s.

But if you wish to travel around the world to see some "wild life" without really leaving Wisconsin, the *Milwaukee County Zoological Gardens* is a worthwhile stop. Among the 2,500 growling, barking, munching, humming, swimming, sniffing, and snuffling animals are leopard sharks, Chinese alligators, King penguins, ring-tailed lemurs, gorillas, snow leopards, Bactrian camels, and Thomson's gazelles, plus almost another 300 species. The sprawling park is located at 10001 West Blue Mound Road. For information, call (414) 771–5500. The zoo is open from 9:00 A.M. to 4:30 P.M. daily January 1 to April 30. From May 1 to September 30, it is open from 9:00 A.M. to 5:00 P.M. Monday to Saturday, and 9:00 A.M. to 6:00 P.M. Sunday and holidays. From October 1 to April 29, hours are 9:00 A.M. to 4:30 P.M. Animal buildings close fifteen minutes prior to zoo closing time. Admissions vary throughout the year, so check the zoo Web site at www.milwaukeezoo.org.

To learn more about Wisconsin's ethnic community, read one of the several publications focusing on Old World heritages. You can easily pick up a copy of any of these Milwaukee-based newspapers or magazines.

For a calendar of Gaelic goings-on in Wisconsin (as well as throughout the Midwest), the **Irish American Post** has it all. The monthly online magazine goes one step further with reportage by top journalists in Ireland, Britain, and the United States.

Contact the *Post* at 1815 West Brown Deer Road, (414) 540–6636; e-mail: editor@irishamericanpost.com. You can check out the Web site at www.irish americanpost.com.

The **Spanish Journal** gives the latest on the state's Hispanic community. The *Journal* is published at 152 West Wisconsin Avenue, Suite 613 (414–271–5683). Subscriptions are $45 for fifty-two weeks. An online edition is found at www.spanishjournal.com. Individual copies are free. The free **Italian Times** can be found throughout the city at newsstands and at the Italian Community Center. Call (414) 223–2807. The Italian Community Center is located at 631 East Chicago Avenue. The ***Vremia,*** a national Russian newspaper, 11520 North Port Washington Road, Mequon, is also available (262–241–1655).

For African-American coverage, secure copies of the **Milwaukee Courier** (2003 West Capitol Drive, 414–449–4860). Subscriptions are $25 a year, while

Take a Cruise

The Milwaukee skyline looks very different when viewed from one of the city's cruise boats. All are kid-safe, but you should still keep an eye on the tykes. Each vessel offers onboard beverages, rest rooms, and plenty of deck space. Their well-informed crews can answer questions about the height of the harbor's Daniel Webster Hoan Memorial Bridge and how many freighters visit during the city's shipping season. Boats leave from one of several docks in the downtown area. Call to confirm schedules. Tours are generally April through October. The **Iroquois,** (414) 332–4194, docks downtown on the Milwaukee River between the Michigan and Clybourn Street bridges. **Celebration of Milwaukee,** (414) 272–2628, departs from 502 North Harbor Drive. The **Edelweiss,** (414) 272–3769, departs from 1110 North Old World Third Street. Reservations are required for this boat, which serves lunch, brunch, and dinner. Many have been the comfortable summer hours when we lazed away a Saturday afternoon aboard a harbor cruise on one of these vessels. Shades of Captain Ahab and pirates and the *Queen Mary* . . . the dreams of a relaxing off-the-beaten-waterway expedition!

FOR MORE INFORMATION

Greater Milwaukee Convention and Visitors Bureau,
101 West Wisconsin Avenue,
Milwaukee 53203,
(414) 273–7222 or
(800) 231–0903

individual copies are free. Another weekly covering the African-American scene is the **Milwaukee Times** (1938 North Martin Luther King Jr. Drive, 414–263–5088). Subscriptions are $45 for a year's worth of reading and are free individually.

Copies of all these publications can usually be picked up at area newsstands.

The Wisconsin Jewish Chronicle is located at 1360 North Prospect Avenue (414–390–5888). The weekly newspaper covers Jewish activities throughout Wisconsin and is available only via subscriptions ($36 per year).

Milwaukee is an easy city in which to drive, even with the seemingly endless construction. Laid out by straight-thinking German engineers, most roads run east to the lake or due north and south. Seldom does an out-of-town driver get lost, except possibly while trying to find an on-ramp to I–94. If you spend too much time spinning around blocks, ask a patrol officer (yes, Milwaukee still has beat cops) or hole up in a Milwaukee hotel.

Lodgings range from the grande dames of Milwaukee's accommodations world at the Pfister Hotel (424 East Wisconsin Avenue, 800–558–8222 or 414–273–8222) and her sister, the former Marc Plaza, now a Hilton (509 West Wisconsin Avenue, 414–271–7250), to the usual collection of chain motels.

The Pfister, a AAA four-diamond award winner and member of Preferred Hotels and Resorts Worldwide, was named Hotel of the Year in 1991 by the Wisconsin Innkeepers Association. The venerable hotel celebrated its one hundredth anniversary in 1993.

You'll need such a rest stop after galloping around town.

Places to Stay in Milwaukee and Environs

Ambassador Hotel,
2308 West Wisconsin Avenue,
(414) 347–8400
Moderate

County Clare,
1234 North Astor Street,
(414) 27–CLARE (25273)
Moderate to expensive.

Hilton Milwaukee City Center,
509 West Wisconsin Avenue,
(414) 271–7250 or
(800) 558–7708
Moderate

Park East Hotel,
916 East State Street,
(414) 276–8800 or
(800) 328–7275
Moderate

Pfister Hotel,
424 East Wisconsin Avenue,
(414) 273–8222 or
(800) 558–8222
Moderate to expensive.

Places to Eat in Milwaukee and Environs

African Hut Restaurant,
1107 North Old World Third Street,
(414) 785–1110
For an array of authentic African dishes, including delectable peanut soup and jollof rice, the so-called "king of rice" that dates back to the Mali Empire. Diners-in-the-know flock to the African Hut for its primarily western and east African dishes, such as fried plantains as an appetizer (the largest of all the bananas). Zanzi fries are similar to french fries in shape but made from sweet yams coated in spices. Entrees include Cameroonian-style collard greens, Kenyan chicken curry, and beef froyi from Ghana. Owners Yinka and Moji Adedokun offer samples to first-timers. Open daily for lunch and dinner, except Sunday. Moderate.

Beans & Barley,
1901 East North Avenue,
(414) 278–7878
This is the best place in town for the vegetarian crowd, with its meatless items that are tasty, well prepared, and worth returning for more. A legend for almost two decades in the city, everybody knows "Beans," which also has a deli and food store attached. Perch on a front stool and read the local alternative newspapers or choose a booth or table for heady conversation. An attentive waitstaff is always ready. Be prepared for a wait however around noon or an early dinner hour because of the crowd. Yet the turn-around is generally fast. Open daily. Inexpensive to moderate.

Bjonda,
7754 Harwood Avenue,
(414) 431–1444
Bjonda has become known for being one of the Milwaukee area's most sophisticated restaurants. Women even get a small stool for placing next to their seat to hold their purses. Well-trained, white-gloved waitstaff are extremely attentive in the dining area, while the lounge bar is much more casual. The Skylight Lounge, a small side room, seats about ten persons, making for a cozy starter place to hover over drinks before dinner. Wild Norwegian salmon and beef short ribs braised in Sprecher root beer are among the main items. The Maine blue crab sandwiches are exceptional. Located in the suburb of Wauwatosa, Bjonda is open for lunch and dinner daily. Moderate to expensive.

Calderone Club,
8001 North Port Washington Road,
(414) 352–9303
Owner Tony Fazzari runs a tight ship, watching every step of preparation and serving of his numerous Italian dishes that include dishes primarily from Rome south into Sicily. His simple spaghetti is heavy with sauces. Add a meatball the size of a basketball and you have a meal and a half. It also takes several dozen strong, hungry eaters to carry out one of his pizzas, they are so loaded with goodies. Well, almost anyway. Open daily for lunch and dinner. Moderate.

Gil's Cafe,
2608 North Downer Avenue,
(414) 964–4455
Featuring gourmet pizzas, plus husky burgers, pasta, and homemade soup, Gil's has become an East Side staple. Located near the Downer Theatre and a number of clubs, Gil's is a favorite for a pre-show, pre-party dinner. An upstairs dining area doubles as a stage for touring musicians such as country-folk great Tom Russell and others. Each summer, the restaurant sponsors Gilfest, featuring some of the best musicians in Texas and the Southwest, who come to Milwaukee for a real musical blowout on the adjacent streets. OBP co-author Dan Hintz was a chef here for a time between travel stints to exotic locales. Moderate.

Lulu's Cafe,
2921 North Oakland Avenue,
(414) 962–1183
In a city known for its ethnic eateries, Lulu's always stands out with its mix of Ethiopian, Somali, and Italian fare, reminding diners of a colonial past. Many of Milwaukee's East African cabbies eat here, which vouches for its authenticity. Many of the stews and meat dishes are served family-style on a large pizza-like bread placed in the center of the table. Open daily for lunch and dinner. Moderate.

Poco Loco,
4134 West River Lane,
(414) 355–9550
Tiny, with only twenty stools, Poco Loco is more than just a North Shore neighborhood joint. Fine Mexican fare, such as lobster quesadillas, draws patrons from all over Milwaukee. Be prepared to rub shoulders with race car drivers, corporate magnates, rock musicians, school teachers, doctors, auto mechanics, and just about anyone else who appreciates a good South-of-the-Border beer with a platter full of fish tacos. Fresh eggs from a farm down the road ensures quality mayo and are used in other dishes. Mike the bartender serves a mean margarita, along with a wide variety of tequilas. Open daily for lunch and dinner. Inexpensive.

The Safe House,
779 Front Street,
(414) 271–2007
For almost thirty years, the Safe House has been drawing delighted customers who need to know a password to gain entrance through a cleverly concealed door. Folks at the inside bar laugh as newcomers try to enter, watching via video camera. But no one is ever turned away and eventually a staff member will help out the newcomers. With its still fun and funky James Bond interior, guests can be anybody they want to be. Whenever a president or other world leader is in town, their security staffs often wind up here. Pub grub, steaks, and pastas are on the menu. Another secret entrance takes guests back and forth to the Milwaukee Press Club, with hundreds of autographs of notable personages dating back to the 1800s adorning the walls. The club is the nation's oldest continually existing organization for journalists and wannabes. The Safe House is open daily for lunch and dinner. Moderate.

Trocadero,
1758 North Water Street,
(414) 272–0205
Reminiscent of a French *tabac,* a tobacco shop (the Troc even carries French-language publications and cigarettes) around the bar up front, the interior dining room becomes a cozy space. It also has a bar on one side where denizens of Milwaukee's East Side like to congregate. Nightly wine specials are posted on a huge board behind the bar. Patio dining is a must in the summer. The place serves dinner Monday through Saturday, as well as a hearty Sunday brunch. An upstairs room is always available for parties and special events, used primarily by the city's hip and trendies. Moderate to expensive.

General Index

ACCOMMODATIONS/RESTAURANTS

ATTRACTIONS

FESTIVALS/EVENTS

MUSEUMS

About the Authors

Martin Hintz, a member of the Society of American Travel Writers, has been a travel writer for three decades. Hintz has more than sixty books to his credit, some of which are other travel-related books published by Globe Pequot, and he has written hundreds of magazine and newspaper articles. He also publishes *The Irish American Post,* an international online news magazine (www .irishamericanpost.com), and is director of the Mountjoy Writers Group, an international news syndicate. In addition to his oldest son, Daniel, son Stephen and daughter Kate have collaborated with him on writing projects.

Daniel Hintz is an experienced world traveler who lived for a time in the former Soviet Union and worked with a construction crew in Venezuela. He has also visited numerous other countries and traveled extensively in the United States. Hintz was a volunteer for Americorps, directing a youth arts project in Washington State. A trained chef, Hintz worked in the Denver area and in several other major cities, and he had his own catering company. He is also a poet, filmmaker, and drama teacher. Hintz was director of youth development for the Downtown YMCA in Seattle and now directs a Tax Incremental Finance (TIF) District, concentrating on the arts and downtown development, in Fayetteville, Arkansas.